Reading
STREET
Grade 2

Scott Foresman

Reader's and Writer's Notebook

Glenview, Illinois • Boston, Massachusetts • Chandler, Arizona •
Upper Saddle River, New Jersey

Copyright © by Pearson Education, Inc., or its affiliates. All Rights Reserved.
Printed in the United States of America. This publication is protected by copyright,
and permission should be obtained from the publisher prior to any prohibited
reproduction, storage in a retrieval system, or transmission in any form or by any
means, electronic, mechanical, photocopying, recording, or likewise. The publisher
hereby grants permission to reproduce these pages, in part or in whole, for classroom
use only, the number not to exceed the number of students in each class. Notice of
copyright must appear on all pages. For information regarding permissions, write to
Pearson Curriculum Group Rights & Permissions, One Lake Street, Upper Saddle River,
New Jersey 07458.

Pearson, Scott Foresman, and Pearson Scott Foresman are trademarks, in the U.S.
and/or other countries, of Pearson Education, Inc., or its affiliates.

ISBN 13: 978-0-328-47670-1
ISBN 10:   0-328-47670-6
19 V011 18 17 16
CC1

Unit 1: Exploration

© Pearson Education, Inc., 2

Unit 2: Working Together

© Pearson Education, Inc., 2

iv

Unit 3: Creative Ideas

© Pearson Education, Inc., 2

v

Unit 4: Changes

© Pearson Education, Inc., 2

Unit 5: Responsibility

© Pearson Education, Inc., 2

Unit 6: Traditions

© Pearson Education, Inc., 2

Name _____

Unit I Reading Log

Reading Time	Title and Author	What is it all about?	How would you rate it?	Why?
From ____ to ____			Great OK Awful	
From ____ to ____			Great OK Awful	
From ____ to ____			Great OK Awful	
From ____ to ____			Great OK Awful	
From ____ to ____			Great OK Awful	

© Pearson Education, Inc., 2

Name _____

Unit 2 Reading Log

Reading Time	Title and Author	What is it all about?	How would you rate it?	Why?
From _____ to _____			Great OK Awful	
From _____ to _____			Great OK Awful	
From _____ to _____			Great OK Awful	
From _____ to _____			Great OK Awful	
From _____ to _____			Great OK Awful	

RR2   **Independent Reading**

© Pearson Education, Inc., 2

Name _____

Unit 3 Reading Log

Reading Time	Title and Author	What is it all about?	How would you rate it?	Why?
From ____ to ____			Great OK Awful	
From ____ to ____			Great OK Awful	
From ____ to ____			Great OK Awful	
From ____ to ____			Great OK Awful	
From ____ to ____			Great OK Awful	

© Pearson Education, Inc., 2

Name _____

Unit 4 Reading Log

Reading Time	Title and Author	What is it all about?	How would you rate it?	Why?
From ____ to ____			Great OK Awful	
From ____ to ____			Great OK Awful	
From ____ to ____			Great OK Awful	
From ____ to ____			Great OK Awful	
From ____ to ____			Great OK Awful	

© Pearson Education, Inc., 2

Name _____

Unit 5 Reading Log

Reading Time	Title and Author	What is it all about?	How would you rate it?	Why?
From ____ to ____			Great OK Awful	
From ____ to ____			Great OK Awful	
From ____ to ____			Great OK Awful	
From ____ to ____			Great OK Awful	
From ____ to ____			Great OK Awful	

© Pearson Education, Inc., 2

Name _____

Unit 6 Reading Log

Reading Time	Title and Author	What is it all about?	How would you rate it?	Why?
From ____ to ____			Great OK Awful	
From ____ to ____			Great OK Awful	
From ____ to ____			Great OK Awful	
From ____ to ____			Great OK Awful	
From ____ to ____			Great OK Awful	

© Pearson Education, Inc., 2

RR6   **Independent Reading**

Name _____

Story Title _____

Author _____

Write why it is important to **monitor** your comprehension while you read. Then write what you can do to **clarify** something that you do not understand.

_____
_____
_____
_____
_____
_____
_____

Look again at the story. Were there parts you did not understand? **Write** the questions you asked yourself to better understand the story. **Write** what you did to clarify your understanding.

_____
_____
_____
_____
_____
_____
_____
_____
_____
_____

© Pearson Education, Inc., 2

Name _____

Story Title _____

Author _____

Draw a picture of yourself in a spacecraft. What would you wear? What would you do? **Write** a sentence telling about your clothing or equipment.

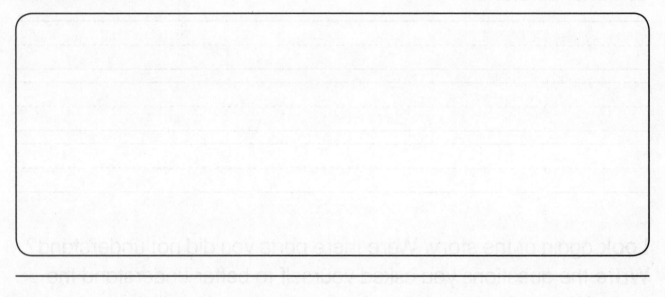

You can use the organization of the **text** to remember or understand what you read.

Write another heading that asks a question about astronauts. Then use the text to **write** an answer.

Heading:

Answer:

© Pearson Education, Inc., 2

Name _____

Story Title _____

Author _____

Circle the sentences that are true about realistic fiction.

It has animals that act like people.

There are characters.

It is story that is supposed to be acted out.

It has a setting.

It is a made-up story that could happen in real life.

Draw pictures to show what happened at the beginning, the middle, and end of the story. Write a short sentence about each picture. Make sure you include the characters and the setting.

© Pearson Education, Inc., 2

Name _____

Story Title _____

Author _____

What do you know about the desert? **Draw** a picture showing what a person should wear for a walk through a hot, dry desert. **Draw** what a person should carry in a backpack, too. **Label** the clothing and things. Then **write** a sentence to describe the desert.

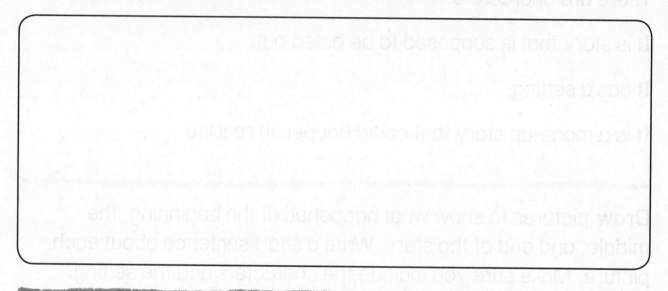

What did you learn about the desert? **Write** two or three facts about the desert. **Draw** pictures.

© Pearson Education, Inc., 2

Name _____

Story Title _____

Author _____

Look at the title and the pictures of the story. **Predict** what will happen in the story. **Set a purpose** for reading. **Write** or **draw.**

[empty box]

Check your predictions. Were your predictions correct? Was your purpose for reading met? **Explain.**

© Pearson Education, Inc., 2

Name _____

Story Title _____

Author _____

Draw a picture that shows a way dogs can help people. Then **write** a sentence about your picture.

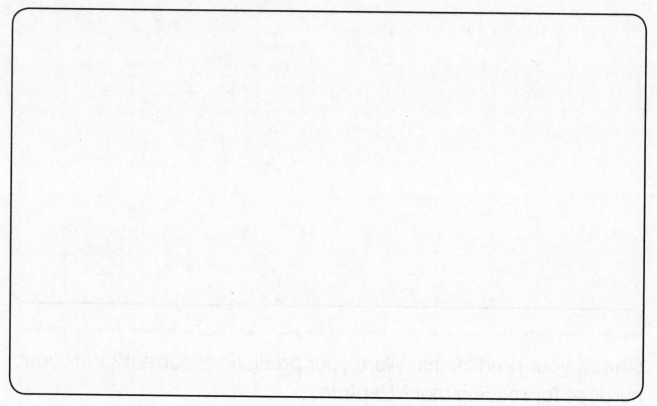

- -

Add to your picture. **Draw** and **write** how Tara and Tiree worked together to rescue Jim. **Summarize.**

- -

- -

© Pearson Education, Inc., 2

Name _____

Story Title _____

Author _____

Circle the sentences that are true about informational text.

It has make-believe characters.

The text informs readers.

It gives facts and details.

It is a made-up story that could happen in real life.

It can be about real places and events.

You can pay attention to how a **text is organized** to better understand what you read.

Look again at this story. **Write** how the text was organized. Did the organization of this story help you to better understand what you read? Explain.

_____
- -
_____
_____
- -
_____

© Pearson Education, Inc., 2

Name _____

Story Title _____

Author _____

Draw a picture of your favorite kind of fruit. **Write** a sentence telling whether you can buy this fruit all year long or only at certain times of the year.

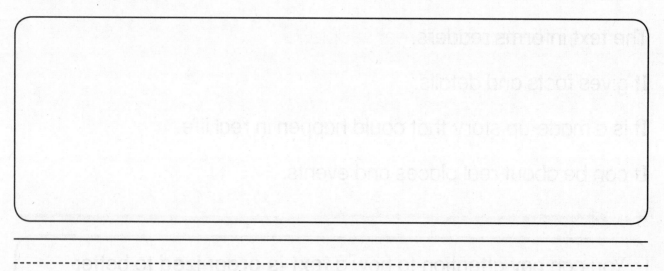

_____
- -
_____

What would you do if you were not able to get your favorite fruit? **Write.**

_____
- -
_____
- -
_____
- -
_____
- -
_____

© Pearson Education, Inc., 2

Name _____

Story Title _____

Author _____

Underline the sentences that are true about drama.

It is supposed to be acted out.

It informs readers about real people.

It has dialogue.

It gives facts and details.

It has characters, setting, and a plot.

It explains how to make something.

―――――――――――――――――――――――――――――――

Write about one feature of drama. Tell how it helped tell the story.

_____

_____

_____

_____

_____

_____

_____

© Pearson Education, Inc., 2

Name _____

Story Title _____

Author _____

Underline the sentences that are true about a folk tale.

The characters are always animals.

It is a story that was told long ago.

It states a moral, or lesson, about life.

It has rhyme.

It often has repeated words.

It tells about an historical event.

> You can use clues in the text and picture clues **to figure out more** than what is stated in the text. This is known as **inferring.**

Think about one of the characters from the story. What can you figure out, or infer, from the character's actions or what the character said? **Write.**

_____
_____
_____
_____
_____
_____
_____

© Pearson Education, Inc., 2

Name _____

Story Title _____

Author _____

> You can **ask questions** about the pictures in a story before reading to better understand what you will read.

Look at the pictures. **Write** any questions you may have before you read.

_____
- -
_____
_____
- -
_____

Now **answer** your questions. Look again at the story if you need help.

_____
- -
_____
_____
- -
_____
_____
- -
_____
_____
- -
_____

© Pearson Education, Inc., 2

Name _____

Story Title _____

Author _____

Look at the title and the pictures of the story. **Predict** what will happen in the story. **Set a purpose** for reading. **Write.**

_____
- -
_____
- -
_____
- -
_____
- -
_____
- -
_____

Check your predictions. Were your predictions correct? Was your purpose for reading met? **Explain.** What surprised you and why? **Write.**

_____
- -
_____
- -
_____
- -
_____
- -
_____
- -
_____
- -

© Pearson Education, Inc., 2

Name _____

Story Title _____

Author _____

Draw pictures of a seed and what might happen if the seed was planted. Write a sentence that tells one way this plant could change over time.

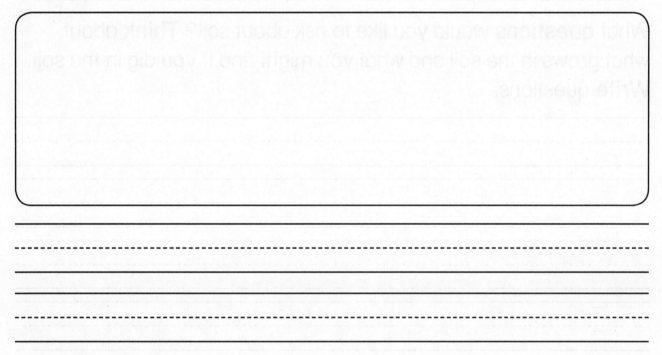

_____

- -

_____

- -

_____

Think about what happens when a pumpkin seed is planted. **Draw** pictures that show the stages in the life cycle of a pumpkin. **Write** a short sentence under each picture telling about the stage.

© Pearson Education, Inc., 2

Name _____

Story Title _____

Author _____

Read the title of the story and **look** at the pictures. Use what you know to **predict** what the story will tell about the American flag. **Write.**

_____
- -
_____
- -
_____
- -
_____

Check your predictions. Were your predictions correct? **Write** a sentence or **draw** a picture that tells about an important fact you learned from the story.

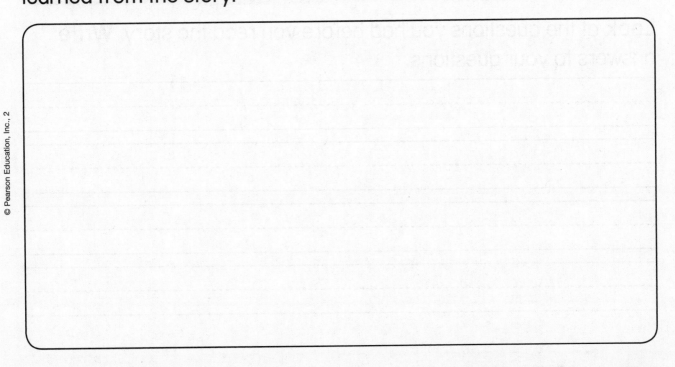

© Pearson Education, Inc., 2

Name _____

Story Title _____

Author _____

Think about the folk tale *One Good Turn Deserves Another*. Then complete the sentences to tell about a folk tale.

_____

A folk tale is a story that was told _____ .

A folk tale often gives a _____ about life.

It often has repeated _____ .

Now compare *Anansi* and *One Good Turn*. **Complete** the chart.

	One Good Turn	Anansi
Characters		
Plots		

© Pearson Education, Inc., 2

Name _____

Story Title _____

Author _____

Look at the title and the pictures of the story. **Predict** what will happen in the story. **Set a purpose** for reading. **Write.**

_____

_____

_____

_____

_____

_____

Check your predictions. **Circle** the predictions that were correct. Was your purpose for reading met? **Explain** why or why not. Was there something in the story that surprised you and why? **Write.**

_____

_____

_____

_____

_____

_____

© Pearson Education, Inc., 2

Name _____

Story Title _____

Author _____

Write two characteristics of a biography.

_____
- -
_____
- -
_____
_____
- -
_____
_____
- -
_____
_____

Look again at the text. Were there parts of the text that were hard to understand? **Write** the questions you asked yourself. Then **write** what you did to clarify your understanding of what you read.

- -
_____
_____
- -
_____
_____
- -
_____
_____
- -
_____
_____
- -
_____

© Pearson Education, Inc., 2

Name _____

Story Title _____

Author _____

Draw a picture that shows what a frog's home might look like.
Write a sentence that tells why this would be a good place for a
frog to live.

_____

- -

_____

- -

_____

Look at the picture you drew of a frog's home. **How** do you think
Frog might change this home in the future? **Add** to your picture to
show the changes Frog might make.

© Pearson Education, Inc., 2

Name _____

Story Title _____

Author _____

Draw pictures of a seed and what might happen if the seed was planted. Write a sentence that tells one way this plant could change over time.

```
┌─────────────────────────────────────────┐
│                                           │
│                                           │
│                                           │
│                                           │
│                                           │
└─────────────────────────────────────────┘
```

_____

- -

_____

_____

- -

_____

Think about what happens when a pumpkin seed is planted. **Draw** pictures that show the stages in the life cycle of a pumpkin. **Write** a short sentence under each picture telling about the stage.

```
┌─────────────────────────────────────────┐
│                                           │
│                                           │
│                                           │
│                                           │
│                                           │
└─────────────────────────────────────────┘
```

© Pearson Education, Inc., 2

Name _____

Story Title _____

Author _____

> You can **ask questions** about what you are going to read to better understand the story.

What **questions** would you like to ask about soil? **Think** about what grows in the soil and what you might find if you dig in the soil. **Write** questions.

_____
_____
_____
_____
_____
_____
_____
_____

Read the questions you had about soil. **Write** an answer to each question that was answered in the story *Soil*.

_____
_____
_____
_____
_____
_____

© Pearson Education, Inc., 2

Name _____

Story Title _____

Author _____

Circle the sentences that are true about a myth.

A myth is a made-up story about something in nature.

A myth is a story that could not happen in real life.

A myth may have characters who are gods or superheroes.

A myth is a story that takes place today.

Look for the characteristics of a myth as you read *The Night the Moon Fell*.

Read the sentences that are characteristics of a myth. **Which** of these characteristics did you find in *The Night the Moon Fell*? **Write** examples of these characteristics from the story.

_____
- -
_____
- -
_____

© Pearson Education, Inc., 2

Name _____

Story Title _____

Author _____

Write the different ways you can **monitor** and **clarify** your understanding of what you read. **Use** these ways as you read *The First Tortilla*.

_____
- -
_____
- -
_____
- -
_____
- -
_____
- -
_____

Read your list of ways you can **monitor** and **clarify** your understanding of what you read. **Write** examples of the ways you used to better understand *The First Tortilla*.

_____
- -
_____
_____
- -
_____
_____
- -
_____
_____
- -

© Pearson Education, Inc., 2

Name _____

Story Title _____

Author _____

Draw a picture of a firefighter working. **Write** a sentence that explains what job the firefighter is doing.

```
┌─────────────────────────────────────────┐
│                                         │
│                                         │
│                                         │
│                                         │
│                                         │
│                                         │
│                                         │
└─────────────────────────────────────────┘
```

_____

- -

_____

Write two or three **facts** you learned about a firefighter's job.

_____

- -

_____

- -

_____

- -

_____

© Pearson Education, Inc., 2

Name _____

Story Title _____

Author _____

Read the title of the story and **look** at the pictures. **Set a purpose** for reading the story. **Write** or **draw.**

```
┌──────────────────────────────────────────────┐
│                                                │
│                                                │
│                                                │
│                                                │
│                                                │
│                                                │
│                                                │
│                                                │
└──────────────────────────────────────────────┘
```

───

```
┌──────────────────────────────────────────────┐
│  When you visualize a story, you form pictures │
│  in your mind based on the details from the    │
│  story.                                        │
└──────────────────────────────────────────────┘
```

Draw a picture of how you **visualize** Carl and his friends playing in the park after 5 P.M.

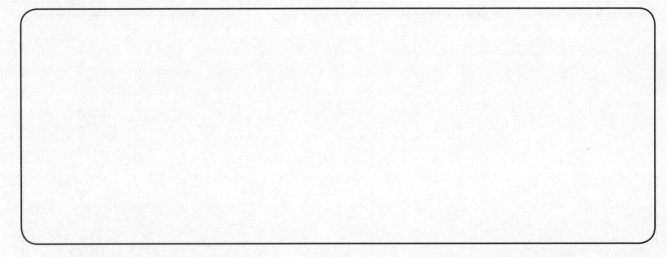

© Pearson Education, Inc., 2

Name _____

Story Title _____

Author _____

Draw two pictures of yourself with a dog. Show a good dog in one picture and a bad dog in the other. **Write** speech balloons showing what you would say to each dog.

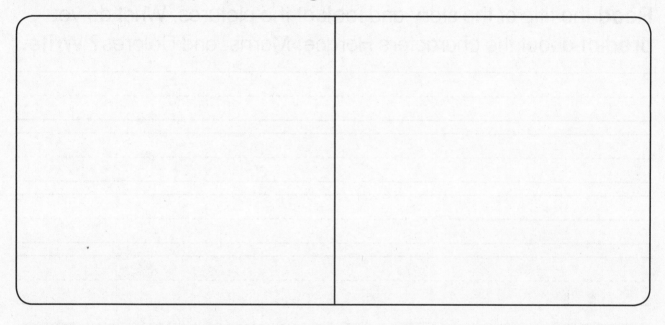

Why do you think Sam's use of treats helped in training Dodger? **Write.**

_____
_____
_____
_____
_____
_____
_____

© Pearson Education, Inc., 2

Name _____

Story Title _____

Author _____

> Before you read a story, you can use what you know to **predict** what the characters in the story might do.

Read the title of the story and **look** at the pictures. What do you **predict** about the characters Horace, Morris, and Dolores? **Write.**

_____
_____
_____
_____
_____
_____
_____
_____
_____

Read what you **predicted** about the characters. Did you predict what really happened? **Write** sentences to **retell** the part of the story that was surprising and why it was surprising.

_____
_____
_____
_____
_____
_____
_____
_____

© Pearson Education, Inc., 2

Name _____

Story Title _____

Author _____

Circle each sentence that is true about humorous fiction.

The characters are never animals.

It has a beginning, a middle, and an end.

Its purpose is to entertain.

It is a made-up story.

Look for the characteristics of humorous fiction as you read *The Signmaker's Assistant*.

Sometimes an author does not tell everything that happens in a story. To figure out more about what happens, you can **infer.** You can use clues in the story and what you already know.

What can you **infer** about Norman? **Write** what you think will become of him in the future.

_____
- -
_____
_____
- -
_____
_____
- -
_____

© Pearson Education, Inc., 2

Name _____

Story Title _____

Author _____

Write why it is important to **monitor** your comprehension while you read. Then **write** what you can do to **clarify** something you do not understand.

_____
_____
_____
_____
_____
_____
_____
_____
_____

Were there parts of the story you did not understand? **Write** a question you asked yourself to better understand the story.

_____
_____
_____
_____
_____

Then **reread** the part of the story that helps you answer the question. **Write** the answer to your question.

_____
_____
_____
_____
_____

© Pearson Education, Inc., 2

Name _____

Story Title _____

Author _____

Read the title of the story and **look** at the pictures. Use what you know to **predict** what the story will tell about the American flag. **Write.**

_____
- -
_____
_____
- -
_____
_____
- -
_____

Check your predictions. Were your predictions correct? **Write** a sentence or **draw** a picture that tells about an important fact you learned from the story.

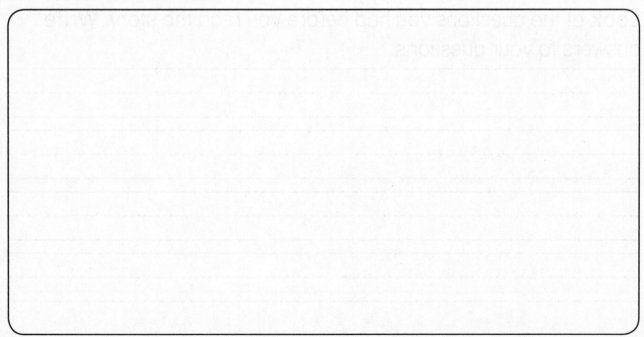

© Pearson Education, Inc., 2

Name _____

Story Title _____

Author _____

> You can **ask questions** about what you are going to read to better understand the story. Then you can look for the answers to your questions as you read.

What **questions** do you have about the story *A Birthday Basket for Tia?* **Write** your questions.

_____
_____
_____
_____
_____
_____
_____

Look at the questions you had before you read the story. **Write** answers to your questions.

_____
_____
_____
_____
_____
_____
_____
_____
_____

© Pearson Education, Inc., 2

Name _____

Story Title _____

Author _____

Circle the correct word to complete each sentence about informational text.

It often tells _____ about real people.   jokes   facts

It often tells about a _____ way of life.   make-believe   true

It often describes events in _____.   history   fantasy

Look for the characteristics of informational text as you read the story.

_____

Think about the characteristics of informational text you might find in the story. **Write** the characteristics you did find.

_____
_____
_____
_____
_____
_____
_____
_____
_____

Were there any characteristics you did not find? If yes, **write** these characteristics.

_____
_____
_____
_____
_____

© Pearson Education, Inc., 2

Name _____

Story Title _____

Author _____

Look at the pictures and **read** the title and topic sentences of the story. Then use these ideas to write your purpose for reading *Grace for President* and to **predict** what will happen in the story.

_____
_____
_____
_____
_____
_____
_____
_____

Check the purpose you set for reading the story and your predictions. Was your purpose met? Were your predictions correct? **Write** to explain.

_____
_____
_____
_____
_____
_____
_____
_____

© Pearson Education, Inc., 2

Name _____

Read Together

Book Talk Tips

- Talk about a book you like.

- Use a loud, clear voice.

- Look at your classmates.

- Don't tell how it ends!

Directions When you talk about a book, answer these questions.

1. What is the title of the book?

2. Who is the author?

3. What kind of book is it?

4. What other book has the author written?

5. Tell what you liked the best.

6. Tell why they should read the book.

© Pearson Education, Inc., 2

Name _____

Read Together

Before You Write

- Think about ideas with a friend.

- Ask questions to help your friend pick a good topic.

When You Revise

- Read your friend's paper out loud. Listen for what you like.

- Tell your friend three things you like. Say: "I like how you ____."

- Read your friend's paper out loud again. Listen for what you do not understand.

- Ask your friend two questions that you have.

It might help to think about the:

- Title

- Beginning

- Ending

- Words that were used

- Use of verbs, nouns, adjectives or adverbs

© Pearson Education, Inc., 2

Name _____

Title of Writing _____

Directions   Answer these questions about what you wrote.

1. What are the two things that are best about this?

_____

_____

_____

_____

2. What is one thing you could have done better?

_____

_____

3. Do you like what you wrote? Why or why not?

_____

_____

_____

_____

© Pearson Education, Inc., 2

Name _____

Title of Writing _____

Directions   Answer these questions about what you wrote.

1. What are the two things that are best about this?

2. What is one thing you could have done better?

3. Do you like what you wrote? Why or why not?

Name _____

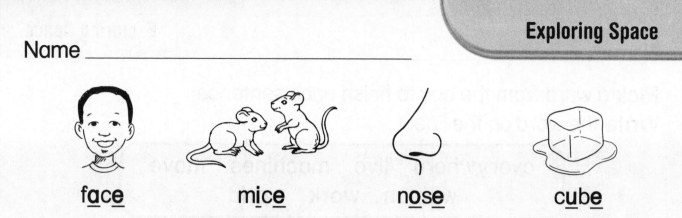

face   mice   nose   cube

Say the word for each picture.
Write a, i, o, or **u** to finish each word.

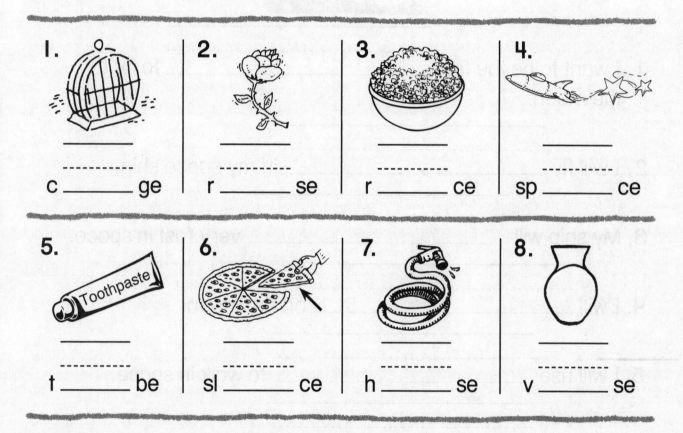

1. c ____ ge

2. r ____ se

3. r ____ ce

4. sp ____ ce

5. t ____ be

6. sl ____ ce

7. h ____ se

8. v ____ se

Find the word that has the same middle sound as the picture.
Mark the space to show your answer.

9. ⬭ cup
   ⬭ cape
   ⬭ cute

10. ⬭ bone
    ⬭ bite
    ⬭ bell

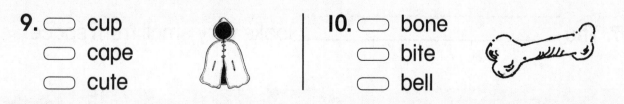

Home Activity Your child wrote words that end with silent *e* and have long vowel sounds in the middle. Give your child practice with words that rhyme with *face, cube, mice,* and *nose.* Take turns writing and reading rhyming words.

© Pearson Education, Inc., 2

Name _____

Pick a word from the box to finish each sentence.
Write the word on the line.

everywhere live machines move
woman work world

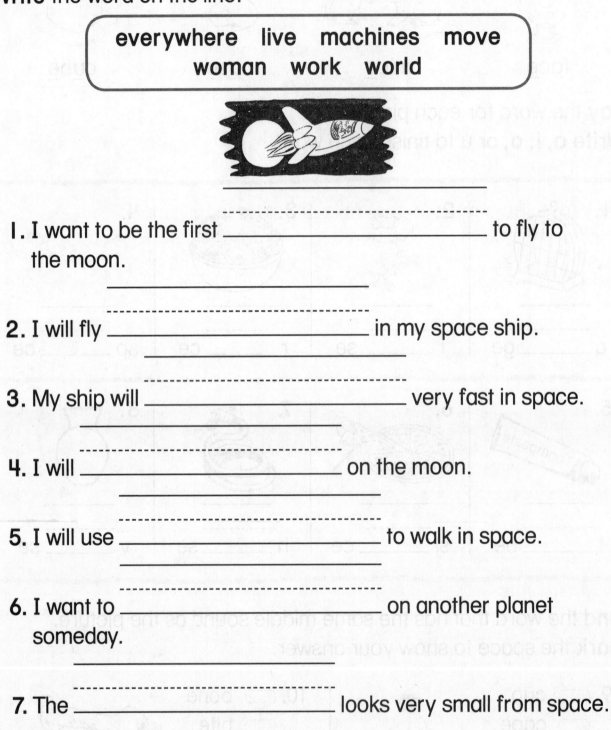

1. I want to be the first _____ to fly to the moon.

2. I will fly _____ in my space ship.

3. My ship will _____ very fast in space.

4. I will _____ on the moon.

5. I will use _____ to walk in space.

6. I want to _____ on another planet someday.

7. The _____ looks very small from space.

© Pearson Education, Inc., 2

Home Activity Your child learned to read the words *everywhere, live, machines, move, woman, work,* and *world*. Select books or magazine articles about working women. Tell your child to look for these words in the selections you read.

Name _____

Read each story. **Follow** the directions.

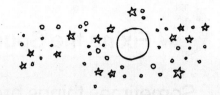

We know a lot about the moon. It orbits Earth. It reflects the light of the sun. It has craters on its surface. Wouldn't it be fun to hop on a ship and go to the moon?

1. Write the sentence that tells the main idea.

_____

- -

_____

2. Write one detail that tells more about the main idea.

_____

- -

_____

We know that Mars is red. We also know there was once water on the planet. Mars is a place we want to learn more about.

3. Write the sentence that tells the main idea.

_____

- -

_____

4. Write one detail that tells more about the main idea.

_____

- -

_____

School + Home **Home Activity** Your child described the main idea and supporting details in two selections. Tell your child about your childhood. Ask your child to tell you the important parts. Together, brainstorm a good title.

© Pearson Education, Inc., 2

Name _____

Fixing the Space Station

Sometimes things break on the space station and astronauts have to fix them. Astronauts need to fix things that break inside the space station. This is tricky. Why? The astronaut and the astronaut's tools float around. Sometimes astronauts must fix things on the outside of the space station. They put on big space suits. They tie their tools to their suits. Then the tools won't float away and get lost in space. They tie themselves to the space station. They don't want to float away either!

Key Features of Expository Nonfiction

• Expository nonfiction gives information about a topic.

• Expository nonfiction tells about real people, places, and events.

• Expository nonfiction uses facts and details.

© Pearson Education, Inc., 2

Name _____

Long Vowels VCe

Spelling Words					
page	nose	space	size	fine	huge
mice	late	race	blaze	vote	rice

Write the list word that makes sense in both phrases.

the human ____
____ against time

ten shirt
____ it to fit

turn the ____
get a ____

1. _____

2. _____

3. _____

coming ____
a ____ news bulletin

paid a ____
looks ____

outer ____
____ for one more

4. _____

5. _____

6. _____

Write a list word that rhymes.

7. note _____

8. slice _____

9. maze _____

10. nice _____

11. rose _____

12. luge _____

© Pearson Education, Inc., 2

Home Activity Your child spelled words that contain long vowels. Ask your child how all the spelling words are alike. (All have a long vowel sound and end with vowel-consonant-e.)

Name _____

Look at the picture.
Pick a word from the box that
tells about the picture.
Write the word on the line.

behind   around   outside   over

1. The boy is _____ the table.

2. You have to walk _____ the table to get to the front.

3. The tree is _____ of the room.

4. The bird is flying _____ the tree.

Read these directions. Draw the objects in the picture.

5. Draw a ball **below** the table.

6. Draw a cat **beside** the chair.

7. Draw a hat **inside** the box.

8. Draw a clock **above** the boy.

Home Activity Your child practiced using position words. Play "Simon Says" with your child. Use the same words on this page in your directions. For example: Simon Says, "Put your hands above your head." Simon Says, "Stand beside the chair."

© Pearson Education, Inc., 2

Name _____

Look at the picture. **Circle** or **write** the answers.

1. What source would you use to find facts about the moon?

2. What source would you use to tell about the moon's phase today?

3. What source would you use to find the meaning of **crater**?

4. List two more topics that would be of interest to you and your classmates.

_____

- -

_____

- -

_____

© Pearson Education, Inc., 2

 Home Activity Your child learned about choosing reference sources. Discuss resources you use when you need information. Ask your child what two resources he or she could use to find out about space exploration.

Name _____

Long Vowels VCe

Read the note Jeff wrote about his pets.
Circle three spelling mistakes. **Write** the words
correctly. Then write the last sentence and
add the missing subject.

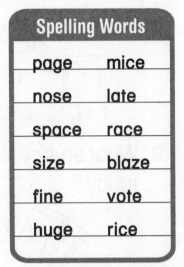

Spelling Words	
page	mice
nose	late
space	race
size	blaze
fine	vote
huge	rice

> Some people do not lik mice, but I do. I have
> two pet mice. One has a black knows. The other
> mouse is huje. Think mice make fine pets.

1. _____   2. _____   3. _____

_____

_____

Frequently Misspelled Words
nice
like
baseball

Circle the word that is spelled correctly. **Write** it.

5. blaze _____
blaiz

6. voat _____
vote

7. raice _____
race

8. page _____
paje

9. ryce _____
rice

10. space _____
spase

© Pearson Education, Inc., 2

Home Activity Your child has been learning to spell words with long vowels. Have your child write a
paragraph using some of the spelling words.

Name _____

Pick a word from the box to match each clue.
Write the words in the puzzle.

astronaut   experiment   everywhere   gravity   live
machines   move   telescope   woman   work   world

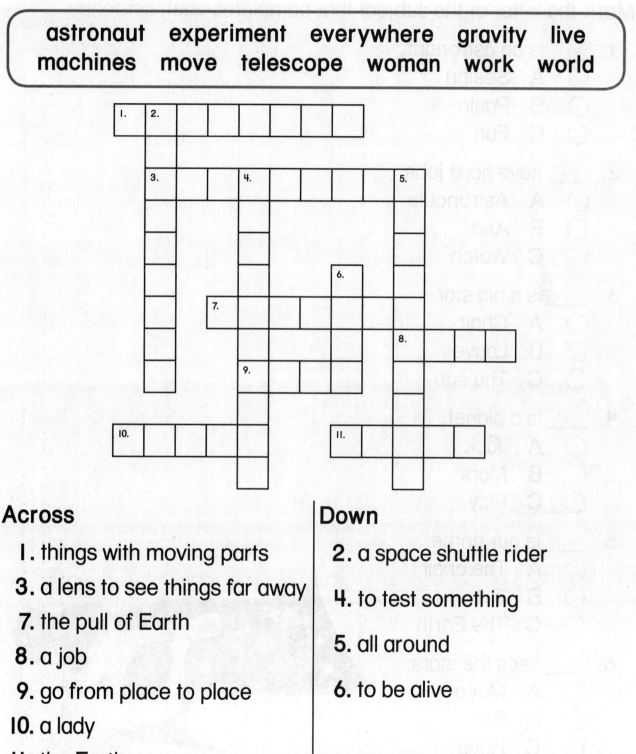

Across

1. things with moving parts

3. a lens to see things far away

7. the pull of Earth

8. a job

9. go from place to place

10. a lady

11. the Earth

Down

2. a space shuttle rider

4. to test something

5. all around

6. to be alive

Home Activity Your child completed a crossword puzzle using high-frequency and selection words learned this week. Find other simple crossword puzzles for your child to do. Or create your own word puzzles using your child's high-frequency and selection words.

© Pearson Education, Inc., 2

Name _____

Subjects

Mark the letter of the subject that completes each sentence.

1. _____ is an astronaut.
   - ○ **A** Seeing
   - ○ **B** Paula
   - ○ **C** Fun

2. _____ have hard jobs.
   - ○ **A** Astronauts
   - ○ **B** And
   - ○ **C** Watch

3. _____ is a big star.
   - ○ **A** Chair
   - ○ **B** Leaves
   - ○ **C** The sun

4. _____ is a planet.
   - ○ **A** Jack
   - ○ **B** Mars
   - ○ **C** Play

5. _____ is our home.
   - ○ **A** The chair
   - ○ **B** Tell
   - ○ **C** The Earth

6. _____ sees the stars.
   - ○ **A** Maya
   - ○ **B** Sit
   - ○ **C** Have

© Pearson Education, Inc., 2

 School + Home **Home Activity** Your child prepared for taking tests on the subjects of sentences. Say simple sentences such as *The moon is full. The sun is hot. The Earth is round.* Then ask your child to tell you the subjects of the sentences.

Name _____

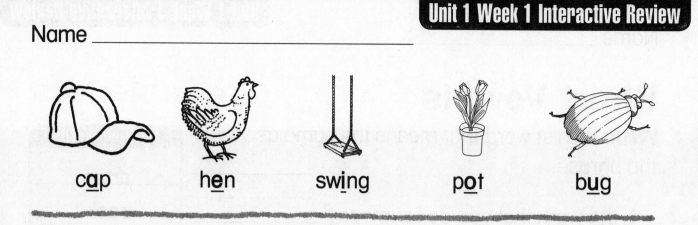

cap　　hen　　swing　　pot　　bug

Look at the first word.
Circle the word that rhymes with the first word.

1. rocket	pocket	packet	right
2. sadness	sudden	stories	gladness
3. sink	sank	rink	ring
4. neck	peck	nick	nest
5. hung	hunk	sung	hang

Read the story.

Nan is a black duck. She can swim in the pond. She had a snack, but the snack sank in the pond. Nan was sad. Ted said, "Do not be sad. I will bring you a snack, and we will have a picnic." Now Nan has a snack again, and she is happy.

© Pearson Education, Inc., 2

School + Home　**Home Activity** Your child read words that have the short vowel sounds in *cap, hen, swing, pot,* and *bug.* Say one of these words. Have your child name words that rhyme with it. Repeat with another word with a different short vowel sound.

Phonics　61

Name _____

Short Vowels

Write the list word that means the same as the phrase.

1. the work that you do for money _____

2. a paper or plastic bag _____

3. a bone that protects your heart _____

4. to cut into small pieces _____

5. unhappy _____

6. a card tied to something _____

7. words, names, or numbers written one below the other _____

Spelling Words
drum
rock
list
desk
job
sad
chop
sack
tag
rib
mess
dust

Read the clues. **Write** the list words. The letters in the boxes will complete the riddle. **Write** the mystery word on the line below.

8. a piece of furniture with a flat top for writing ☐ __ __ __

9. any piece of stone ☐ __ __ __

10. fine, dry, powdery earth ☐ __ __ __

11. a place or group of things that is not clean ☐ __ __ __

Question: What did the _____ say to the trumpet?

Answer: "I'm really beat!"

Mystery Word: _____

School + Home **Home Activity** Your child is learning to spell words with short vowels and these consonant/vowel patterns: CVC, CVCC, CCVC. Have your child write a short story using some of the spelling words.

© Pearson Education, Inc., 2

Name _____

Pick a word from the box to match each clue.
Write the words in the puzzle.

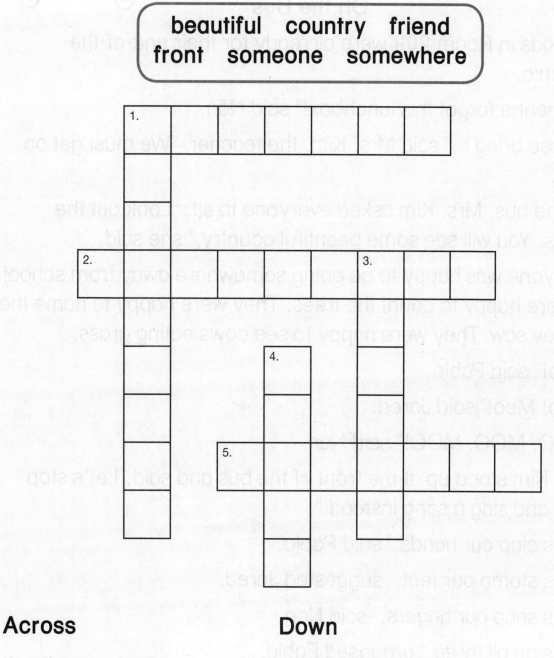

beautiful   country   friend
front   someone   somewhere

Across

1. a human being

2. opposite of **ugly**

5. where farms are

Down

1. an unknown place

3. a buddy

4. opposite of **back**

Home Activity Your child completed a crossword puzzle using high-frequency words learned in this unit. Ask your child to draw a picture to illustrate each word. Have him or her write the word below each drawing.

© Pearson Education, Inc., 2

Name _____

Read the story. **Answer** the questions.

On the Bus

The kids in Room 204 were all ready for their end-of-the-year picnic.

"Someone forgot this lunchbox!" said Nan.

"Please bring it," said Mrs. Kim, the teacher. "We must get on the bus."

On the bus, Mrs. Kim asked everyone to sit. "Look out the windows. You will see some beautiful country," she said.

Everyone was happy to be going somewhere away from school. They were happy to count the trees. They were happy to name the birds they saw. They were happy to see cows eating grass.

"Moo!" said Pablo.

"Moo! Moo!" said Jared.

"MOO, MOO, MOO!" said Nan.

Mrs. Kim stood up at the front of the bus and said, "Let's stop mooing and sing a song instead."

"Let's clap our hands," said Pablo.

"Let's stomp our feet," suggested Jared.

"Let's snap our fingers," said Nan.

"Let's do all three," proposed Pablo.

"Stop!" said Mrs. Kim. "That would be too many things to do at once."

© Pearson Education, Inc., 2

Home Activity Your child identified the setting of a story and some of the characters and what they did. Read a short story with your child. Have your child tell you about the characters and describe where the story takes place.

Name _____

Everyone was quiet. Soon the bus stopped. Mrs. Kim stood and said, "Here we are. The picnic table is over there by the lake."

"It is time to eat," said Pablo. "I do not have my lunchbox!"

"Here it is, my friend," said Nan.

"Thanks," said Pablo. "I will share my apple with you."

"You can have some of my rice cakes," said Nan.

It was the best picnic ever. On the way back to school no one mooed. Everyone napped. Mrs. Kim smiled. She was happy too.

1. Where does most of this story take place?

_____

_____

2. Who is Mrs. Kim?

_____

_____

3. What do you think Pablo is like? Circle the answer below.
   He is sad and cries a lot.
   He is happy and likes to have fun.
   He is very quiet and doesn't talk much.

4. Which two characters seem to be good friends?

_____

_____

5. What happens in the story that tells you they are friends?

_____

_____

© Pearson Education, Inc., 2

Sentences

Find the sentence. **Underline** the sentence.

1. In the small town.
   We went to the fair in the small town.

2. They like to run together.
   like to run together.

3. The boys will always be friends.
   The boys.

4. Lives on a farm.
   Juan Ramón lives on a farm.

5. Walk around their.
   The boys walk around their neighborhoods.

Write each sentence on the line.
Begin and **end** the sentence correctly.

6. summer was almost over

   _____
   -
   _____

7. the boys write to each other

   _____
   -
   _____

8. they changed the club name

   _____
   -
   _____

© Pearson Education, Inc., 2

Name _____

Day 1 Unit 1 Week 1   **The Twin Club**

Copy the sentences. Make sure you use the proper size when writing tall and small letters.

Don and Ann drag a rock.

_____
- -
_____

Dan has red socks.

_____
- -
_____

Day 2 Unit 1 Week 2   **Exploring Space**

Copy the sentences. Make sure you form the letters correctly.

Gus and I are cousins.

_____
- -
_____

Cal gave his dog a bone.

_____
- -
_____

Home Activity: Your child practiced writing the letters *Aa, Dd, Oo, Gg, Cc, Ee, Ss, Ff, Bb, Ll, Tt, Hh,* and *Kk.* Have your child look in his or her favorite book and copy two sentences using his/her best handwriting. After writing the sentences, have your child circle any of the letters from the list above.

© Pearson Education, Inc., 2

Name _____

Day 3 Unit 1 Week 3   **Henry and Mudge**

Copy the sentences. Make sure your letters are all straight.

She lives on Essex Street.

_____

- -

_____

Day 4 Unit 1 Week 4   **A Walk in the Desert**

Copy the sentences. Check the spacing of the letters in each word.

Fran likes baking.

_____

- -

_____

Dad and Bill like fishing.

_____

- -

_____

Day 5 Unit 1 Week 5   **The Strongest One**

Copy the sentences. Make sure you use
proper spacing between the words in each sentence.

Tom has an itch.

_____

- -

_____

Karl can see that shark.

_____

- -

_____

© Pearson Education, Inc., 2

Name _____

lace   page   slice   hose   cube

Pick a word to match each clue. **Circle** the word.

1. You can ride it.

    bake   bike

2. You put it in food.

    spice   space

3. You ask friends to come.

    invite   instead

4. It is a flower.

    rise   rose

5. It helps men walk.

    cane   cone

6. You can wear it.

    cape   cage

7. You can swim in it.

    like   lake

8. It means "put back."

    replace   ready

Read the story.

  Tony is in Jane's class. His desk is next to her desk. Yesterday, Jane had to lend Tony a pen and paper. Later, they rode home together. Today, Jane will put on her cape and ride her bike to school. Jane will take her lunch in the basket on her bike. She will invite Tony to ride with her. They will not be lonely.

Home Activity Your child identified words that end with silent e and have long vowel sounds in the middle of a syllable. Point to words that your child circled. Ask your child to read each word aloud and use the word in a sentence.

© Pearson Education, Inc., 2

Name _____

Long Vowels VCe

Spelling Words					
huge	mice	page	late	nose	race
space	blaze	size	rice	fine	vote

Find the list words. Look across and down. **Circle** the words.

```
f   r   w   s   p   a   r   e   e   g
n   b   v   i   s   p   a   c   e   r
b   l   a   z   e   r   c   r   p   i
q   a   j   e   k   x   e   m   l   c
z   h   u   g   e   e   p   a   g   e
l   e   n   d   y   p   o   y   f   t
a   v   o   t   e   l   h   e   i   i
t   k   s   c   i   k   j   a   n   l
e   x   e   r   l   m   i   c   e   s
```

Write the list words when you find them in the puzzle.

1. _____   2. _____   3. _____

4. _____   5. _____   6. _____

7. _____   8. _____   9. _____

10. _____   11. _____   12. _____

Home Activity Your child has been learning to spell words with long vowels. Give clues about a word from the word list. Have your child guess and spell the word.

© Pearson Education, Inc. 2

Name _____

Pick a word from the box to finish each sentence.
Write the word on the line.

> everywhere   live   machines
> move   woman   work   world

_____
----

1. A _____ who works at a wildlife park
   spoke to our class.

2. Wildlife parks have animals from all
   _____
   over the _____.

3. The park has room for the animals to
   _____
   _____ about.

4. The animals live outside, and you can see them
   _____
   _____
   _____.

5. I would like to be a vet and _____
   in a wildlife park.

6. Different _____ help a vet find
   out why an animal is sick.

7. With good health care, animals will _____ longer.

School + Home **Home Activity** Your child learned to read the words *everywhere, live, machines, move, woman, work,* and *world*. Select books or magazines about animal parks. Ask your child to look for these words in the selections you read.

© Pearson Education, Inc., 2

High-Frequency Words 71

Name _____

Read the story.
Follow the directions.

Brr! It's Cold!

It is a big animal. It has black skin you cannot see, but you can see its white fur. Sometimes its fur looks yellow. Its legs are big and fat. This huge animal lives near the top of the world. It lives in or near the North Pole. Brr! It is cold up there. But ice is nice for this animal. Do you know what animal it is? It is the polar bear.

A polar bear has 42 teeth. It needs them to eat its food. Sniff, sniff. It can smell dinner. It is time to dive and swim. It is time to hunt for food. It may be a fish. It may be a whale! Those 42 teeth are sharp and can easily cut up a meal.

The polar bear moves its food to the ice. It naps on the ice. It keeps its cubs warm on the ice. It is good that ice is everywhere!

There is trouble going on in the world of the polar bear. The sun is very hot. The sun melts the ice. Sometimes the bear is on a sheet of ice, but the ice is too small. Some of it has melted. The bear cannot nap on this ice. It cannot feed on this ice. It cannot care for its cubs on this ice. What will happen to the polar bear?

© Pearson Education, Inc., 2

Home Activity Your child identified the main idea and details in some paragraphs. Read a story with your child and pause after an interesting paragraph. Ask your child to tell you the main idea. Then help your child list some details that support the main idea.

Name _____

    Some people want to help the polar bears. They want to work to keep them safe. We want the polar bears to be safe so they can live on and on.

_____

1. Look at the second paragraph. Underline the sentence that tells the main idea.

2. Look at the second paragraph again. List three details that tell about the main idea.

_____
_____
_____
_____
_____
_____

3. Look at the fourth paragraph. Underline the sentence that tells the main idea.

4. Look at the fourth paragraph again. List two details that tell about the main idea.

_____
_____
_____
_____
_____
_____

© Pearson Education, Inc., 2

Name _____

Subjects

Underline the subject in each sentence.

1. Astronauts go into space.

2. Six people are on the space shuttle.

3. Earth is a planet.

Write a subject to complete each sentence.
Use a subject from the box.

> **Many stars**   **Saturn**   **Space shuttles**

4. _____ go very fast.

5. _____ has rings around it.

6. _____ twinkle at night.

© Pearson Education, Inc., 2

Name _____

Say the word for each picture.
Write the letters from the box to finish each word.

| bl | sl | nt | spr | nd | sk | st | str | fr | spl |

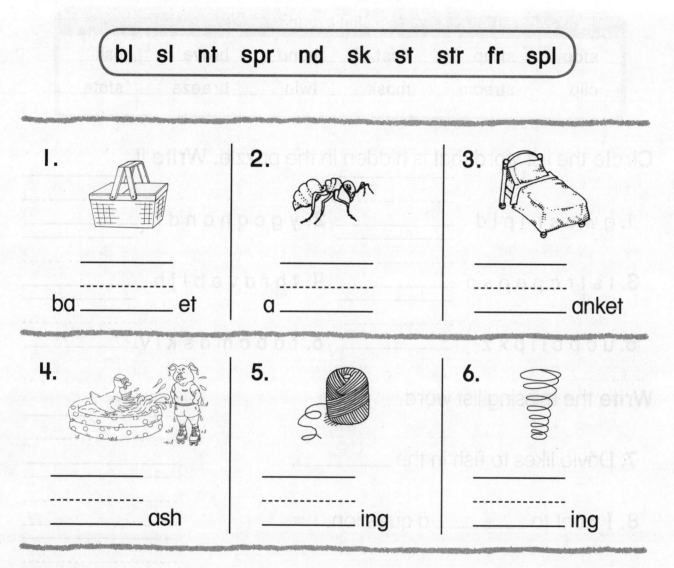

1. ba _____ et

2. a _____

3. _____ anket

4. _____ ash

5. _____ ing

6. _____ ing

Read the story.

Blanca is so strong she can split logs with an ax. She is also fast. She can sprint faster than any other kids in her class. This spring, her class will plant a tree. Then the kids will run in a race. Blanca will not finish last. After the race, the kids in her class will play games.

Home Activity Your child wrote words that started or ended with consonant blends, such as _stop, hand,_ and _strap._ Ask your child to circle words in the story with these blends.

Phonics   75

© Pearson Education, Inc., 2

Name _____

Consonant Blends

Spelling Words					
stop	strap	nest	hand	brave	ask
clip	stream	mask	twin	breeze	state

Circle the list word that is hidden in the puzzle. **Write** it.

1. g w o s t o p l d _____

2. y g c q h a n d f _____

3. t s t r a p e o s c _____

4. t b r a v e b l j h _____

5. u c p c l i p x z _____

6. r d b c m a s k l v _____

Write the missing list word.

_____

7. David likes to fish in the _____.

_____

8. I want to _____ a question.

_____

9. Lucy is my _____. We look the same.

_____

10. It is not hot today. There is a cool _____.

_____

11. There are three birds in the _____.

_____

12. My cousin lives far away in another _____.

 School + Home **Home Activity** Your child has been learning to spell words with consonant blends. To practice at home, divide a sheet of paper into two columns. Write a list word in one column and say the word with your child. Then cover the word and have your child write the word in the second column.

© Pearson Education, Inc., 2

Name _____

Pick a word from the box to match each clue.
Write the letters of each word in the puzzle.

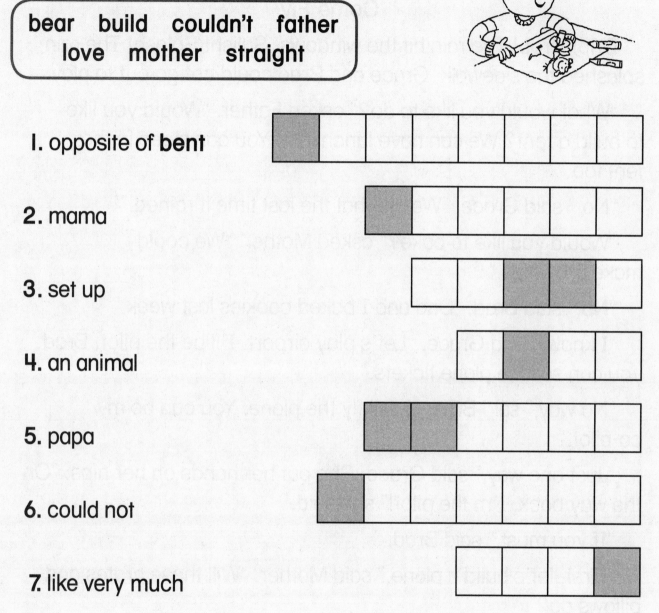

bear   build   couldn't   father
love   mother   straight

1. opposite of **bent**

2. mama

3. set up

4. an animal

5. papa

6. could not

7. like very much

Read the letters in the gray squares to find two hidden words.

Hidden Words: _____

Home Activity Your child is learning to read the words *bear, build, couldn't, father, love, mother,* and *straight*. Point to each word. Ask your child to read the word aloud and use it in a sentence.

© Pearson Education, Inc., 2

Name _____

Read the story. **Answer** the questions.

Come Fly

Drip! Drop! The rain hit the windows. Splish! Splash! The rain splashed the sidewalk. Grace and Brad could not go out to play.

"What would you like to do?" asked Father. "Would you like to build a tent? We can have lunch in it. You can sleep in the tent too."

"No," said Grace. "We did that the last time it rained."

"Would you like to bake?" asked Mother. "We could make brownies."

"No," said Brad. "Dad and I baked cookies last week."

"I know," said Grace. "Let's play airport. I'll be the pilot. Brad, you can sell the plane tickets."

"No way," said Brad. "I will fly the plane. You can be my co-pilot."

"Just one way," said Grace. She put her hands on her hips. "On the way back, I'm the pilot!" she said.

"If you must," said Brad.

"First, let's build a plane," said Mother. "Will these crates and pillows do?"

The family got busy building the plane. "Make sure the crates line up straight," said Mother.

They all helped build the plane. Then Grace said, "We have the plane. We have the pilot and co-pilot, but we have no riders."

© Pearson Education, Inc., 2

Home Activity Your child identified and described the characters and setting of a story. Read a short story with your child. Have your child identify the characters and setting and tell something about them.

Mother looked at Father. Father winked at Mother. "I guess you have two riders," said Mother. "Here are our tickets."

"Fasten your seatbelts," said Brad.

"Ay, ay, Captain," said Grace.

1. Who are the characters in this story? Write their names below.

_____

_____

_____

2. What is the setting of the story?

_____

_____

_____

3. How did Mother and Father help Brad and Grace?

_____

_____

_____

4. How do you think Mother, Father, Grace, and Brad feel at the end of the story?

_____

_____

_____

© Pearson Education, Inc., 2

Name _____

Predicates

Write the predicate of each sentence.

1. Henry and Mudge hear something.

_____

_____

2. Henry looks outside.

_____

_____

3. A big bear walks by.

_____

_____

4. The bear sees Henry.

_____

_____

5. Mudge barks.

_____

_____

6. The bear runs away.

_____

_____

© Pearson Education, Inc., 2

Name _____

Read each word. **Find** the base word.
Write the base word on the line.

1. helps _____

2. stacked _____

3. dusting _____

4. stopped _____

5. fixed _____

6. dropped _____

7. smiling _____

8. gives _____

Read the story.

Lola likes to toss balls at the basket. Phillip likes to tell her how to get them into the basket. A few days ago, Lola was jumping to get the ball into the basket. Phillip jumped even higher, but he did not get the ball into the basket. Lola did. Now she can do it better than Phillip. Phillip asked her to help him, and Lola said yes. Now she helps him all the time.

© Pearson Education, Inc., 2

Home Activity Your child wrote words that ended with -s, -ed, or -ing, such as *kicks, stacked, hopping,* and *riding.* Ask your child to reread the story and circle the words that end with -s, -ed, and -ing.

Name _____

Inflected Endings

Spelling Words					
talked	talking	dropped	dropping	excited	exciting
lifted	lifting	hugged	hugging	smiled	smiling

Write the list word that completes each sentence.

1. I am _____ the heavy box.

2. The happy baby _____ when he saw the toy.

3. The movie was very _____ !

4. Please stop _____. It is time to go to sleep.

5. The monkey at the zoo _____ its baby close.

6. Oh no! I _____ my glass of milk!

Circle the list word that completes each sentence.

7. Paul was **excited exciting** about the class field trip.

8. I am **smiled smiling** because I got a good grade on my test.

9. We **talked talking** about starting a baseball team.

10. The squirrel is **dropping dropped** nuts from the tree.

11. Maria is **hugged hugging** her grandmother.

12. My sister **lifted lifting** the box of toys and put it on the shelf.

Home Activity Your child has been learning to spell words with -ed and -ing. To practice at home, name a base word and have your child explain how to add the ending.

© Pearson Education, Inc., 2

Name _____

Pick a word from the box to answer each question.
Write the word on the line.

> animals   early   eyes
> full   warm   water

1. Where do sharks live?

_____
_____

2. What are turtles and snails?

_____
_____

3. What does the sun feel like
   on your skin?

_____
_____

4. If you get to school before
   the bell rings,
   what are you?

_____
_____

5. What do you call a glass of
   milk filled to
   the top?

_____
_____

6. Which part of your head has lids?

_____

Home Activity Your child learned the words *animals, early, eyes, full, warm,* and *water* and used them to answer questions. Take turns with your child making up other questions that have these words as answers.

© Pearson Education, Inc., 2

High-Frequency Words   83

Name _____

Read the story. **Follow** the directions.

Saving the Turtles

One warm day, a big leatherback turtle swims ashore. It lays its eggs in the sand. There may be 60 to 100 eggs. Only some of these eggs will hatch. The turtles that hatch can be seen crawling to the sea and swimming away. They will swim very far. They may swim across an ocean. They may stay in the water until they are ready to lay eggs, as their mothers did.

The leatherback is the largest sea turtle. Its shell is not like other turtles. Its back is rough, like leather.

The leatherback turtle is in danger. There are many reasons why. One reason is because this turtle eats jellyfish. It may see a plastic bag in the water and think it is a jellyfish. When it eats the bag, the turtle dies. Here are some other reasons these animals are in danger. Many people like to eat turtle eggs. The turtles get caught in fishing nets. People build homes on the shores and the turtles lose their nesting places.

© Pearson Education, Inc., 2

School + Home

Home Activity Your child identified the main idea and details of a paragraph. Read another story together. Then have your child tell you the main idea of one of the last paragraphs. Then have your child tell details about the main idea.

In one country, a group of people wanted to help the turtles. Now people there get paid to watch over the turtles' eggs. They get paid to keep hunters away. These helpers earn money, and the turtles stay safe. The group's plan has worked well.

1. Look at the third paragraph. Underline the main idea.

2. Look at the third paragraph again. List three details that tell about the main idea.

_____

- -

_____

- -

_____

- -

_____

3. Look at the fourth paragraph. Underline the main idea.

4. Look at the fourth paragraph again. List two details that tell about the main idea.

_____

- -

_____

- -

_____

© Pearson Education, Inc., 2

Declarative and Interrogative Sentences

Put a **period** at the end if the sentence is a statement.
Put a **question mark** at the end if the sentence is a question.

1. Do plants grow in the desert _____

2. The saguaro has red fruit _____

3. What did the coyote do _____

4. Woodpeckers can live in the desert _____

Write each sentence correctly.

5. a cactus stores water

   _____

   -

   _____

6. which cactus is tall

   _____

   -

   _____

7. do lizards like the sun

   _____

   -

   _____

8. the tortoise has a shell

   _____

   -

   _____

© Pearson Education, Inc., 2

Name _____

Say the first word for each picture.
Write the letters from the box to finish each word.

ch   sh   th   wh   tch

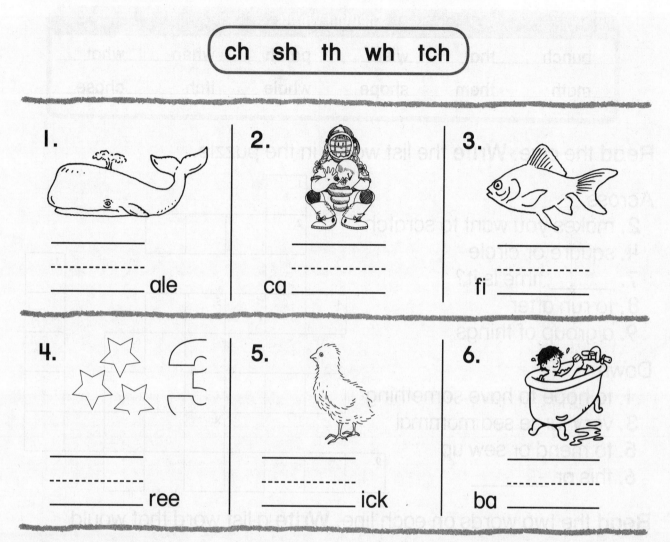

1. _____ ale

2. ca _____

3. fi _____

4. _____ ree

5. _____ ick

6. ba _____

Read the story.

Chen chatted with his pal Chad in the shade. "I wish I could pitch as well as you," he said. Chad was a fine pitcher. Chad said, "Let us practice. When you throw the ball, I will catch it." Chen threw the ball to the left, and it went into the brush. A chipmunk ran out of the brush. "You will throw better next time," said Chad. Chen did throw the ball well the next time and each time after that.

School + Home **Home Activity** Your child wrote words that begin or end with the consonant digraphs *ch, tch, sh, th,* and *wh.* Ask your child to circle words in the story with these digraphs. Work with your child to write a new story using some of these words.

© Pearson Education, Inc., 2

Name _____

Consonant Digraphs

Spelling Words					
bunch	that	wish	patch	when	what
math	them	shape	whale	itch	chase

Read the clue. **Write** the list words in the puzzle.

Across
2. makes you want to scratch
4. square or circle
7. _____ time is it?
8. to run after
9. a group of things

Down
1. to hope to have something
3. very large sea mammal
5. to mend or sew up
6. this or _____

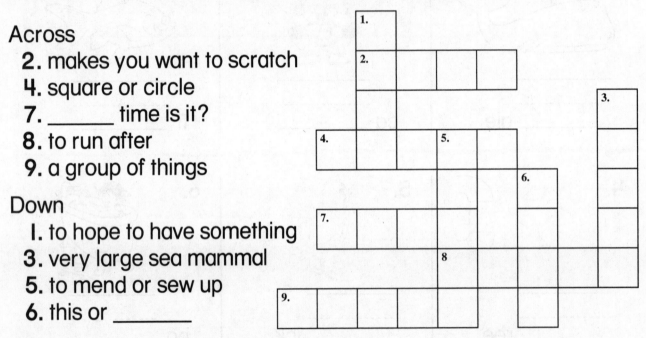

Read the two words on each line. **Write** a list word that would come between them in a dictionary.

10. van _____ yellow

11. rock _____ under

12. lamp _____ park

math
when
them

Home Activity Your child has been learning to spell words with *ch*, *tch*, *sh*, *th*, and *wh*. Look at a magazine or newspaper with your child. Have your child point to words with these letter combinations. Say them with your child.

© Pearson Education, Inc., 2

Name _____

Pick a word from the box to complete each sentence.
Write the word on the line.

> gone   learn   often   pieces
> though   together   very

1. My tooth was missing. It was _____.

2. In the summer, it is hot. Some days, it is
   _____
   _____ hot.

3. I like to walk in the rain. I go walking even
   _____
   _____ it's raining.

4. I will study hard. I want to _____.

5. My friends and I are a team. We work _____.

6. In the summer, I water my garden many times because it
   _____
   doesn't rain _____.

7. I will tear the paper into bits. I'll tear it into little
   _____
   _____.

Home Activity Your child completed sentences using the words *gone, learn, often, pieces, though, together,* and *very*. Gather a selection of favorite books. Have your child look for these words in the books as you read together.

© Pearson Education, Inc., 2

Name _____

Read the play.
Answer the questions.

Let's Go Shopping

Characters: Mrs. Goose   Mr. Toad, a sales clerk   Mrs. Hen
Setting: The mall

Mrs. Goose: I need a new skirt. What can you show me?

Mr. Toad: Try this red one with the blue stripes.
It will match your red shoes.

Mrs. Goose: No thanks. I shall keep looking.

Mr. Toad: Then how about this white skirt?
Feel this piece of cloth. It is very smooth.
Just touch it. It is so soft. It is the last white skirt
in the store.

Mrs. Goose: No, I think I want something green.

Mr. Toad: I have nothing green, but I have a blue shirt.
It goes well with the white skirt.

Mrs. Goose: I do not want a blue shirt or a white skirt with red
shoes. I will look like a flag! I must keep looking.

Mr. Toad: I am going to help Mrs. Hen then.

Mrs. Goose: Sure. Okay.

Mrs. Hen: What a nice piece of cloth this is. I think I will buy
this white skirt. I will buy that blue shirt, too.
You so often have just what I am looking for.

© Pearson Education, Inc., 2

Home Activity Your child reviewed finding facts and details in a play. Research information about one or
more of the animals (goose, hen, toad). List some of the facts and details with your child.

Name _____

Mr. Toad:	So glad, so glad! I will put both together. Then I will put them in a shopping bag.
Mrs. Goose:	Mr. Toad, I changed my mind. I want that white skirt.
Mr. Toad:	Sorry, I just sold it. It is gone. Mrs. Hen thought it was a very good buy.
Mrs. Goose:	Oh, maybe I can buy it from her. Mrs. Hen! Mrs. Hen!
Mr. Toad:	Will she ever learn?

1. Circle the words in the play that name things people wear.

2. How are red, white, blue, and green alike?

_____

- -

_____

3. How are Mrs. Goose and Mrs. Hen alike?

_____

- -

_____

- -

_____

4. Look at the names of all the characters. How are they alike?

_____

_____

_____

© Pearson Education, Inc., 2

Name _____

Imperative and Exclamatory Sentences

Write *C* if the sentence is a command.
Write *E* if it is an exclamation.

1. Come with me.

----

2. I am so excited!

----

3. Wait here.

Write each sentence correctly.

4. watch the ant

_____

- - - - - - - - - - - - - - - - - - - -

_____

5. that is amazing

_____

- - - - - - - - - - - - - - - - - - - -

_____

6. he is the strongest ant of all

_____

- - - - - - - - - - - - - - - - - - - -

_____

© Pearson Education, Inc., 2

Name _____

Story Chart

Fill out this story chart to help you organize your ideas. **Write** your ideas in sentences.

Title _____

Beginning

↓

Middle

↓

End

© Pearson Education, Inc., 2

Name _____

Use Words That Tell How You Feel

Write a word from the box to tell how the writer feels.

nervous	mad	scared	excited

1. I am _____ .

   _____ .

   I am getting a new puppy.

2. José is _____ .

   _____ .

   Tim took his favorite toy car.

3. The boys are _____ .

   _____ .

   They heard a strange sound.

4. Jackie feels _____ .

   _____ .

   She is trying out for the play.

© Pearson Education, Inc., 2

Name _____

Adding Words, Phrases, or Sentences

When you revise, add words, phrases, and sentences to give more details and to make your writing more vivid.

Follow the directions to revise the sentence.

This park has trees.

1. Add the word **huge** to describe the park. Write the new sentence.

   _____
   _____
   _____
   _____

2. Add the phrase **many kinds of** to describe the trees. Write the new sentence.

   _____
   _____
   _____
   _____

3. Show how the narrator feels about the park. Add the sentence **I like to hike here.** Write both sentences.

   _____
   _____
   _____
   _____

© Pearson Education, Inc., 2

Name _____

Self-Evaluation Guide

Check **Yes** or **No** about voice in your story.

	Yes	No
1. I used words that tell how I feel.		
2. I used one or more words that describe.		
3. I used one or more words that show action.		

Answer the questions.

4. What is the best part of your story?

_____

_____

_____

_____

_____

_____

5. What is one thing you would change about this story if you could write it again?

_____

_____

_____

_____

_____

_____

© Pearson Education, Inc., 2

Name _____

arm   horn   core   oar

Pick a word from the box to match each picture.
Write the word on the line.

artist   bark   garden   roar   score
short   start   store   stork   storm

1.

2.

3.

4.

5.

6.

7.

8.

Pick a word that is the opposite of each word below.
Write the word on the line.

9. stop _____

10. tall _____

School + Home **Home Activity** Your child wrote words that contain the vowel sounds in *arm*, *horn*, *core*, and *oar*. Ask your child to name words that rhyme with *arm*, *horn*, *core*, or *oar*. Write the words your child names. Ask your child to read the list of words.

© Pearson Education, Inc., 2

Name _____

Pick a word from the box to match each clue. **Write** the letters of the word in each puzzle. **Read** the circled letters to find two hidden words.

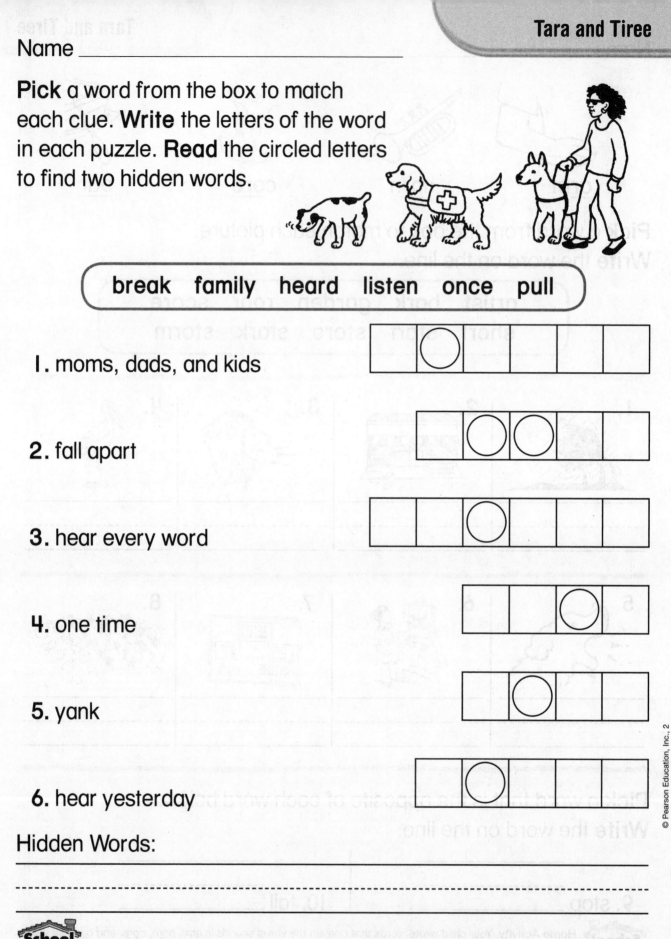

break	family	heard	listen	once	pull

1. moms, dads, and kids

2. fall apart

3. hear every word

4. one time

5. yank

6. hear yesterday

Hidden Words: _____

© Pearson Education, Inc., 2

School + Home **Home Activity** Your child is learning to read the words *break, family, heard, listen, once,* and *pull.* Point to each word. Have your child read the word and use it in a sentence.

Name _____

Read the story. **Answer** the questions.

Koalas

Koalas are mammals that live in forests in Australia. It is not correct to call them koala bears because they are not bears. They do have soft thick fur and ears with long white hairs on the tips. Koalas sleep during the day and eat at night. Koalas eat leaves and bark from different trees, but eucalyptus leaves are their favorite. Because koalas eat so many eucalyptus leaves, they often smell like certain kinds of cough drops. Female koalas have a pouch where a baby koala lives. A baby koala is called a joey.

I. What is the subject of this story?

_____

_____

2. What causes koalas to smell like cough drops?

_____

_____

_____

_____

3. Why do koalas eat at night?

_____

_____

© Pearson Education, Inc., 2

Home Activity Your child identified causes and effects in a nonfiction story. Look for another nonfiction story about animals. Read a section of the story together. Help your child find a cause (reason for something happening) and an effect (the result of a cause).

Comprehension Cause and Effect **99**

Writing • Narrative Nonfiction

 Marta to the Rescue

Marta is a lifeguard at the beach. Most of the time, things are quiet. However, last week, Marta's friend, Jack, swam too far out. The tide was strong, and he couldn't swim back.

Marta spotted him and jumped in the ocean. Soon she was pulling Jack in. Then they were back on the beach.

Jack felt a little shaky. But he was fine. He was also very grateful. Marta did a wonderful thing when she saved Jack's life!

Key Features of Narrative Nonfiction

• It tells about real people and events.

• It usually tells events in the order they happened.

© Pearson Education, Inc., 2

Name _____

Vowels: *r*-Controlled, *ar, or, ore*

© Pearson Education, Inc., 2

Spelling Words

part	hard	born	horse	before	more
smart	farm	porch	corn	chore	score

Add a list word to each group.

1. beans, peas, _____

2. city, town, _____

3. bright, clever, _____

4. pig, cow, _____

5. firm, solid, _____

6. door, roof, _____

7. piece, portion, _____

8. job, task, _____

Write the list word to finish each sentence.

9. I put on my socks _____ my shoes.

10. The _____ was 21 to 14.

11. The kittens were _____ last week.

12. May I have _____ pizza?

School + Home **Home Activity** Your child wrote words with *ar, or,* and *ore.* Take turns with your child spelling the words and using them in sentences.

Name _____

Read the sentence.
Write the letter of the correct meaning on the line.
Use other words in the sentence to help.

1. The window was <u>ajar</u>, so the rain came into the house. _____

   a. closed tight   b. a little opened   c. a little wet

2. The <u>shrill</u> sound of the siren hurt our ears. _____

   a. loud and piercing   b. soft and silent   c. long and thin

3. It was a <u>boring</u> day because we had nothing to do. _____

   a. dull   b. exciting   c. surprising

Read the sentence. **Write** the meaning of the underlined word.
Use other words in the sentence to help.

4. Because he wasn't looking where he was going, Ben <u>collided</u>
   with the tree.

   _____

   _____

5. When you are asked a question you should <u>respond</u>.

   _____

   _____

School + Home **Home Activity** Your child used context clues to figure out the meaning of unfamiliar words. Read some sentences from a book your child enjoys. Replace a word in a sentence with a nonsense word. See if your child can guess what your nonsense word means.

© Pearson Education, Inc., 2

Name _____

Nouns

A **common noun** names a person, place, animal, or thing.

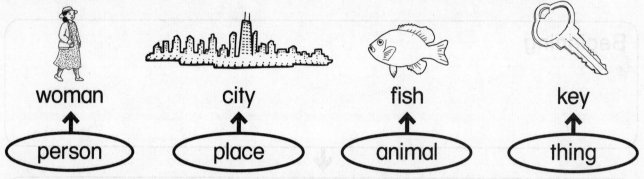

| woman | city | fish | key |
| person | place | animal | thing |

Write the noun in each sentence. **Say** a sentence with the noun.

1. The man fell down. _____

2. The ice cracked. _____

3. The dog barked. _____

Write the two nouns in each sentence.

4. The cat is in a tree.

_____ _____

5. The boy gets a ladder.

_____ _____

Home Activity Your child learned about nouns. Take a walk with your child. Point to people, places, animals, and things without naming them. Have your child tell you each noun.

© Pearson Education, Inc., 2

Name _____

Story Chart

Title _____

┌─────────────────────────────────────┐
│ **Beginning**   │
│   │
│   │
└─────────────────────────────────────┘
                    ↓
┌─────────────────────────────────────┐
│ **Middle**   │
│   │
│   │
│   │
└─────────────────────────────────────┘
                    ↓
┌─────────────────────────────────────┐
│ **End of Story**   │
│   │
│   │
│   │
└─────────────────────────────────────┘

Home Activity Your child is learning to write stories, poems, brief reports, nonfiction paragraphs, letters, and other products this year. Ask what your child is writing this week.

© Pearson Education, Inc., 2

Name _____

Read this important announcement.

Fire Drills

Fire drills can happen at any time. Follow these rules to stay safe. Stop what you are doing. Even if you are doing math or spelling, you must stop. Find your partner if you have one. Leave your classroom. Walk calmly and quietly down the hall. You must never run. Meet the rest of your class in the special meeting place. When your teacher announces "all clear," you may return to your classroom.

FIRE
●
↓ PULL DOWN ↓
ALARM

Take notes about the announcement. **List** four things to remember for staying safe during a fire drill.

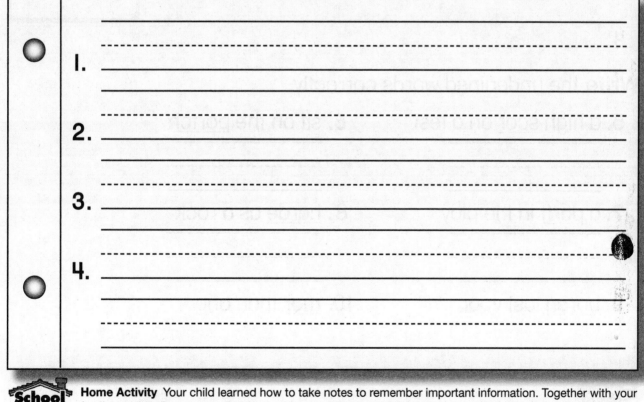

1. _____

2. _____

3. _____

4. _____

© Pearson Education, Inc., 2

School + Home **Home Activity** Your child learned how to take notes to remember important information. Together with your family, create a fire escape plan for your home. Ask your child to take notes of the important steps of your fire escape plan. Then post the plan in a prominent place in your home.

Name _____

Vowels: *r*-Controlled

Read Adam's article. **Circle** three spelling mistakes. **Write** the words correctly. Then **write** the sentence that does not belong.

Spelling Words

part	smart
hard	farm
born	porch
horse	corn
before	chore
more	score

Second-Grade News

Our Class Trip
Monday our class visited a farm. We fed corne to a hors. Tim is smart in math. A new colt was born just befor we got there.

_____   _____

I. _____   2. _____

3. _____

4. _____

Frequently Misspelled Words

started

before

Write the underlined words correctly.

5. a high <u>scor</u> on a test

_____

6. sit on the <u>portch</u>

_____

7. a <u>partt</u> in the play

_____

8. <u>harde</u> as a rock

_____

9. <u>boren</u> last year

_____

10. <u>mor</u> than one

_____

© Pearson Education, Inc., 2

School + Home **Home Activity** Your child has identified misspelled words with *ar*, *or*, and *ore*. Ask your child to say the sound of each letter combination. (Note: The letter combinations *or* and *ore* have the same sound.)

Name _____

Pick a word from the box to finish each sentence.
Write the word on the line.

> brave   break   collar   family   heard
> listen   once   pull   slipped

_____

1. I _____ helped save a hurt seal.

2. My sister _____ the seal crying out.

3. My _____ and I rode on a rescue boat.

4. We held the net so it would not _____ .

5. The seal _____ over the side of the boat.

6. We had to _____ to know what to do next.

7. We put a bandage on its neck like a _____ .

8. Dad had to _____ the seal from the water.

9. We all felt _____ .

School + Home **Home Activity** Your child used clues to write high-frequency and selection words learned this week.
Challenge your child to write a story about rescuing an animal using some of the words in the box.

© Pearson Education, Inc., 2

Name _____

Nouns

Mark the letter of the word that completes each sentence.

1. Mike wants a ____.
   - ○ **A** eat
   - ○ **B** pet
   - ○ **C** where

2. He got a ____.
   - ○ **A** puppy
   - ○ **B** nice
   - ○ **C** when

3. They walk in the ____.
   - ○ **A** here
   - ○ **B** tell
   - ○ **C** park

4. They play ____ in the yard.
   - ○ **A** with
   - ○ **B** feed
   - ○ **C** games

5. The puppy is a ____ for Mike.
   - ○ **A** then
   - ○ **B** friend
   - ○ **C** count

Say other sentences. **Tell** which words are nouns.

Home Activity Your child prepared for taking tests on nouns. Read a book together. Point out several simple sentences. Have your child identify the nouns in the sentences.

© Pearson Education, Inc., 2

Name _____

Read the contractions in the box.
Pick the contraction that is formed
from each pair of words.
Write the contraction on the line.

It is happy.
It's happy.

| can't   haven't   he's   I'm   she's   they'll   we'll   who's |

1. have + not

_____
- - - - - - - - - - - - - - - -
_____

2. I + am

_____
- - - - - - - - - - - - - - - -
_____

3. can + not

_____
- - - - - - - - - - - - - - - -
_____

4. they + will

_____
- - - - - - - - - - - - - - - -
_____

5. who + is

_____
- - - - - - - - - - - - - - - -
_____

6. we + will

_____
- - - - - - - - - - - - - - - -
_____

Circle the contraction in each sentence.

7. He's her little brother.

8. She's his big sister.

9. Lisa hasn't eaten lunch yet.

Home Activity Your child practiced forming contractions, such as *hasn't, she's, we'll,* and *I'm.* Read one of the contractions shown in the box above. Ask your child to tell you the words that make up the contraction. Work with your child to practice the contractions shown on the page.

© Pearson Education, Inc., 2

Name _____

Pick a word from the box to match each clue.
Write the word on the line.

| certainly either great laugh |
| second worst you're |

1. giggle

_____
- - - - - - - - - - - - - - - - - -
_____

2. surely

_____
- - - - - - - - - - - - - - - - - -
_____

3. one or the other

_____
- - - - - - - - - - - - - - - - - -
_____

4. most awful

_____
- - - - - - - - - - - - - - - - - -
_____

5. follows the first

_____
- - - - - - - - - - - - - - - - - -
_____

6. very important

_____
- - - - - - - - - - - - - - - - - -
_____

7. you are

_____
- - - - - - - - - - - - - - - - - -
_____

Home Activity Your child learned to read the high-frequency words *certainly, either, great, laugh, second, worst,* and *you're.* Write sentences using each of these words, but leave blanks for the words. Have your child use the high-frequency words to complete the sentences.

© Pearson Education, Inc., 2

Name _____

Read the text below. **Answer** the questions.

Thomas Jefferson
by Virginia Mann

Thomas Jefferson was the third President of the United States. Jefferson lived in Virginia and made the plans for his house there. It was a beautiful house. Jefferson invented many useful things for his house. Some of the things Jefferson invented are listed in the chart below.

What Jefferson Invented	What It Was Like
bookstand	Held five books at once Could be turned to each book
great clock	Could see its face from inside and outside his house
ladder	Made of wood Could be folded up

I. What is the author's name? _____

_____

2. What is the topic of this text? _____

3. What did you learn by reading the chart?

_____

_____

4. What do you think the author's purpose was for writing this story?

_____

_____

Home Activity Your child answered questions about a nonfiction text and told why the author wrote it. Read a newspaper or magazine article with your child. Have your child identify who wrote the text and why the writer might have written it.

© Pearson Education, Inc., 2

Name _____

Writing • Biography

 Helen Keller

Helen Keller was born in 1880 in Alabama. When she was a baby, she got very sick. After that, Helen could not see, hear, or speak.

Helen's parents hired a teacher for her. The teacher's name was Annie Sullivan. She taught Helen how to "speak" and "hear" with her hands.

Helen learned fast. She was very smart. When she grew up, she went to college. After college, Helen wrote books and gave speeches. In 1903 she wrote a book about her life. Helen Keller taught people that they should never give up.

Key Features of a Biography

• It tells about a real person's life.

• It tells important facts about the person.

© Pearson Education, Inc., 2

Contractions

Spelling Words					
haven't	it's	he's	I'm	didn't	who's
she's	can't	isn't	aren't	hadn't	I'll

Write the contraction that can be made from the underlined words.

1. We <u>have not</u> started practicing yet.

2. It <u>is not</u> snowing.

3. Do you know <u>who is</u> riding the bus today?

4. I think <u>she is</u> at the nature center.

5. I <u>can not</u> go to the show.

6. We <u>are not</u> done until afternoon.

Write the contractions for the words below.

7. it is

8. did not

9. had not

10. I will

11. he is

12. I am

Home Activity Your child wrote contractions. Have your child name the words that were combined to make each contraction.

© Pearson Education, Inc., 2

Name _____

Look at the dictionary pages. **Write** the words from the box that you would find on each page. **Use** the Guide Words to choose the correct page.

rant   structure   sample   television
pleasant   sentence   traffic   tunnel

1. **over**

rapid

2. **raw**

settle

3. **soy**

today

4. **tomorrow**

under

School + Home **Home Activity** Your child learned how to use guide words in a dictionary. Have your child name one more word that could be found on each page using the guide words above.

© Pearson Education, Inc., 2

Name _____

Proper Nouns

Proper nouns are special names for people, places, animals, and things. They begin with capital letters. **Days of the week, months of the year,** and **holidays** also begin with capital letters. **Titles** and **initials** for people begin with capital letters. Many titles end with a **period (.).**

Noah and **Maya** learned about **Abraham Lincoln. Ms. Grant** told the children the story of **Mr. Lincoln. Abraham Lincoln** was born on **February** 12, 1809, in **Kentucky.**

Write the proper nouns in each sentence on the line.

1. Noah and Maya ripped the map on Monday.

   _____

   _____

2. Abraham Lincoln was a lawyer in Springfield, Illinois.

   _____

   _____

3. On November 6, 1860, Mr. Lincoln was elected President.

   _____

   _____

4. The Civil War ended on April 9, 1865.

   _____

   _____

© Pearson Education, Inc., 2

Home Activity Your child learned about proper nouns. Go through a piece of mail with your child and have him or her point out all the proper nouns in the addresses.

Name _____

Web

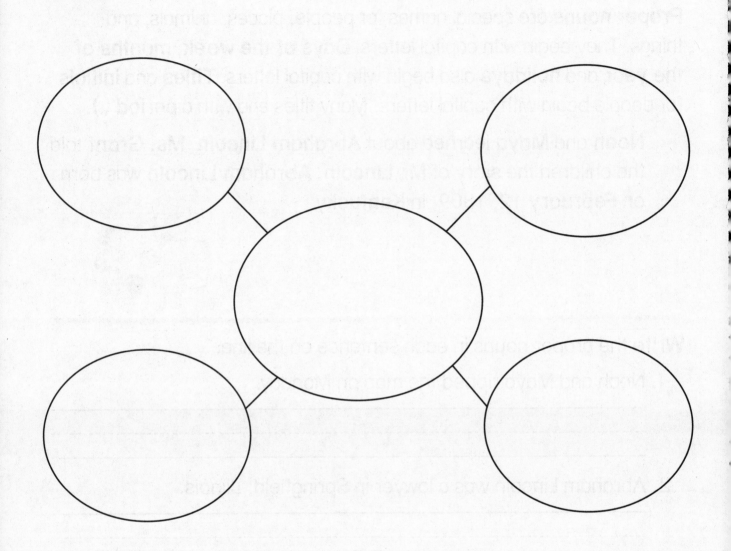

© Pearson Education, Inc., 2

 School + Home

Home Activity Your child is learning to write stories, poems, brief reports, nonfiction paragraphs, letters, and other products this year. Ask what your child is writing this week.

116 Writing Plan

Name _____

You will be presenting a visual display to help answer the Question of the Week, *How has working together changed history?* Use the following steps to help you plan your visual display.

Step 1- Write the information you would most like to share with the class.

_____
- -
_____
- -
_____
- -
_____
- -
_____

Step 2- Organize the information into chronological order.

_____
- -
_____
- -
_____
- -
_____

Step 3- Choose which events show how working together changed history.

_____
- -
_____
- -
_____
- -
_____

Step 4- Place the information in the appropriate area of the time line. Include a short description with each date. Circle which events are examples of people working together.

© Pearson Education, Inc., 2

Home Activity Your child found information on a time line. Have your child create a time line about special events in his or her life. Help your child write a year for each event and describe each event with a short sentence.

Name _____

Contractions

Spelling Words					
haven't	it's	he's	I'm	didn't	who's
she's	can't	isn't	aren't	hadn't	I'll

Read Emmet's letter. **Circle** two spelling mistakes.
Circle the word with the capitalization mistake. **Write**
the words correctly.

> Dear Grandpa,
> That was a great game on friday. I
> did't think you could come, but I'm
> glad you did! Mom says its time for
> dinner, so I have to go.
> Love, Emmet

1. _____

2. _____

3. _____

Fill in the circle to show the correct spelling.
Write the word.

4. ○ are't   ○ aren't

5. ○ can't   ○ cann't

6. ○ she's   ○ shes

7. ○ whos'   ○ who's

8. ○ haven't   ○ havn't

4. _____

5. _____

6. _____

7. _____

8. _____

Home Activity Your child identified misspelled contractions. Have your child point to each apostrophe (')
and tell what letter or letters the apostrophe replaced.

118 **Spelling** Contractions

© Pearson Education, Inc., 2

Name _____

Read the story.

Write in the correct words from the box to finish the sentences.

| certainly either great laugh |
| second worst you're |

My sister is learning to be a lawyer. I think she will be a

_____ _____

_____ lawyer. She is always _____

reading or writing. She _____ has to read a lot

of books.

One time I noticed that she dropped a book. Then she dropped

_____

a _____ book. It wasn't her fault. She says the

_____

_____ part of learning to be a lawyer is that the books

are so heavy.

Today I left a picture on her desk. It showed her dropping books.

"Now, who drew this?" she asked. I was honest. I told her that I did it.

_____

"Joe, _____ a funny boy," she said to me. "And your

_____

picture made me _____ ."

School + Home **Home Activity** Your child used high-frequency words learned this week to complete sentences in a story. Have your child write about a favorite book. Encourage your child to use some of these high-frequency words.

© Pearson Education, Inc., 2

Name _____

Proper Nouns

Mark the letter of the word or words that correctly complete each sentence.

1. Abraham's last name was _____.
   - ○ **A** lincoln
   - ○ **B** grant
   - ○ **C** Lincoln

2. Abraham lived in _____.
   - ○ **A** Kentucky, indiana, and Illinois
   - ○ **B** Kentucky, Indiana, and Illinois
   - ○ **C** kentucky, Indiana, and illinois

3. Abraham's wife was _____.
   - ○ **A** Mrs. lincoln
   - ○ **B** mrs. lincoln
   - ○ **C** Mrs. Lincoln

4. Abraham's nickname was _____.
   - ○ **A** abe
   - ○ **B** Abe
   - ○ **C** ABE

5. President Lincoln lived in the _____.
   - ○ **A** white house
   - ○ **B** White House
   - ○ **C** white House

Choose other proper nouns. **Say** a sentence for each proper noun.

Home Activity Your child prepared for taking tests on proper nouns. Read a story together. Have your child identify the proper nouns on a page.

120 Conventions Proper Nouns

© Pearson Education, Inc., 2

Name _____

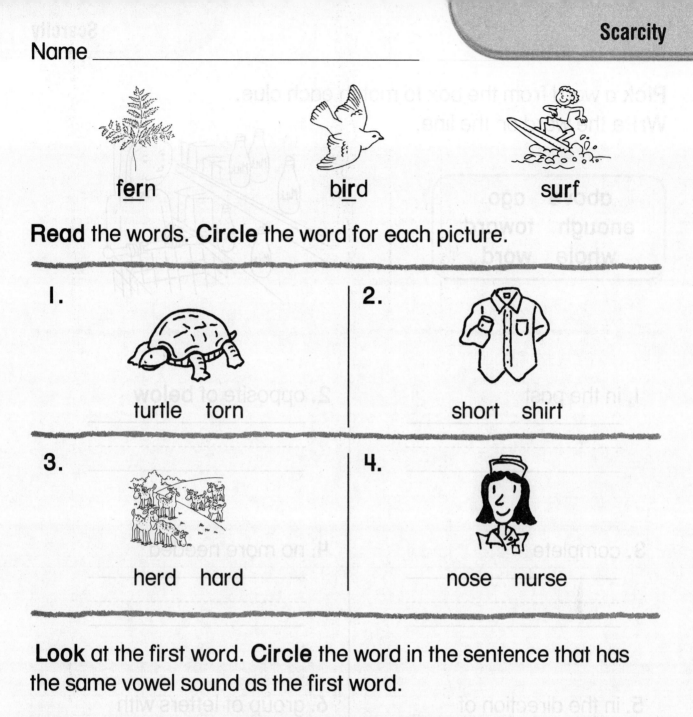

fern   bird   surf

Read the words. **Circle** the word for each picture.

1. turtle   torn

2. short   shirt

3. herd   hard

4. nose   nurse

Look at the first word. **Circle** the word in the sentence that has the same vowel sound as the first word.

her   5. I live around the corner from Amy.

burn   6. My mom puts her keys in her purse.

dirt   7. Liam was first in line for lunch.

perch   8. We like to watch monster movies.

© Pearson Education, Inc., 2

Home Activity Your child identified words with *er, ir,* and *ur* that have the same vowel sound as in *fern, bird,* and *surf.* Have your child use the circled words in the above exercise in his or her own sentences. Encourage your child to write the sentences and illustrate them.

Name _____

Pick a word from the box to match each clue.
Write the word on the line.

| above   ago |
| enough   toward |
| whole   word |

1. in the past

_____

- - - - - - - - - - - - - - - - - - -

_____

2. opposite of **below**

_____

- - - - - - - - - - - - - - - - - - -

_____

3. complete

_____

- - - - - - - - - - - - - - - - - - -

_____

4. no more needed

_____

- - - - - - - - - - - - - - - - - - -

_____

5. in the direction of

_____

- - - - - - - - - - - - - - - - - - -

_____

6. group of letters with meaning

_____

- - - - - - - - - - - - - - - - - - -

_____

© Pearson Education, Inc., 2

Home Activity Your child is learning to read the high-frequency words *above, ago, enough, toward, whole,* and *word*. Ask your child to look at the picture at the top of the page. Discuss what people might do if there were a scarcity of milk. Have your child write sentences about the picture, using as many of the high-frequency words as he or she can.

Name _____

Read the text. **Write** the answer to each question.

Hurricanes

What Is a Hurricane?

A hurricane is a huge storm. It is made up of rain and very strong winds that spin around in circles. Hurricanes begin over an ocean and may travel over land.

What Are the Parts of a Hurricane?

The center of a hurricane is called the eye. It is calm in the eye, but in the area around the eye, the winds move at very high speeds. This area of the storm is called the eyewall.

Why Is a Hurricane Dangerous?

The winds in a hurricane are strong enough to blow down buildings and trees and lift up cars. The heavy rains from hurricanes can cause floods and mudslides.

1. Under which heading do you find a definition of a hurricane?

_____

- -

_____

2. What are two facts about the eye of a hurricane?

_____

- -

_____

3. What is a detail about the eyewall?

_____

- -

_____

© Pearson Education, Inc., 2

School + Home **Home Activity** Your child learned to find facts and details in an informational article. Read an article with your child. Tell them to listen to the article to find facts. When you have finished reading, ask your child to name three facts from the article.

Name _____

Writing • Informational Paragraph

 A New Student

Writing Prompt: Write an informational paragraph about how you and others helped someone at school.

Last month, a new student came to our second grade class. Her name is Suki. Suki's family moved from Tokyo, Japan, all the way to Austin, Texas! Suki speaks English very well. But she was a little scared at first. Everything was new to her. So the kids in our class helped her out. We showed her where to find things in the classroom. We showed her what to do in the lunchroom and the library. During recess, we taught her how to play T-ball. Our teacher said she was proud of us.

© Pearson Education, Inc., 2

Vowels: *r*-Controlled *er, ir, ur*

Spelling Words					
her	person	nurse	dirt	turn	birth
serve	curb	curl	skirt	purse	turtle

Find two list words that fit the clues. **Write** them.

They have **ur**. They rhyme. I. _____ 2. _____

They have **ir**. They rhyme. 3. _____ 4. _____

They have **ur**. They have **c**. 5. _____ 6. _____

Write the list word that fits each clue.

7. This person works with a doctor. 7. _____

8. This animal is a reptile. 8. _____

9. This is what waiters do. 9. _____

10. This is the opposite of **him**. 10. _____

11. This is what doorknobs do. 11. _____

12. It is when you were born. 12. _____

School + Home **Home Activity** Your child wrote words with *er, ir,* and *ur*. Have your child circle *er, ir,* and *ur* in the spelling words.

© Pearson Education, Inc., 2

Name _____

The words in the box tell about time-order.
Write the correct word from the box in each sentence.

> before   after   first

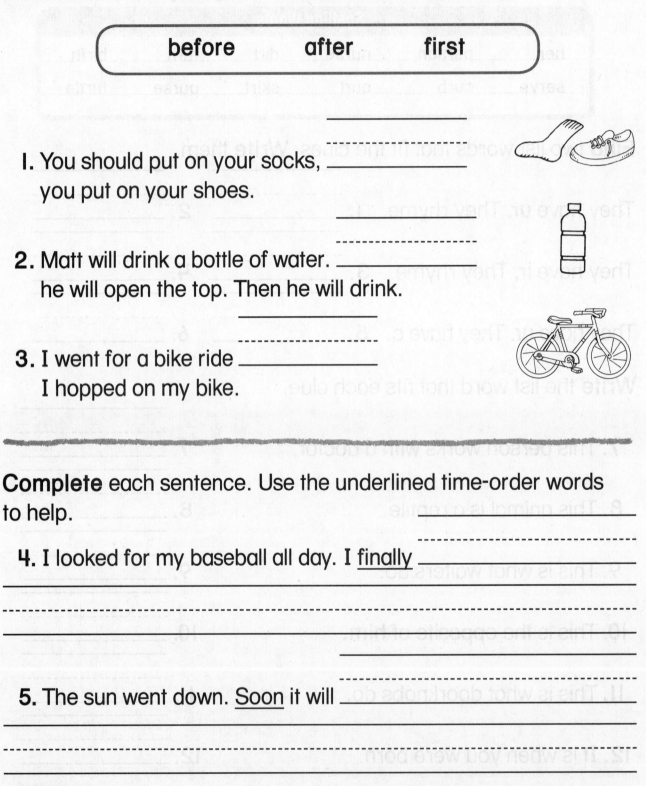

1. You should put on your socks, _____
   you put on your shoes.

2. Matt will drink a bottle of water. _____
   he will open the top. Then he will drink.

3. I went for a bike ride _____
   I hopped on my bike.

Complete each sentence. Use the underlined time-order words
to help.

4. I looked for my baseball all day. I <u>finally</u> _____
   _____
   _____

5. The sun went down. <u>Soon</u> it will _____
   _____
   _____

Home Activity Your child used time-order words to tell when events happened. Have your child tell you directions for something he or she knows how to do, such as make a sandwich. Ask your child to use the words *first, then, next,* and *finally* in the directions.

© Pearson Education, Inc., 2

Name _____

Singular and Plural Nouns

A **singular noun** names one person, place, animal, or thing.
A noun that names more than one is called a **plural noun.**

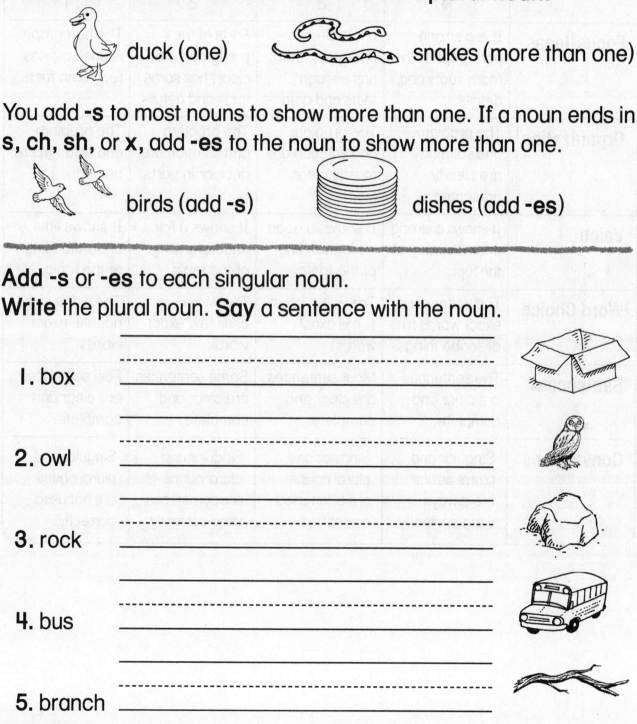

duck (one)   snakes (more than one)

You add **-s** to most nouns to show more than one. If a noun ends in
s, ch, sh, or **x,** add **-es** to the noun to show more than one.

birds (add **-s**)   dishes (add **-es**)

Add -s or **-es** to each singular noun.
Write the plural noun. **Say** a sentence with the noun.

1. box _____

2. owl _____

3. rock _____

4. bus _____

5. branch _____

Home Activity Your child learned about singular and plural nouns. Point out things in your home. Name each one and ask your child to say the plural form of the word.

© Pearson Education, Inc., 2

Name _____

Scoring Rubric: Expository Nonfiction/ Informational Paragraph

	4	3	2	1
Focus/Ideas	It is a strong paragraph with many facts and details.	It is a clear paragraph that has enough facts and details.	Parts of the paragraph are clear; has some facts and details.	The paragraph is unclear; has few or no facts.
Organization	The problem and solution are clearly presented.	The problem and solution are mostly clear.	The problem and solution are unclear in parts.	The problem and solution are unclear.
Voice	It shows a strong understanding of the topic.	It shows a good understanding of the topic.	It shows a fair understanding of the topic.	It shows little understanding of the topic.
Word Choice	The writer uses exact words to describe things.	The writer uses some exact words.	The writer uses few exact words.	The writer does not use exact words.
Sentences	The sentences are clear and complete.	Most sentences are clear and complete.	Some sentences are clear and complete.	Few sentences are clear and complete.
Conventions	Singular and plural nouns are always used correctly.	Singular and plural nouns are often used correctly.	Singular and plural nouns are sometimes used correctly.	Singular and plural nouns are not used correctly.

© Pearson Education, Inc., 2

Home Activity Your child is learning to write an informational paragraph. Ask your child to describe the kind of paragraph he or she is writing. Your child's writing will be evaluated based on this four-point scoring rubric.

Name _____

Look at the chapter headings and picture dictionary of this book.
Write the answer to each question.

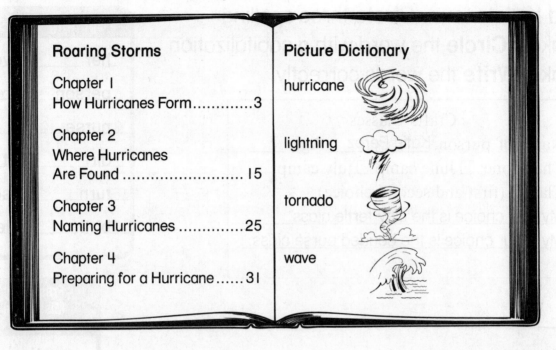

Roaring Storms

Chapter 1
How Hurricanes Form............3

Chapter 2
Where Hurricanes
Are Found 15

Chapter 3
Naming Hurricanes 25

Chapter 4
Preparing for a Hurricane......31

Picture Dictionary

hurricane

lightning

tornado

wave

1. In which chapter would you
find out about hurricane names?
_____
_____
_____

2. What is this ?
_____

3. What will be discussed in Chapter 2?
_____
_____
_____

4. What is this 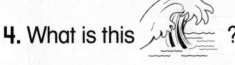 ?
_____

5. Which chapter would have
information about staying
safe in a hurricane?
_____
_____

Home Activity Your child learned about chapter headings. With your child, look at a nonfiction book. Ask
your child what information can be found in specific chapters. Then look at a fiction book. Ask your child to
predict what each chapter is about based on the chapter heading.

© Pearson Education, Inc., 2

Name _____

Vowels: *r*-Controlled *er, ir, ur*

Read Katie's form. **Circle** three spelling mistakes. **Circle** the word with a capitalization mistake. **Write** the words correctly.

Spelling Words

her	serve
person	curb
nurse	curl
dirt	skirt
turn	purse
birth	turtle

Crafts Classes
Name of purson: <u>Katie Perez</u>   Age: <u>7</u>
Check one: ☐ June camp ☐ july camp
Classes (first and second choice):
<u>My first choice is the clay tertle class.</u>
<u>My othur choice is the beaded purse class.</u>

Frequently Misspelled Words

another

other

heard

were

1. _____

2. _____

3. _____

4. _____

Circle the word that is spelled correctly.
Write it.

her	hir	hur	5. _____
skert	skirt	skurt	6. _____
nerse	nirse	nurse	7. _____
tern	tirn	turn	8. _____

Home Activity Your child has identified misspelled words with *er*, *ir*, and *ur*. Remind your child that *er*, *ir*, and *ur* often have the same sound so each spelling word must be memorized.

© Pearson Education, Inc., 2

Name _____

Pick a word from the box to finish each sentence.
Write the word on the line.

> above   ago   enough   scarce
> toward   whole   word

1. Bad weather can harm our food resources and make some

   _____

   foods _____.

2. Not long _____, hurricanes hurt a lot of pecan trees.

3. Some growers almost lost their _____ crop.

4. The growers didn't have _____ nuts to sell,
   so there was a scarcity of pecans.

5. When a hurricane moves _____ land, people
   need to get out of the way.

6. Hurricanes can push waves _____ the roofs
   of some houses.

7. Can you think of another _____ for
   trade-off?

 Home Activity Your child is learning to read the words *above, ago, enough, scarce, scarcity, hurricanes, resources, toward, trade-off, whole,* and *word*. Write a sentence using one of these words, but leave a blank for the word. Have your child use one of the words from the box to complete the sentence. Continue for each word.

© Pearson Education, Inc., 2

Name _____

Singular and Plural Nouns

Mark the letter of the word that correctly completes each sentence.

1. There are not enough ____.
   - ○ **A** resource
   - ○ **B** resources
   - ○ **C** resourceses

2. Hurricanes can harm fruit ____.
   - ○ **A** trees
   - ○ **B** tree
   - ○ **C** treeses

3. The prices rose on ____.
   - ○ **A** orange
   - ○ **B** orangeses
   - ○ **C** oranges

4. People pay hundreds of dollars for some ____.
   - ○ **A** toy
   - ○ **B** toyes
   - ○ **C** toys

5. Some people stopped driving and rode ____.
   - ○ **A** bikes
   - ○ **B** bikeses
   - ○ **C** bike

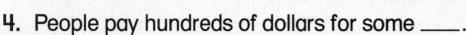

Choose other nouns. **Say** a sentence for each noun.

School + Home **Home Activity** Your child prepared for taking tests on singular and plural nouns. Read a book together. Have your child find plural nouns that end in *-s* or *-es*.

© Pearson Education, Inc., 2

Name _____

Write the word for each picture. **Use** the words in the box to help you. **Add -s, -es,** change the **y** to **i** and add **-es,** or change the **f** to **ve** and add **-s.**

bunny   bush   calf   fork   fox
house   leaf   candy   shelf   spoon

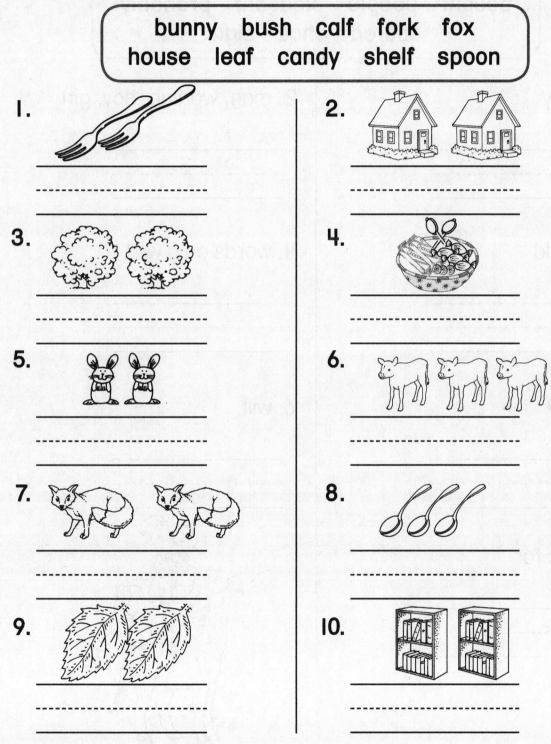

1.

2.

3.

4.

5.

6.

7.

8.

9.

10.

School + Home   **Home Activity** Your child formed plural nouns by adding *-s, -es,* changing the *y* to *i* and adding *-es,* or changing the *f* to *ve* and adding *-s.* Ask your child to name objects in a room, closet, or drawer and then list the words. Have your child write the plural form of a word when needed.

© Pearson Education, Inc., 2

Name _____

Pick a word from the box to match each clue.
Write the word on the line.

> bought   people   pleasant   probably
> scared   shall   sign

1. likely

_____

- - - - - - - - - - - -

_____

2. man, woman, boy, girl

_____

- - - - - - - - - - - -

_____

3. afraid

_____

- - - - - - - - - - - -

_____

4. words on a wall

_____

- - - - - - - - - - - -

_____

5. nice

_____

- - - - - - - - - - - -

_____

6. will

_____

- - - - - - - - - - - -

_____

7. paid for

_____

- - - - - - - - - - - -

_____

© Pearson Education, Inc., 2

Home Activity This week your child learned to read the words *bought, people, pleasant, probably, shall,* and *sign.* On small pieces of paper, write each word. Then write clues on other papers. Have your child match the word with the clue.

Name _____

Read the fairy tale. **Answer** the questions.

One Morning in Dragonville

Long ago in the land of Dragonville, there lived a friendly dragon named Spots. Spots had brown spots all over his body. One morning, Spots was sad because he noticed one of his spots was missing. His friend Sparrow said he would help Spots look for the missing spot.

"I see my spot!" Spots cried. No, it was just a brown stone.

"I see your spot!" Sparrow exclaimed. No, it was just an acorn.

The two friends walked on. Suddenly Sparrow chirped, "Lift up your foot, Spots." There was the missing spot stuck to the bottom of the dragon's foot.

I. Why is this a fairy tale?

_____

- -

_____

2. Why is Spots sad at the beginning of the fairy tale?

_____

- -

_____

3. Why did the two friends walk on?

_____

- -

_____

© Pearson Education, Inc., 2

Home Activity Your child identified causes and effects in a fairy tale. Read a fairy tale with your child. Have your child identify the make-believe characters, setting, and series of events using cause and effect.

Name _____

Writing • Fairy Tale

 ## The Farmer's Daughters

Once upon a time, there lived a farmer and his three daughters. The family had a pretty garden. They grew many fruits and vegetables.

One morning, a troll came into their garden. He ate lots of plants! After that, he came back every day. The farmer and his daughters were very upset.

So the three daughters came up with a plan. That night, they sprinkled hot pepper on all their plants.

The next day, the troll was back. He picked a tomato and took a bite. Then he howled and ran away! The farmer and his daughters laughed and laughed. And they never, ever, saw the troll again.

Key Features of a Fairy Tale

- It tells a story about magical characters and events.

- The characters usually are either very good or very bad.

© Pearson Education, Inc., 2

Name _____

Plurals

Spelling Words					
note	lunch	story	tune	switch	baby
notes	lunches	stories	tunes	switches	babies

Write the missing list words.

1. I will eat my _____ now.

2. She told a _____ about a lost prince.

3. We packed _____ to eat on the hike.

4. My sister wrote two _____ .

5. Your _____ loves to eat bananas.

6. The _____ can play in the shade.

Write the list word that rhymes. Then write the word adding **-s** or **-es**.

dune   ditch   vote

7. _____   8. _____   9. _____

10. _____   11. _____   12. _____

School + Home **Home Activity** Your child wrote plurals with and without -s and -es. Name a singular word and have your child explain how the plural is formed.

Name _____

Read each pair of sentences.
Write the correct word from the box on the line.

I. a. I use _____ to bake a cake.

b. I picked a _____ from my garden.

flour /flower

2. a. My sister is _____ years old.

b. The boy walks _____ school.

2

to /two

3. a. I read the _____ book in a week.

b. The _____ in the ground was very deep.

hole /whole

4. a. The dolphins swam in the _____.

b. I use my eyes to _____.

sea /see

© Pearson Education, Inc., 2

Home Activity Your child learned about words that sound the same but are spelled differently. Have your child make up silly sentences that have both homophones in the same sentence.

Plural Nouns That Change Spelling

A **plural noun** names more than one person, place, animal, or thing. Some nouns change spelling to name more than one.

Singular	Plural	Singular	Plural
child	children	leaf	leaves
man	men	wolf	wolves
woman	women	mouse	mice
tooth	teeth	goose	geese
foot	feet		

Choose the correct plural noun in ( ).
Write the noun on the line.

1. A bird has two (foots, feet).

_____

- -

_____

2. The bugs crawl through the (leaves, leafs).

_____

- -

_____

3. All the (children, childs) listen to the music.

_____

- -

_____

4. The (gooses, geese) are noisy.

_____

- -

_____

© Pearson Education, Inc., 2

School + Home

Home Activity Your child learned about plural nouns that change spelling. Together, look through several of your child's favorite books. Have your child point out plural nouns that change spelling.

Name _____

Story Chart

Title _____

Characters

Setting

Beginning

↓

Middle

↓

End of Story

Home Activity Your child is learning to write stories, poems, brief reports, nonfiction paragraphs, letters, and other products this year. Ask what your child is writing this week.

© Pearson Education, Inc., 2

Name _____

Today, you reviewed the concept web that explored the Question of the Week, *Why is it a good idea to work together?* Use the following steps to help you add your interests to the list that the class started and create questions that you have about why it is good to work together.

Step 1- Ask yourself the following questions:

• What good experiences have I had working with others? What have I accomplished by working with others?

• What stories have I read or movies have I seen about people working together? Why was it a good experience for the characters, or people in the stories?

Step 2- Discuss these questions and your answers with a partner. What new ideas does your partner's responses lead to?

Step 3- Write down your new ideas and interests about the class topic.

_____   _____
_____   _____
_____   _____
_____   _____

Step 4- What do you want to know about why it is good to work together? Write four questions you have about why it is good to work together.

_____   _____
_____   _____
_____   _____
_____   _____

© Pearson Education, Inc., 2

School + Home **Home Activity** Your child learned how to generate a list of interests and create questions about topics that interest them. Discuss with your child your experiences working with others and have your child add new ideas and questions to the lists.

Name _____

Plurals

Read the journal entry. **Circle** three spelling mistakes. **Circle** the word with a capitalization mistake. **Write** the words correctly.

Spelling Words	
note	tune
notes	tunes
lunch	switch
lunches	switches
story	baby
stories	babies

My Journal

Monday

I ate lunch with my freinds. Then Mrs. perez read a story about a mother raccoon and her babys. I like storys.

Frequently Misspelled Words

friends

presents

1. _____   2. _____

3. _____   4. _____

Fill in the circle to show the correctly spelled word.

5. The ◯ baby ◯ beby ◯ babys   is crying.

6. Turn the ◯ switche ◯ switch ◯ swich   off.

7. Dad whistled some ◯ tunes ◯ tunies ◯ tuns.

8. We can eat our ◯ lunchs ◯ lunches ◯ lunchies   outside.

9. He wrote a ◯ note ◯ not ◯ noties   to his friend.

10. The light ◯ switchies ◯ switchs ◯ switches   are broken.

School + Home

Home Activity Your child has identified misspelled words with and without -s and -es. Ask your child to explain why -es is added to *lunch* and *switch*. (The words end with *ch*.)

© Pearson Education, Inc., 2

Name _____

Read the story.
Write in the correct words
to finish the sentences.

> bought   excitement
> pleasant   probably
> robbers   scared   sign

Carlos crept up to the old mill. There was a _____
that said "Keep Out!" Carlos still wanted to see if there were really

monsters inside. Would they think there were _____
breaking in?

Just as Carlos got close, he heard a racket. Carlos was

_____ . He would _____ be eaten.
What would people say if he turned back, though? Carlos stepped
inside.

What was inside? It was an old man playing a horn! The

_____ was gone.

"What was that horrid sound?" asked Carlos.

"I don't know what you mean," the musician sniffed.

"I just _____ this horn. I think my playing is very

_____. Wait! I shall play you another tune!"

© Pearson Education, Inc., 2

School + Home **Home Activity** Your child completed sentences in a story using high-frequency and selection words learned this week. Work with your child to write a story using these words.

Name _____

Plural Nouns That Change Spelling

Mark the letter of the word that correctly completes each sentence.

I. A flock of ____ flew by.
   - ○ **A** goose
   - ○ **B** geeses
   - ○ **C** geese

2. All the ____ ate the cheese.
   - ○ **A** mice
   - ○ **B** mices
   - ○ **C** mouse

3. The three ____ wear hats.
   - ○ **A** men
   - ○ **B** man
   - ○ **C** mens

4. People tapped their ____.
   - ○ **A** foots
   - ○ **B** feet
   - ○ **C** feets

5. Men and ____ danced.
   - ○ **A** women
   - ○ **B** woman
   - ○ **C** womans

6. Does a rooster have ____?
   - ○ **A** tooth
   - ○ **B** tooths
   - ○ **C** teeth

Choose a plural noun. **Say** a sentence for the noun.

Home Activity Your child prepared for taking tests on plural nouns that change spelling. Have your child look through a newspaper or magazine article and find plural nouns that change spelling. Ask him or her to circle the words.

© Pearson Education, Inc., 2

Name _____

Read each sentence.
Circle the word with the **long a** sound.
Write the word on the line.

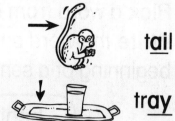

t<u>ai</u>l

tr<u>ay</u>

1. The ducklings play in the water.

----

2. The baby ducks do not see the cat.

----

3. It is waiting in the grass.

----

4. The big ducks are not afraid of the cat.

----

5. The cat runs away as fast as it can.

----

6. We bought a new table.

© Pearson Education, Inc., 2

School + Home

Home Activity Your child identified words with common vowel patterns spelled *a, ai,* or *ay (tail, tray)*. Have your child read sentences to find words with the *long a* sound. Ask your child to tell how the *long a* sound is spelled in each word.

Name _____

Pick a word from the box to finish each sentence.
Write the word on the line. **Remember** to use a capital letter at the beginning of a sentence.

> behind   brought   door   everybody
> minute   promise   sorry

_____

1. _____ went to see desert animals today.

2. Dad made sure we _____ water to drink.

3. I sat in the back of the car _____ my father.

4. We locked each _____ and wore our seat belts.

5. My sister made me _____ to be good.

6. I enjoyed every _____ of the trip.

7. I was so _____
when we had to go home.

Horned Lizard

Home Activity Your child learned to read the words *behind, brought, door, everybody, minute, promise,* and *sorry*. Together, write a description of a family or school trip your child has taken. Encourage your child to include some of these words.

© Pearson Education, Inc., 2

Name _____

Read each story.
Follow the directions.

Why Turtles Live in Water
(African tale)

Long ago, turtles lived only on land. One day, some people were about to break the shell of a turtle to kill and cook it. The turtle stopped them and said that drowning him would work much better. So the people threw the turtle in the river. The turtle laughed and swam away. After that, turtles always lived safely in water.

Bear's Race with Turtle
(Native American tale)

Bear and Turtle agreed to have a race to see who was the fastest animal in the woods. Turtle said he was. The two had a race. Bear ran around a frozen lake while Turtle swam in it. Turtle poked his head through holes in the ice so Bear could see him. But Turtle fooled Bear. He had other turtles ready at each hole so Bear would think each head popping up was Turtle's. Bear got very tired and Turtle won the race. Bear was so tired that he slept all winter. That is why bears sleep during the winter.

1. What character trait describes the turtles in both stories?

_____

----

2. What do both stories explain about animals?

_____

_____

_____

_____

3. Underline the sentence below that tells how the turtle's problem in *"Why Turtles Live in Water"* is different from Turtle's problem in *"Bear's Race with Turtle."*

The turtle's life is in danger.   The turtle is a good swimmer.

School + Home **Home Activity** Your child compared and contrasted two folk tales. Point out to your child that one story is set in the woods. Have your child compare and contrast this story setting to a story set in a desert. Ask your child to describe the things that are the same and different.

Comprehension Compare and Contrast **147**

© Pearson Education, Inc., 2

Name _____

Writing • Folk Tale

 The Little Red Hen

Once there was a Little Red Hen that found some grains of wheat. She asked Dog, Pig, and Cat to help her plant it. But they were too busy to help. So she planted the wheat by herself.

Soon the wheat was ready to be cut. "Who will help me cut the wheat?" she asked.

"Not I," said Dog, Pig, and Cat. So Little Red Hen cut the wheat by herself.

After she ground the wheat into flour, she asked Dog, Pig, and Cat to help her bake the bread. But they were too tired to help. So Little Red Hen baked the bread by herself.

Soon the bread was done, and it smelled delicious! Dog, Pig, and Cat ran into Little Red Hen's kitchen. "We would love a slice of bread!" they said.

"I don't need your help now!" said Little Red Hen. "I did all the work by myself. Now I will enjoy this bread by myself!" And she did.

Key Features of a Folk Tale

· It is like a story from long ago.

· Good ways of acting usually are rewarded.

· Bad ways of acting usually are punished.

© Pearson Education, Inc., 2

Name _____

Vowel Digraphs *ai, ay*

Spelling Words					
tail	main	wait	say	away	play
raise	brain	paint	stay	today	tray

Write a list word to complete each phrase or sentence.

1. worth the _____

2. _____ the house.

3. wag a _____

4. Use your _____.

5. _____ put.

6. have the final _____

7. _____ the flag.

8. _____ is the day.

Write a list word to finish each sentence.

9. The bird flew _____ .

10. I can _____ after school.

11. Put your cup on the _____ .

12. The _____ road is closed.

Home Activity Your child spelled words with *long a* spelled *ai* and *ay*. Ask your child to explain the meanings of the sayings on this page.

© Pearson Education, Inc., 2

Name _____

Read the sentence. **Circle** the meaning of the underlined word in each sentence. Use other words in the sentence to help.

1. Hanna made a <u>pledge</u> to her mom that she would clean her room by the end of the week.

    a. a question   b. a silly joke   c. a promise

2. The dog was <u>appreciative</u> for the kindness the stranger showed it.

    a. grateful   b. angry   c. sorry

3. The soldier's brave actions <u>merit</u> an award.

    a. put in danger   b. deserve   c. surprise

4. The kitten felt <u>anxious</u> when she saw the big dog.

    a. happy   b. worried   c. furry

Read each sentence. **Write** the meaning of the *italicized* word. Use other words in the sentence to help.

5. Sara could not *visualize* her new house because she still had not seen it.

    _____

    -

    _____

6. Henry was *timid*. He did not want to stand on stage in front of so many people.

    _____

    -

    _____

© Pearson Education, Inc., 2

Home Activity Your child used context clues to figure out the meaning of unfamiliar words. Have your child tell you how he or she figured out the meaning of the words in sentences 5 and 6.

Possessive Nouns

A noun that shows who or what owns something is a **possessive noun**. To show ownership, add an **apostrophe (')** and **-s** when the noun is singular. Add just an **apostrophe (')** when the noun is plural.

the goat**'s** legs

the bear**s'** paws

Add 's to each singular noun in ( ).
Write the words on the line.

1. the (snake) hole

_____
- -
_____

2. the (mouse) tail

_____
- -
_____

Add ' to each plural noun in ( ).
Write the words on the line.

3. the (grasshoppers) meals

_____
- -
_____

4. the (coyotes) howls

_____
- -
_____

© Pearson Education, Inc., 2

School + Home **Home Activity** Your child learned about possessive nouns. Read a story together. Have your child point tut possessive nouns and tell what belongs to each person, animal, or thing.

Name _____

Story Chart

Title _____

Beginning

⬇

Middle

⬇

End of Story

© Pearson Education, Inc., 2

School + Home

Home Activity Your child is learning to write stories, poems, brief reports, nonfiction paragraphs, letters, and other products this year. Ask what your child is writing this week.

Name _____

Today, you will review your topic to check that you have found the answers to your original research topic. Use the following steps to help you review your topic and revise it if necessary.

Step 1- Make sure it is clear what you originally set out to learn about your topic. Write your research topic below.

_____

I want to know _____ .

Step 2- Review the list of questions you created about this topic and the answers from your research. Ask yourself the following questions:

• Do I have many unanswered questions?

• Did I learn something surprising that affects what I originally wanted to know?

• Based on what I learned, do I have new questions?

Step 3- Did you answer *yes* to any of the questions in Step 2? If so, you might want to consider revising your topic.

Step 4- Use your new questions and the surprising information you learned to revise your topic. You might need to just change a few words or you might need to rewrite the entire topic. Write your new topic and go back to Step 2. Can you answer *no* to all of the questions?

_____

My new topic is _____ .

Home Activity Your child learned how to revise a topic if needed. Discuss why it is important to revise a topic as a result of new information.

© Pearson Education, Inc., 2

Name _____

Vowel Digraphs *ai, ay*

Read the poster. **Circle** three spelling mistakes.
Write the words correctly. Then rewrite the last
sentence, using correct grammar.

Spelling Words	
tail	raise
main	brain
wait	paint
say	stay
away	today
play	tray

Fire Safety Tips

• Stay awai from fires.
• Replace worn electric cords
  because thay can start fires.
• Store paynt away from heat.
• Don't never play with
  matches.

1. _____

2. _____

3. _____

**Frequently
Misspelled
Words**

favorite

they

4. _____

Circle the word in each pair that is spelled correctly.
Write the word.

5. tial   _____
   tail

6. main   _____
   mian

7. brain   _____
   brian

8. raise   _____
   rase

Home Activity Your child has been spelling words with *long a* spelled *ai* and *ay*. Have your child underline these letter combinations in the list words.

154   Spelling Vowel Digraphs *ai, ay*

© Pearson Education, Inc., 2

Name _____

Pick a word from the box to finish each sentence.
Write the word on the line.
Remember to use a capital letter at the beginning of a sentence.

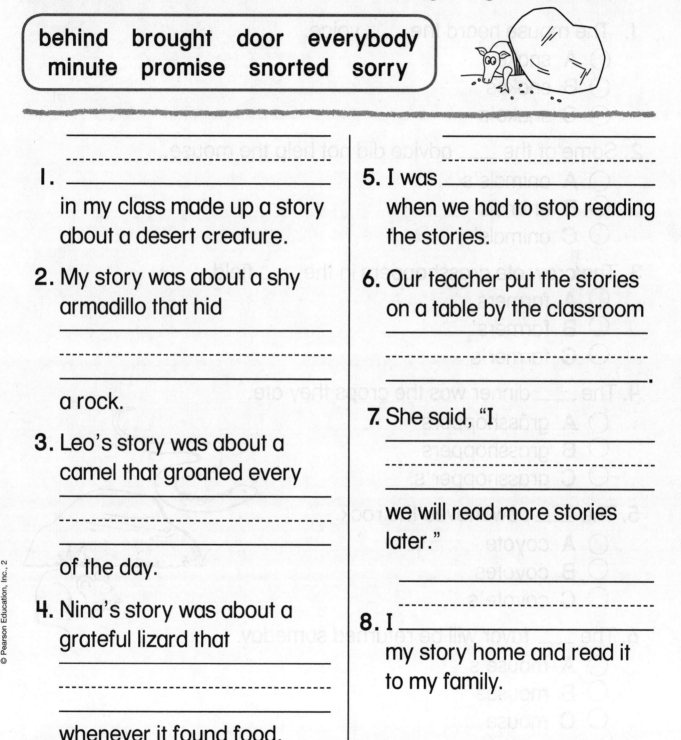

> behind brought door everybody
> minute promise snorted sorry

1. _____ in my class made up a story about a desert creature.

2. My story was about a shy armadillo that hid _____ a rock.

3. Leo's story was about a camel that groaned every _____ of the day.

4. Nina's story was about a grateful lizard that _____ whenever it found food.

5. I was _____ when we had to stop reading the stories.

6. Our teacher put the stories on a table by the classroom _____.

7. She said, "I _____ we will read more stories later."

8. I _____ my story home and read it to my family.

Home Activity Your child is learning to read the high-frequency words *behind, brought, door, everybody, minute, promise, snorted,* and *sorry*. Write each word on an index card or slip of paper. Then have your child pick a card, read the word aloud, and use it in an oral sentence.

© Pearson Education, Inc., 2

Name _____

Possessive Nouns

Mark the letter of the word that completes each sentence.

1. The mouse heard the ___ voice.
   - ○ **A** snake
   - ○ **B** snakes'
   - ○ **C** snake's

2. Some of the ___ advice did not help the mouse.
   - ○ **A** animals's
   - ○ **B** animals
   - ○ **C** animals'

3. The crow ate grasshoppers in the ___ field.
   - ○ **A** farmers
   - ○ **B** farmers'
   - ○ **C** farmer's

4. The ___ dinner was the crops they ate.
   - ○ **A** grasshoppers'
   - ○ **B** grasshoppers
   - ○ **C** grasshopper's

5. The ___ paw moved the rock.
   - ○ **A** coyote
   - ○ **B** coyotes
   - ○ **C** coyote's

6. The ___ favor will be returned someday.
   - ○ **A** mouse's
   - ○ **B** mouses'
   - ○ **C** mouse

© Pearson Education, Inc., 2

Home Activity Your child prepared for taking tests on possessive nouns. Write the words *mouse, snakes, crow, armadillo,* and *coyotes* on paper. Have your child add either *'s* or *'* and something that could belong to the animals, for example, *snakes' hole.*

Name _____

Read the words.
Circle the word for each picture.

1. farmer former	**2.** marching morning
3. oar are	**4.** stare store

Read the story.

Dan went with his mother to her store this morning. His mom is in a car pool, so they rode in Barney's car. First, they drove along the shore and listened to the roar of the sea. They had to drive around some fresh tar on the road. Then they passed a farm. The farmer was harvesting corn in his garden. At last, they came to the store Dan's mother owns.

© Pearson Education, Inc., 2

Home Activity Your child identified words with *ar, or, ore,* and *oar* that have the same vowel sound as in *barn, stork, store,* and *board*. Have your child use the circled words from the above exercise in his or her own sentences. Encourage your child to write the sentences and illustrate them.

Name _____

Vowels: *r*-Controlled *ar, or, ore*

Spelling Words					
part	hard	born	horse	before	more
smart	farm	porch	corn	chore	score

Read the two words. **Write** a list word that would come between them in a dictionary.

1. new _____ rice

2. apple _____ desk

3. little _____ next

4. gave _____ ice

5. rest _____ trunk

6. egg _____ gave

```
corn
farm
more
porch
hard
score
```

Unscramble the list word. **Write** it.

7. m s t r a _____

8. r t p a _____

9. e f b e r o _____

10. h e c r o _____

11. s e h o r _____

12. b r o n _____

School + Home **Home Activity** Your child has been learning to spell words with *ar, or,* and *ore*. Give clues about a word. Say, for example, "This is what you do when you clean your room." Have your child guess and spell the word. (chore)

© Pearson Education, Inc., 2

Name _____

Write the correct word from the box below each clue.

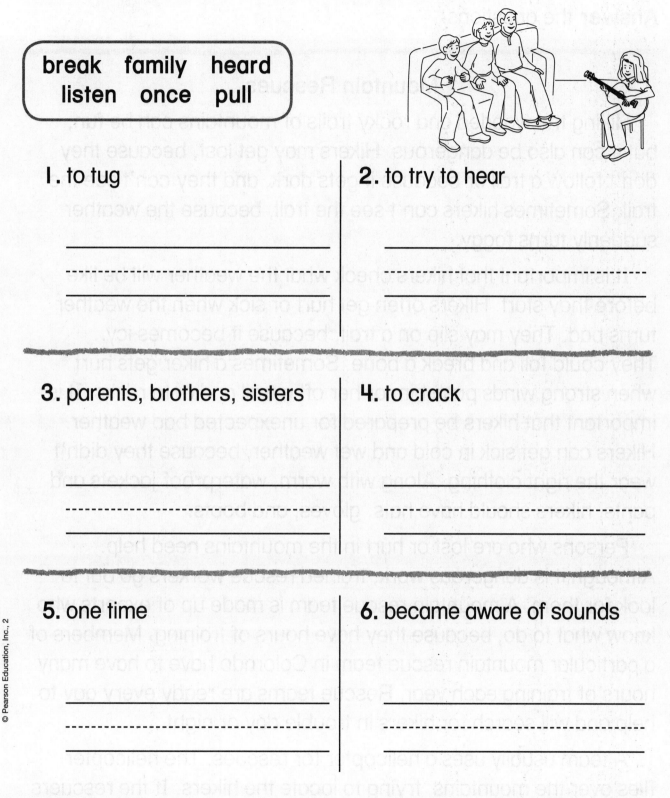

> break   family   heard
> listen   once   pull

1. to tug

_____

- -

_____

2. to try to hear

_____

- -

_____

3. parents, brothers, sisters

_____

- -

_____

4. to crack

_____

- -

_____

5. one time

_____

- -

_____

6. became aware of sounds

_____

- -

_____

© Pearson Education, Inc., 2

School + Home

Home Activity Your child reviewed the words *break, family, heard, listen, once,* and *pull.* Ask your child to read the words aloud and give an example for each. *What can break? Who is part of a family? What have you heard at night? What music do you listen to? What animal have you seen only once? What can you pull?*

High-Frequency Words   159

Name _____

Read the story.
Answer the questions.

Mountain Rescues

Hiking the wooded and rocky trails of mountains can be fun, but it can also be dangerous. Hikers may get lost, because they don't follow a trail or because it gets dark, and they can't see the trail. Sometimes hikers can't see the trail, because the weather suddenly turns foggy.

It is important that hikers check what the weather will be like before they start. Hikers often get hurt or sick when the weather turns bad. They may slip on a trail, because it becomes icy. They could fall and break a bone. Sometimes a hiker gets hurt when strong winds push him or her off a trail and onto rocks. It is important that hikers be prepared for unexpected bad weather. Hikers can get sick in cold and wet weather, because they didn't wear the right clothing. Along with warm, waterproof jackets and pants, hikers should have hats, gloves, and boots.

Persons who are lost or hurt in the mountains need help. Although it is dangerous work, trained rescue workers go out to look for them. A mountain rescue team is made up of experts who know what to do, because they have hours of training. Members of a particular mountain rescue team in Colorado have to have many hours of training each year. Rescue teams are ready every day to help and will search for hikers in trouble day or night.

A team usually uses a helicopter for rescues. The helicopter flies over the mountains, trying to locate the hikers. If the rescuers

© Pearson Education, Inc., 2

School + Home **Home Activity** Your child recognized causes and effects in a nonfiction story. Read a favorite story or watch a favorite children's video with your child. Pause every so often to ask about cause and effect relationships in the book or movie's story.

Name _____

are searching at night, they wear goggles that allow them to see in the dark. The team may have to airlift a hiker, because it's the only way to get him or her out of the mountains. For example, the hiker may be trapped on a ridge. During an airlift, the helicopter drops the rescuers on the ridge and then lowers a cable with a basket attached. The rescuers get the hiker into the basket, and the helicopter pulls the basket back up.

Rescued hikers are taken to a nearby hospital. Because brave rescue workers find lost or hurt persons as quickly as possible, they save many lives.

I. What could happen if a hiker doesn't follow a trail?

_____

_____

2. What effect could not wearing the right clothing have on hikers?

_____

_____

3. What is the reason rescue workers know what to do?

_____

_____

4. Why might a rescue team need to airlift a hurt hiker?

_____

_____

5. What effect do rescue workers have on lost or hurt hikers?

_____

_____

© Pearson Education, Inc., 2

Name _____

Nouns

Underline the noun in each sentence.

1. Two dogs barked.

2. A man fell.

3. The wind blew.

4. The snow was deep.

Write the noun in each sentence.

5. The water was cold.   _____

6. The ice cracked.   _____

7. The animals helped.   _____

8. That fire was warm.   _____

© Pearson Education, Inc., 2

Name _____

Day 1 Unit 2 Week 1   **Tara and Tiree**

Copy the sentences. Make sure you use the proper size when writing tall and small letters.

I go into your store.

_____
- -
_____

Ron Lion can roar.

_____
- -
_____

Day 2 Unit 2 Week 2   **Abraham Lincoln**

Copy the sentences. Make sure you use the proper size when writing tall and small letters.

Manny can't swim.

_____
- -
_____

She's my Aunt Nan.

_____
- -
_____

© Pearson Education, Inc., 2

Home Activity Your child practiced writing these letters: *Ii, Uu, Rr, Nn, Mm, Jj, Pp, Ww, Yy, Qq, Vv.* Have your child write two sentences about what he or she likes to do. After writing the sentences, have your child circle any of the letters from the list above.

Name _____

Day 3 Unit 2 Week 3   **Scarcity**

Copy the sentence. Make sure you form the letters correctly.

Pat and Jack serve pear juice.

_____

- -

_____

Day 4 Unit 2 Week 4   **Bremen Town Musicians**

Copy the sentences. Make sure your letters are all straight.

We want watches.

_____

- -

_____

My bike has yellow wheels.

_____

- -

_____

Day 5 Unit 2 Week 5   **One Good Turn**

Copy the sentences. Check the spacing of the letters in each word.

Val quits playing.

_____

- -

_____

Jay is very quiet.

_____

- -

_____

© Pearson Education, Inc., 2

Name _____

Pick the contraction that is formed from each pair of words.
Write the word on the line.

doesn't	don't	he'll	I'm
it's	she'll	haven't	won't

1. will not

_____
- - - - - - - - - - - -
_____

2. it is

_____
- - - - - - - - - - - -
_____

3. does not

_____
- - - - - - - - - - - -
_____

4. I am

_____
- - - - - - - - - - - -
_____

5. he will

_____
- - - - - - - - - - - -
_____

6. she will

_____
- - - - - - - - - - - -
_____

Read the story.

It's a fine morning, and I'm on my way to Charles's party. He'll have popcorn, hot dogs, and juice. There won't be any cake at the party. His mother doesn't like him to eat sweets, so she'll have fruit instead. I don't mind not having cake. The party will be in the back yard. That's where his garden is. I haven't seen his garden since the corn grew. It'll be a fun day.

Home Activity Your child practiced forming contractions such as *won't, she'll* and *I'm*. Write the contractions from the box on separate index cards. On other cards, write the pairs of words that form the contractions. Have your child match the contractions and word pairs.

© Pearson Education, Inc., 2

Name _____

Contractions

Read the clues. **Write** the list word that fits each clue.

1. Write a word that rhymes with **hid,** but starts like **dog.** Add **n't.** _____

2. Write a word that rhymes with **bad,** but starts like **home.** Add **n't.** _____

3. Write a word that rhymes with **tree,** but starts like **ship.** Add **'s.** _____

4. Write a word that rhymes with **see,** but starts like **hat.** Add **'s.** _____

5. Write a word that rhymes with **bit,** but starts like **inn.** Add **'s.** _____

Spelling Words	
I'll	haven't
it's	he's
I'm	didn't
who's	she's
can't	isn't
aren't	hadn't

Draw a path through the maze. **Follow** the words with the apostrophe (') in the right place. **Write** each word you pass on the path.

6. _____

7. _____

8. _____

9. _____

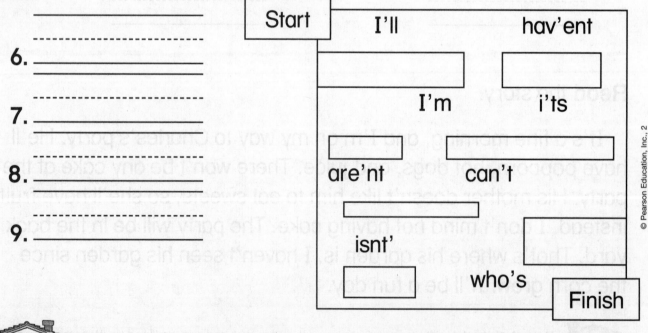

© Pearson Education, Inc., 2

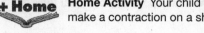

School + Home

Home Activity Your child has been learning to spell contractions. Write two words that can be combined to make a contraction on a sheet of paper. Have your child say the contraction and write it next to the words.

Name _____

Pick a word from the box to match each clue.
Write the letters of each word in the puzzle.
Read the letters in the gray squares to find two hidden words.

> certainly   either   great   laugh
> second   worst   you're

1. important

2. a contraction

3. opposite of **cry**

4. between first and third

5. opposite of **best**

6. for sure

7. one or the other

Hidden Words: _____

© Pearson Education, Inc., 2

School + Home   **Home Activity** Your child used high-frequency words to match clues. Write sentences using each of the words in the box, but leave a blank for the word. Ask your child to write the missing word to complete each sentence.

Name _____

Read the story.
Answer the questions.

Have you ever heard of Amelia Earhart? She was a great pilot. She did many amazing things.

As a child, Amelia didn't like flying. Then she went to an air show. She watched the planes. She got very excited about what she saw. She wanted to learn to fly.

So Amelia took flying lessons. Then she bought her own plane. It was bright yellow. Amelia named it *Canary* after yellow canary birds.

Soon, people heard about Amelia. They heard she was a good pilot. One day, she got a phone call. Some people wanted her to fly across the Atlantic Ocean. Amelia said yes.

She flew in a plane with two other pilots. Amelia was the only woman. The plane made it across the Atlantic Ocean. The pilots had set a new record. They were famous!

Then Amelia decided to fly across the Atlantic a second time. This time, she wanted to fly alone. She barely made it. She had many problems during the flight. She had to land her plane in a field!

Still, Amelia had done something amazing. She was the first woman to fly alone across the Atlantic. Now she was even more famous. She received many awards.

© Pearson Education, Inc., 2

Home Activity Your child read a biography and identified the author's purpose in writing it. Have your child tell you why he or she thinks the author told readers about Amelia Earhart's life before she became famous.

Name _____

Amelia wasn't done flying. She wanted a bigger challenge. So she decided to fly around the world. She almost made it. She flew across the Atlantic Ocean to Europe. Then she flew from Europe to Asia. Now she had only one part left. She needed to fly over the Pacific Ocean. She would do it in two flights, or legs.

Amelia took off on the first leg of her trip. She was supposed to land on a Pacific island, but she never made it. No one knows what happened. Her plane has never been found.

1. What do you think was the author's purpose in writing this story? Circle the answer below.

to tell a funny story

to give information about someone

to explain something

2. Why do you think the author told the reader that Amelia Earhart didn't like flying as a child?

_____
_____
_____
_____

3. What did you learn as you read the story? Tell three things that you learned about Amelia Earhart.

_____
_____
_____
_____

© Pearson Education, Inc., 2

Comprehension 169

Name _____

Proper Nouns

Circle the proper nouns in the sentences.

1. We learned about Abraham Lincoln on Monday.

2. Mr. Lincoln grew up in Indiana.

3. Did you know the Civil War ended on April 9, 1865?

Write the sentences.
Capitalize the proper nouns.

4. abraham lincoln married mary todd.

_____

- -

_____

- -

5. president lincoln lived in the White House.

_____

- -

_____

- -

_____

6. The students taped the united states map together.

_____

- -

_____

- -

_____

© Pearson Education, Inc., 2

Name _____

Pick a word from the box to match each clue.
Write the word on the line.

circus   girl   turkey   herd

1.

_____

2.

_____

3.

_____

4.

_____

Read the story.

   Shirley stroked her cat's fur. The bird looked at the cat as though she were a scary monster. Shirley gave some water to her fern and put it in the corner. Then she fed her turtle. It was time to dress for school. She put on her green skirt. It looked perfect with her white shirt. She looked at the sore on her finger. It looked like it might get worse. When she got to school, she asked the nurse to look at her sore. The nurse said it would be fine.

Home Activity Your child identified words with *er, ir,* and *ur* that have the same vowel sound as in *fern, bird,* and *surf.* Have your child use the written words in the above exercise in his or her own sentences. Encourage your child to write the sentences and illustrate them.

© Pearson Education, Inc., 2

Phonics   171

Name _____

Vowels: *r*-Controlled *er, ir, ur*

Spelling Words					
her	serve	person	curb	nurse	curl
dirt	skirt	turn	purse	birth	turtle

Find two rhyming words in each box. **Circle** the words. **Write** the words.

curb	turn	skirt
dirt	curl	her
birth	serve	turtle

person	dirt	turtle
turn	nurse	birth
curl	purse	serve

1. _____

2. _____

3. _____

4. _____

Circle the list word that is hidden in each row. **Write** it.

5. h e s e r v e j t g   _____

6. v w c c u r l o w   _____

7. u t r t u r n v b n   _____

8. y b i r t h v s a w   _____

9. p e r s o n e w x   _____

10. r d b c c u r b l v   _____

© Pearson Education, Inc., 2

Home Activity Your child has been learning to spell words with *er, ir,* and *ur*. Write the spelling list words on index cards. Hold up a card and use it in a sentence. Then have your child close his or her eyes and spell the word. Repeat with the other list words.

Name _____

Pick a word from the box to match each clue.
Write the words in the puzzle.

above   ago   enough
toward   whole   word

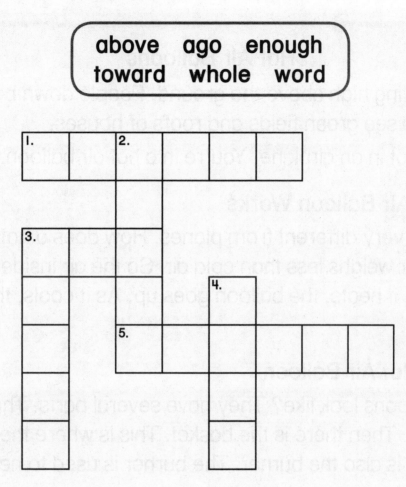

Across

1. headed for

3. in the past

5. plenty

Down

2. not in parts

3. opposite of **below**

4. You learn to spell it.

© Pearson Education, Inc., 2

Home Activity Your child completed a crossword puzzle using high-frequency words learned earlier in this unit. Together, look up the words in a dictionary. Encourage your child to make cards that have a definition on one side and the word on the other side.

Name _____

Read the text.
Answer the questions.

Hot Air Balloons

Imagine floating high above the ground. People down below look like ants. You see green fields and roofs of houses.

No, you're not in an airplane. You're in a hot air balloon.

How a Hot Air Balloon Works

Balloons are very different from planes. How does a hot air balloon work? Hot air weighs less than cold air. So the air inside the balloon is heated. As it heats, the balloon goes up. As it cools, the balloon comes down.

Parts of a Hot Air Balloon

What do balloons look like? They have several parts. There is the balloon itself. Then there is the basket. This is where the people stand. There is also the burner. The burner is used to heat the air inside the balloon.

Operating a Hot Air Balloon

Unlike airplanes, you can't turn hot air balloons. They go wherever the wind takes them. You can only make them go up or come down. You can heat the air inside to make the balloon rise. To make it fall, you can cool the air.

Hot Air Balloon Pilots

Balloon pilots know the best time for a hot air balloon ride. Most rides happen in the morning or evening. That's when the wind is

© Pearson Education, Inc., 2

Home Activity Your child used subheads to locate facts and details in a text about hot air balloons. Reread the text with your child. Have your child tell you one fact or detail provided under each subhead.

Name _____

the calmest. Strong winds are bad for balloon rides.

Would you like to be a hot air balloon pilot someday? You might have to wait a while. Balloon pilots have to be 16 years old or older. They must spend a lot of time in hot air balloons. They need to learn how to do everything. Until then, watching balloons float in the sky is exciting enough.

1. Where would you look to find out what a hot air balloon looks like?

_____

- -

_____

2. What makes a hot air balloon work?

_____

- -

_____

3. What is a hot air balloon basket?

_____

- -

_____

4. If you were operating a hot air balloon, what could you not make it do?

_____

- -

_____

5. How old must a hot air balloon pilot be?

_____

- -

_____

© Pearson Education, Inc., 2

Name _____

Singular and Plural Nouns

Underline the singular nouns in the sentences.
Circle the plural nouns.

1. The oranges grew on the tree.

2. The farmer planted more crops.

3. The boy bought new toys.

4. She shopped at two stores.

Choose the correct plural noun in ( ).
Write the sentence.

5. They put the fruit in (caseses, cases).

_____

- -

_____

6. The (foxs, foxes) ran in the farmer's field.

_____

- -

_____

7. We picked the fruit on the (treeses, trees).

_____

- -

_____

8. Birds perch in the (branches, branchs).

_____

- -

_____

© Pearson Education, Inc., 2

Name _____

Read each word. **Add -s, -es,** change the **y** to **i** and add **-es,** or change the **f** to **v** and add **-s. Write** the new word on the line.

1. cousin

_____

\- -

_____

2. story

_____

\- -

3. bench

_____

\- -

_____

4. elf

_____

\- -

5. wolf

_____

\- -

_____

6. game

_____

\- -

7. penny

_____

\- -

_____

8. sandwich

_____

\- -

Read the story.

Today is my birthday. We'll have sandwiches and cake at my party. There are seven candles and seven candies on my cake. The candies are shaped like mint leaves. First, my friends will go to the punch bowl and serve themselves. Then I'll cut the cake and serve it on dishes. After we eat, we will try to guess how many pennies are in a jar. The person who guesses the correct number will get the pennies. Then I will open my gifts. I think my dad got me some new bookshelves. It will be a great birthday.

© Pearson Education, Inc., 2

Home Activity Your child formed plural nouns by adding *-s, -es,* changing the *y* to *i* and adding *-es,* or changing the *f* to *ve* and adding *-s.* Invite your child to draw pictures to illustrate the plural nouns. Have your child use each plural noun in a sentence.

Name _____

Plurals

Spelling Words					
note	lunch	story	tune	switch	baby
notes	lunches	stories	tunes	switches	babies

Add -s or **-es** to the underlined word. **Write** the new word.

1. One of my favorite <u>tune</u> is playing on the radio. _____

2. We told many <u>story</u> around the campfire. _____

3. Dad put carrots in each of our sack <u>lunch</u>. _____

4. Those <u>baby</u> are learning how to walk. _____

5. Did you remember to turn off both light <u>switch</u>? _____

6. Molly wrote five thank-you <u>note</u> after the party. _____

Read the clues. **Write** the list words.

7. short letter ___ ___ ___ ___ ___   8. a song ___ ___ ___ ___

9. a tale ___ ___ ___ ___ ___   10. on a light ___ ___ ___ ___ ___ ___

11. a child ___ ___ ___ ___ ___   12. noon meal ___ ___ ___ ___ ___

Home Activity Your child has been learning to spell plurals with and without -s and -es. Walk around your home with your child and identify objects such as a door, bench, couch, or plate. Write the word and have your child explain how the plural is formed.

© Pearson Education, Inc., 2

Name _____

Pick a word from the box to answer each riddle.
Write the word on the line.

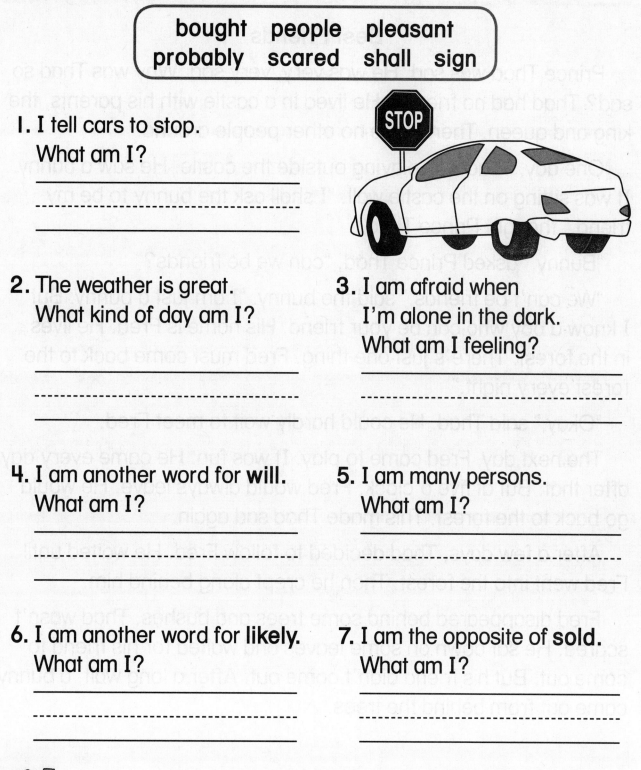

bought   people   pleasant
probably   scared   shall   sign

1. I tell cars to stop.
What am I?

_____
- -
_____

2. The weather is great.
What kind of day am I?

_____
- -
_____

3. I am afraid when
I'm alone in the dark.
What am I feeling?

_____
- -
_____

4. I am another word for **will**.
What am I?

_____
- -
_____

5. I am many persons.
What am I?

_____
- -
_____

6. I am another word for **likely**.
What am I?

- -
_____

7. I am the opposite of **sold**.
What am I?

- -
_____

© Pearson Education, Inc., 2

School + Home

Home Activity Your child answered riddles, using the words *bought, people, pleasant, probably, scared, shall,* and *sign*. Write these words on a sheet of paper. Challenge your child to use the words in a story.

High-Frequency Words 179

Name _____

Read the story.
Finish the sentences.

Best Friends

Prince Thad was sad. He was very, very sad. Why was Thad so sad? Thad had no friends. He lived in a castle with his parents, the king and queen. There were no other people around.

One day, Thad was playing outside the castle. He saw a bunny. It was sitting on the castle wall. "I shall ask the bunny to be my friend," thought Prince Thad.

"Bunny," asked Prince Thad, "can we be friends?"

"We can't be friends," said the bunny. "I am just a bunny. But I know a boy who can be your friend. His name is Fred. He lives in the forest. There's just one thing. Fred must come back to the forest every night."

"Okay," said Thad. He could hardly wait to meet Fred.

The next day, Fred came to play. It was fun. He came every day after that. But at five o'clock, Fred would always leave. He would go back to the forest. This made Thad sad again.

After a few days, Thad decided to follow Fred. He waited until Fred went into the forest. Then he crept along behind him.

Fred disappeared behind some trees and bushes. Thad wasn't scared. He sat down on some leaves and waited for his friend to come out. But his friend didn't come out. After a long wait, a bunny came out from behind the trees.

© Pearson Education, Inc., 2

Home Activity Your child read a story to see what happened and answered questions about the cause of each event. Talk to your child about the events of the day, and what happened and why.

Now Thad understood. The bunny wanted to be Thad's friend. So he turned himself into a boy each day. Finally, Thad was happy. He had a true friend at last. He knew he and Fred the Bunny would be best friends forever.

_____

I. Prince Thad was sad because

_____

- -

_____

2. The Prince talked to the bunny because

_____

- -

_____

3. The bunny turned himself into a boy each day because

_____

- -

_____

4. Prince Thad was finally happy because

_____

- -

_____

© Pearson Education, Inc., 2

Name _____

Plural Nouns That Change Spelling

Underline the plural noun in each row.

1. foot   feet   tooth

2. wolves   wolf   leaf

3. child   goose   children

Choose the plural word in ( ).
Write the word on the line.

4. Many (mouse, mice) build nests in walls. _____

5. Those (goose, geese) are loud! _____

6. You chew with all your (teeth, tooth). _____

7. (Wolves, Wolf) live in packs. _____

8. Did the robbers have (wife, wives)? _____

© Pearson Education, Inc., 2

Name _____

Circle the word in each row with the **long a** sound.
Write the word on the line.

_____

1. badly   banker   baby   _____

2. clam   class   clay   _____

3. bank   bait   bang   _____

4. later   ladder   lamp   _____

Read the story.

Today Katy made boats with paper sails. After it stopped raining we went to the pond to sail them. We put the boats in the pond and they sailed away. The ducks didn't like the boats. They swam away from them. But one duck stayed for a close look. He must have seemed crazy to the other ducks. Then the sky turned gray again. We couldn't see a ray of sunshine. It started to rain and we went home for the day.

© Pearson Education, Inc., 2

School + Home **Home Activity** Your child identified words in which the *long a* sound is spelled *a, ai,* or *ay.* Ask your child to write the *long a* words from above on separate index cards. Then have your child sort the words according to the way the *long a* sound is spelled.

Name _____

Vowel Digraphs *ai, ay*

Spelling Words					
tail	main	wait	say	away	play
raise	brain	paint	stay	today	tray

Read the sentences. **Write** the list word that rhymes with the underlined word and makes sense in the sentence.

1. "Hee-haw!" said the donkey in a long, loud <u>bray</u>. "I hope Farmer Brown will feed us _____!"

   ----

2. "Moo!" said the cow near the big red <u>gate</u>. "He's not here yet. You'll have to _____!"

   ----

3. "Mew!" said the kittens, white, orange, and <u>gray</u>. "When can we go tumble and _____?"

   ----

4. "Meow!" said the mother cat. "What did I <u>say</u>?" "You can run after breakfast, but now you must _____."

   ----

5. "Woof!" said the dog. "There's the farmer with his <u>pail</u>!" He ran up to Farmer Brown, wagging his _____.

   ----

6. "Come and eat!" said the farmer. "It's a wonderful <u>day</u>!" He fed all the animals, and then he went _____.

Unscramble the list word. **Write** it.

7. i n r a b _____

8. e s r i a _____

9. n a m i _____

10. y a r t _____

11. t p i a n _____

12. a y s _____

Home Activity Your child has been learning to spell words with *long a* spelled *ai* and *ay*. Say a word that rhymes with one of the list words. Have your child point to the list word, say it out loud, and then spell it.

© Pearson Education, Inc., 2

Name _____

Find the word that completes the sentence.
Mark the space to show your answer.

1. Did you look _____ the chair?
   - ⬭ behind
   - ⬭ brought
   - ⬭ door

2. Will you _____ to be on time?
   - ⬭ minute
   - ⬭ promise
   - ⬭ sorry

3. I'm _____ you're sick.
   - ⬭ minute
   - ⬭ promise
   - ⬭ sorry

4. The show will begin in one _____.
   - ⬭ everybody
   - ⬭ minute
   - ⬭ promise

5. The _____ is locked.
   - ⬭ brought
   - ⬭ door
   - ⬭ everybody

6. He _____ his dog to school.
   - ⬭ brought
   - ⬭ door
   - ⬭ everybody

7. I drew a picture of _____ in my family.
   - ⬭ brought
   - ⬭ door
   - ⬭ everybody

Home Activity Your child learned to read the words *behind, brought, door, everybody, minute, promise,* and *sorry.* Have your child write sentences using these words. Challenge your child to include two of the words in each sentence.

© Pearson Education, Inc., 2

Name _____

Read the story. **Answer** the questions.

The Fox and the Goat
A Tale from India

Dabbu the fox was happy. And full. He had just eaten a large meal. Now he was walking home in the moonlight. He sang as he walked. He was filled with happy thoughts.

Whoa! Suddenly the fox felt himself falling. He reached out to stop himself. But it was too late. Dabbu the fox had fallen into a shallow well. He often passed the well on his way home. Normally, he would never fall in it. But tonight he had been too happy. He had been singing and not paying attention. Now he was sorry.

Dabbu felt around the well. There wasn't much water in it. That was good. But how was he going to get out? Dabbu tried climbing out. But the walls were muddy and slippery. He couldn't get out. He tried again and again. Finally, he got tired. He sat down to rest. He had to think of a plan.

Not a minute later, he heard a voice. "What are you doing inside that well?" the voice asked.

Dabbu looked up. Standing above him was Laadla the goat. Dabbu studied the goat. He began to make a plan.

"Haven't you heard?" Dabbu asked Laadla. "There is a drought coming. No one will have water. So I jumped into the well to be sure to have some water near me. Why don't you jump down, too?"

The goat looked unsure. "What if you harm me when I jump down?" he asked.

© Pearson Education, Inc., 2

School + Home **Home Activity** Your child compared and contrasted several stories. Read two stories with your child. Have your child tell how the stories are alike and how they are different.

Name _____

"Oh, I promise I won't," the fox said.

"Okay," said Laddla the goat. He jumped into the well.

Suddenly, Dabbu jumped on Laddla's back and leaped out of the well. "So long," he shouted.

Now Laddla was stranded. "Wait!" the goat cried. "You promised not to hurt me!"

The fox laughed as he left. "But I didn't promise to help you, either!"

1. How is this story like "One Good Turn Deserves Another" and "The Ungrateful Tiger"?

_____

_____

_____

_____

2. How is this story different from "One Good Turn Deserves Another" and "The Ungrateful Tiger"?

_____

_____

_____

_____

3. How is this story alike and different from "The Lion and the Mouse"?

_____

_____

_____

_____

© Pearson Education, Inc., 2

Possessive Nouns

Add 's or **'** to each noun in ( ). **Write** the words on the line.

1. the (snake) head

_____

_____

2. the (mouse) squeak

_____

_____

3. the (animals) conversations

_____

_____

4. her (cousin) favor

_____

_____

Add 's or **'** to the underlined word. **Write** the sentence on the line.

5. The <u>creatures</u> words did not help the mouse.

_____

_____

6. The <u>coyote</u> trick caught the snake.

_____

_____

© Pearson Education, Inc., 2

Name _____

Directions Chart

Fill out this directions chart to help you organize your ideas.
Write your ideas in sentences. Draw pictures if it will help.

Title_____

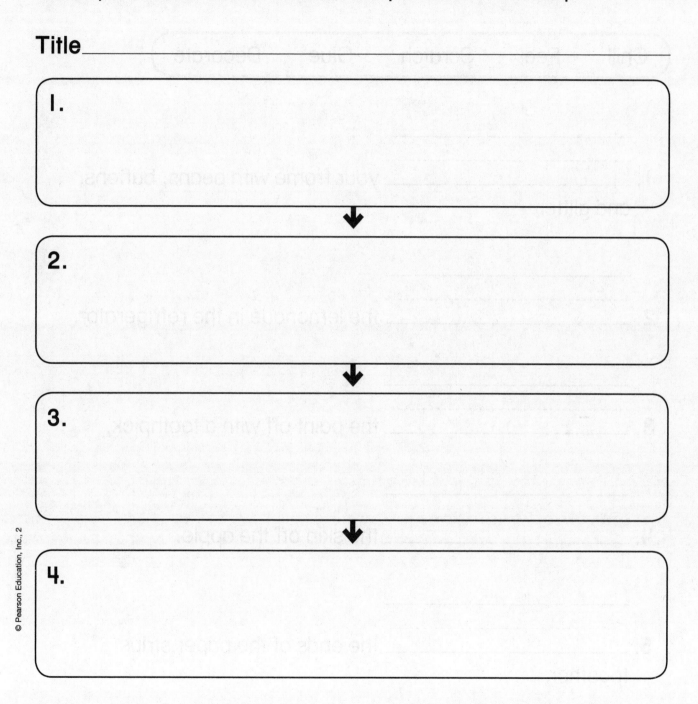

1.

2.

3.

4.

© Pearson Education, Inc., 2

Name _____

Use Strong Verbs

Write a verb from the box that gives a clear picture of what to do.

| Chill | Peel | Scratch | Glue | Decorate |

1. _____ your frame with beans, buttons, and glitter.

2. _____ the lemonade in the refrigerator.

3. _____ the paint off with a toothpick.

4. _____ the skin off the apple.

5. _____ the ends of the paper strips together.

© Pearson Education, Inc., 2

Name _____

Adding Words, Phrases, or Sentences

When you revise, add words, phrases, and sentences to give more details. **Follow** the directions to revise the sentence.

Spread the jam.

1. Add a word that describes the jam. Write the new sentence.

_____
_____
_____
_____

2. Add a phrase that tells what to spread the jam on. Write the new sentence.

_____
_____
_____
_____

3. Add a sentence that tells what to do next. Write both sentences.

_____
_____
_____
_____
_____

© Pearson Education, Inc., 2

Name _____

Editing 1

Proofreading Marks	
Delete (Take out)	ᷧ
Add	^
Spelling	⬭
Uppercase letter	≡
Lowercase letter	/

Edit these sentences. **Look** for errors in grammar, punctuation, capitalization, and spelling. **Use** proofreading marks to show the corrections.

1. Here's a fun game you can allways play with a friend?

2. first use chalk to drew a hopscotch pattern on the sidewalk.

3. A hopscotch pattern have eight squares with numbers in it.

4. Now toss a pebble so that they land in the ferst square.

5. Next, hop onto each square on one foot but dont hop on the square with the pebble.

6. On the next turn, eech player tosses the pebble onto the secund square and hops again.

Now you'll edit the draft of your directions, as your teacher directs you. Then you'll use your draft to make a final copy of your directions. Finally, you'll publish your writing and share it with others.

© Pearson Education, Inc., 2

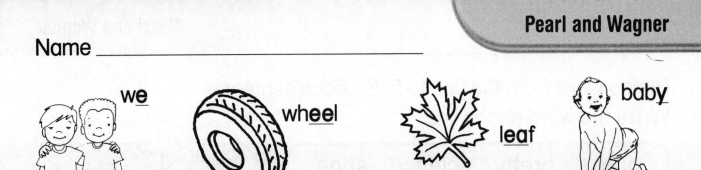

Name _____

we

wheel

leaf

baby

These bees only fly past words with the **long e** sound.
Circle each word with the **long e** sound.
Draw a line to show the path from the bees to the tree.

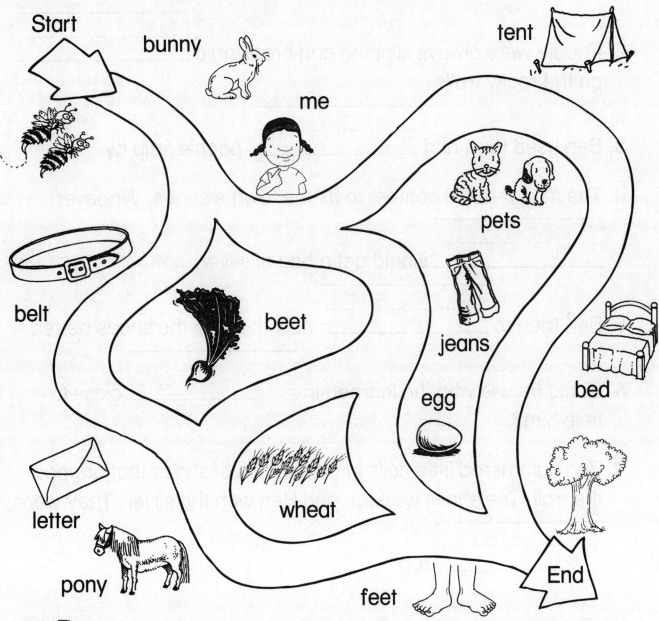

Start

bunny

me

tent

pets

jeans

egg

bed

belt

beet

letter

wheat

pony

feet

End

© Pearson Education, Inc., 2

Home Activity Your child identified words with common vowel patterns spelled *ee* as in *wheel*, *ea* as in *leaf*, *e* as in *we*, and *y* as in *baby*. Work with your child to make picture cards of long e words with a picture on the front and the word for it on the back.

Name _____

Pick a word from the box to finish each sentence.
Write the word on the line.

> guess   pretty   science   shoe
> village   watch   won

1. There was a _____ at the top of a steep hill.

2. People were always slipping and breaking a _____ on the rocky trails.

3. Ben used to sit and _____ people limp by.

4. The mayor had a contest to fix the town's shoes. Whoever _____ would get a bag of silver.

5. Ben tried to _____ how to make the shoes better.

6. Could he use what he learned in _____ class to help him?

7. Ben hammered little nails into the soles of shoes that gripped the trail. The shoes worked, and Ben won the silver. They were _____ too.

Home Activity Your child learned to read the words *guess, pretty, science, shoe, village, watch,* and *won*. Have your child retell the above story in his or her own words while pointing to the words in the box.

© Pearson Education, Inc., 2

Name _____

Read the story.
Follow the directions.

Robert the Robot
by Jake Simmons

Last week I went to the Robot Store. I picked out a cook robot. I named him Robert. Getting Robert is the smartest thing I've ever done. He is great! I showed him how to make my bed. He picks up my stuff from the floor. Next, I am going to teach him how to take out the trash. Robert is the best friend a kid could have!

1. **Circle** the author's name.

2. **Circle** the words that tell what Robert can do.
   go to the store   make my bed

3. **Circle** the words that tell what Robert will learn next.
   take out the trash   pick up stuff

4. **Underline** the sentence that tells where Robert came from.

5. **Write** a sentence that tells why you think the author wrote this story.

_____
- -
_____
_____
- -
_____

© Pearson Education, Inc., 2

School + Home **Home Activity** Your child read a funny story and told why the author wrote it. Select an age-appropriate science fiction story to read with your child. Ask your child to identify who wrote the story and tell why the writer might have written it.

Name _____

Writing • Animal Fantasy

 A Rainy Day

Three friends sit on the porch at Horse's cabin. "The rain stops our fun in the yard," says Horse. "We need something to do." He taps his foot while he thinks. Dog scratches his ear and thinks. Cat swishes her tail back and forth across the bench.

Cat smiles. "Listen to us. We sound like a band!"

The friends decide to make even better music. First they get pans to catch the rain—plink, plunk, plink. Next they tap forks on pots—clink, clink, clank. Then they hum songs they like. At last they sing and make up silly songs.

Now Horse and Dog and Cat like the rain. They make music on every rainy day!

Key Features of an Animal Fantasy

- characters are animals

- events are make-believe

- characters do things that real animals cannot do

© Pearson Education, Inc., 2

Name _____

Vowel Patterns *ee, ea, y*

Spelling Words					
read	feet	easy	deep	seat	party
wheel	leave	windy	sleep	teeth	team

Write the missing list word. It rhymes with the name.

_____

1. Marty couldn't wait for the _____ .

_____

2. Mr. Peep went to _____ .

_____

3. Mrs. Steep dug a hole that is _____ .

_____

4. Mr. Heet asked, "How are your _____?"

_____

5. Cindy said that it was _____ .

_____

6. Mr. Snead likes to _____ .

_____

Write the list word that fits in each group.

_____   _____

7. hood, bumper, _____   8. group, bunch, _____

_____   _____

9. chair, bench, _____   10. lips, tongue, _____

_____   _____

11. simple, basic, _____   12. go, depart, _____

Home Activity Your child spelled words with long *e* spelled *ee, ea,* and *y*. Have your child underline these letter combinations in the list words.

© Pearson Education, Inc., 2

Name _____

Pick the antonym from the box for each word below.
Write the correct antonym on the line.

up	far	funny	strong	empty
stop	hot	shut	break	hard

I. cold _____   2. fix _____

3. down _____   4. soft _____

5. go _____   6. near _____

7. weak _____   8. open _____

9. sad _____   10. full _____

Pick a word from above and its antonym.
Write sentences for the word and its antonym.

II. _____

_____

I2. _____

_____

Home Activity Your child identified and used antonyms. Say three numbered words on this page. Have your child say the antonym without looking at the page.

© Pearson Education, Inc., 2

Name _____

Verbs

A word that shows action is a **verb**.

    The robot **walks** to the door.

The word **walks** is a verb.
It tells what the robot does.

Write the verb in each sentence.

  1. Pearl enters the science fair.

  2. Wagner helps Pearl.

  3. The judge looks at the projects.

  4. The judge picks a winner.

  5. The friends go home.

© Pearson Education, Inc., 2

Home Activity Your child learned about verbs. Read a story with your child. Point to several simple sentences and have your child find the verbs in the sentences.

Conventions Verbs **199**

Name _____

Story Chart

Title _____

> **Characters**

> **Setting**

> **Beginning**

⬇

> **Middle**

⬇

> **End**

© Pearson Education, Inc., 2

Home Activity Your child is learning to write stories, poems, brief reports, nonfiction paragraphs, letters, and other products this year. Ask what your child is writing this week.

Name _____

Look at the picture graph below. **Answer** each question.

Number of Books Read	
Sam	📖 📖 📖 📖
Ella	📖 📖 📖
Hugh	📖 📖 📖
Ted	📖 📖 📖 📖 📖

Each 📖 stands for two books.

1. What does the picture graph show?

_____

----

2. What is the number of books
   each picture represents? _____

   ----

3. Who read the most books?
   How many? _____

   ----

4. Which two children read the same number of books? How many?

_____

_____

5. Add **Lynn** to the chart in the last row. She read 12 books.
   How many pictures should you draw? Complete the chart.

Home Activity Your child learned how to read a picture graph. Together with your child think of a topic for which you could make a picture graph (such as the number of fruits or vegetables eaten in a day or a week). Design a family picture graph and ask your child to add the necessary information.

© Pearson Education, Inc., 2

Name _____

Vowel Patterns ee, ea, y

Read Andy's note. **Circle** three spelling mistakes and an incorrect verb. **Write** the words correctly.

> Mom,
>
> I made the teem! The tryouts was easy.
>
> I have to leav bicause practice starts today.
>
> I'll be home for the party.
>
> Love, Andy

Spelling Words	
read	wheel
feet	leave
easy	windy
deep	sleep
seat	teeth
party	team

Frequently Misspelled Words

because

Easter

1. _____

2. _____

3. _____

4. _____

Fill in the circle to show the correct spelling.

5. ○ tethe   ○ teath   ○ teeth

6. ○ deap   ○ deep   ○ depe

7. ○ party   ○ partie   ○ partee

8. ○ rede   ○ reid   ○ read

9. ○ feat   ○ feet   ○ feit

10. ○ windy   ○ windey   ○ windie

Home Activity Your child identified misspelled words with long *e*: *ee*, *ea*, and *y*. Say a list word. Ask your child how the long *e* sound is spelled.

© Pearson Education, Inc., 2

Name _____

Pick a word from the box to match each clue.
Write the word on the line.

> guess   pretty   science   shoe
> village   wad   watch   won

1. worn on a foot _____

2. to look _____

3. small town _____

4. to try to think of something _____

5. a small bundle of paper _____

6. built a trash-eating robot and got a prize
_____

7. study electricity in this class _____

8. beautiful _____

© Pearson Education, Inc., 2

School + Home

Home Activity Your child matched clues with words learned this week. Write the clues and words on separate slips of paper or index cards. Mix them up and play a matching game with your child.

Name _____

Verbs

Mark the letter of the word that completes each sentence.

1. I _____ Ann at school.
   - ○ **A** with
   - ○ **B** see
   - ○ **C** doll

2. Ann _____ the ball.
   - ○ **A** grabs
   - ○ **B** bells
   - ○ **C** school

3. _____ me the ball.
   - ○ **A** Throw
   - ○ **B** That
   - ○ **C** Tom

4. I _____ the ball.
   - ○ **A** cup
   - ○ **B** sit
   - ○ **C** catch

5. Ann _____ for me.
   - ○ **A** then
   - ○ **B** cheers
   - ○ **C** books

6. I _____ the ball.
   - ○ **A** toss
   - ○ **B** and
   - ○ **C** book

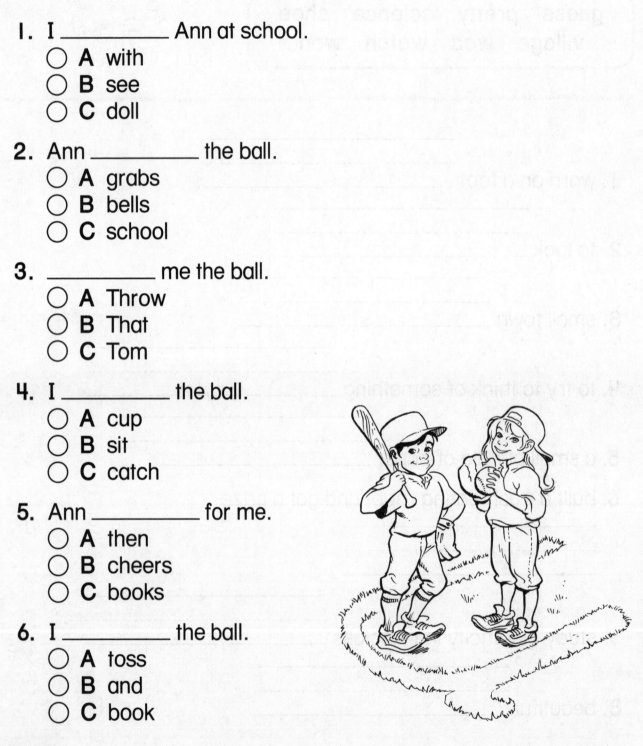

© Pearson Education, Inc., 2

Home Activity Your child prepared to take tests on verbs. Take a walk around the neighborhood and have your child point out verbs that appear on signs and advertisements.

Name _____

 c<u>o</u>bra    b<u>oa</u>t    b<u>ow</u>

Circle the word in each row with the **long o** sound.
Write the word on the line.

1.	toad	top	two
2.	bog	book	bowl
3.	took	toss	toast
4.	out	over	one
5.	most	moss	mop
6.	spoon	show	shoe
7.	hot	hold	hook
8.	play	pot	photo
9.	veto	vet	vane
10.	good	got	grow

_____
_____
_____
_____
_____
_____
_____
_____
_____
_____

© Pearson Education, Inc., 2

 School + Home **Home Activity** Your child identified words with common vowel patterns spelled o, oa, or ow. Write the word endings -ost, -old, -oat, and -ow on slips of paper. Have your child add beginning letters to each ending to form long o words.

Name _____

Pick a word from the box to finish each sentence.
Write the word on the line.

> answer   company   faraway
> parents   picture   school   wash

1. San walked into his new _____. He was
   a little scared.

2. He was with his _____.

3. San had moved here from a _____ country.

4. His dad had a job at a new _____.

5. "How are you today, San?" asked Ms. Larson. San could not
   _____ her question. He felt bad.

6. San brought a _____ book to show the children.

7. One picture showed how some people _____
   their clothes outside. Everyone thought that sounded cool!

Home Activity Your child learned to read the words *answer, company, faraway, parents, picture, school,* and *wash.* Challenge your child to use some of these words to write about family photographs.

© Pearson Education, Inc., 2

Name _____

Read the sentences.
Write your answers on the lines.

1. Jason's mother said, "You will see your grandmother in a few weeks. She will fly here for Thanksgiving." What do you know about where Jason's grandmother lives?

_____

_____

_____

2. Jason sat at the table. Mom was cooking. He had a pen in his hand. There was a piece of paper, an envelope, and a stamp in front of him. Where was he? What was he doing?

_____

_____

_____

3. Jason walked down the street with the envelope in his hand. Where was he going?

_____

_____

_____

4. Jason's grandmother looked at her mail. There was a letter. She knew the letter was from Jason. How did she know who wrote the letter before she opened it?

_____

_____

_____

5. She had a big smile on her face. Why was she smiling?

_____

_____

Home Activity Your child used text to draw conclusions about a story. As you read a story to your child, stop often to ask your child what is happening or why a character is doing something.

© Pearson Education, Inc., 2

Name _____

Writing • Friendly Letter

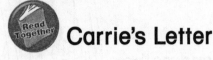 **Carrie's Letter**

November 16, 2011

Dear Roberto,

   Today in school I learned about sign language. It's a way that deaf people communicate. People who live in different places can see one another sign. They use Web cams. I thought learning how to sign would be hard, but it is interesting. I learned to sign "I love you," "Please," and "Thank you." It was fun! I can't wait for you to visit so I can show you.

Your friend,
Carrie

Key Features of a Friendly Letter

- includes the date, a greeting, the body, a closing, and a signature

- the body of the letter has the message

- tells the writer's ideas, feelings, and opinions

© Pearson Education, Inc., 2

Vowel Patterns *o, oa, ow*

Spelling Words					
goat	hold	show	most	bowl	float
toast	ago	open	told	toad	slow

Write two list words that rhyme with each word.

      coat   gold   bow

1. _____ 3. _____ 5. _____

2. _____ 4. _____ 6. _____

Write list words that mean almost the same thing as the underlined words.

7. He has the <u>largest number of</u> marbles.

8. He moved here three years <u>back in time</u>.

9. Put the apples in the <u>dish</u>.

10. Shall I <u>brown</u> some bread for you?

11. The <u>frog</u> jumped into the pond.

12. The store is <u>not closed</u>.

 School + Home   **Home Activity** Your child spelled words with long *o* spelled *o, oa,* and *ow*. Challenge your child to spell *bowl* and think of at least two different meanings for the word. (to knock down pins, a dish, a special football game)

© Pearson Education, Inc., 2

Name _____

Circle the prefix in each word. **Underline** the correct meaning of the word. **Write** a sentence with the word on the line.

1. prepay

    a. pay back   b. pay before   c. pay now

_____

_ _

2. unfair

    a. very fair   b. full of fairness   c. not fair

_____

_ _

3. misinform

    a. give secret   b. give all the   c. give wrong
       information   information   information

_____

_ _

4. reread

    a. read to   b. not read   c. read again

_____

_ _

5. disrespect

    a. to respect   b. to respect   c. to not respect
       again   often

_____

_ _

© Pearson Education, Inc., 2

Home Activity Your child learned about words with prefixes and their meanings. Challenge your child to name other words that begin with the prefixes he or she circled on this page and tell what the words mean.

Verbs with Singular and Plural Nouns

The subject and verb in a sentence must work together, or **agree**.
Add -*s* to a verb to tell what one person,
animal, or thing does.
Do not add -*s* to a verb that tells what
two or more people, animals, or things do.

Juno **writes** a letter.
Max and Pam **write** letters.

Circle the verb in ( ) that completes each sentence.

1. The boy (send, sends) letters to his grandma.

2. His letters (tells, tell) about him.

3. Grandma (like, likes) his pictures.

4. His pictures (makes, make) her happy.

5. Juno (read, reads) a letter from his grandma.

© Pearson Education, Inc., 2

Home Activity Your child learned about verbs with singular and plural nouns. Look for simple sentences in a magazine or newspaper. Have your child point out verbs that are used with singular nouns and verbs that are used with plural nouns.

Name _____

Main Idea Chart

My letter is going to _____

_____

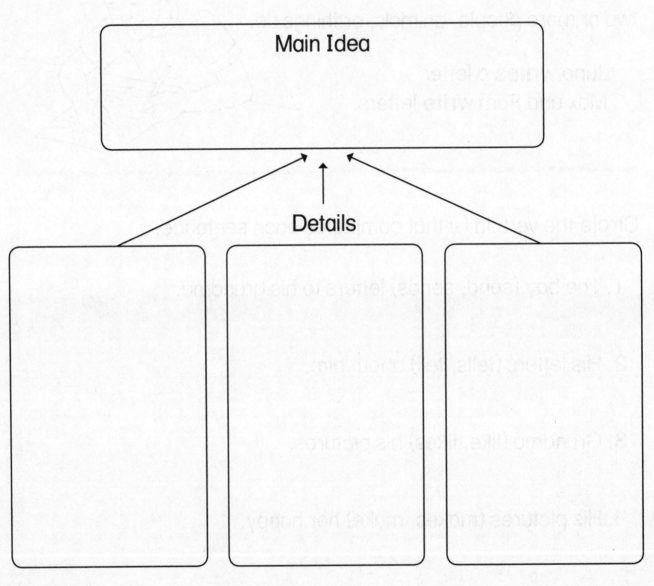

Main Idea

Details

© Pearson Education, Inc., 2

Home Activity Your child is learning to write stories, poems, brief reports, nonfiction paragraphs, letters, and other products this year. Ask what your child is writing this week.

Name _____

You will be presenting a dramatization answering the Question of the Week, *In what creative ways do we communicate?* Use the following steps to help you plan your dramatization.

Step 1 What did you learn that interests you most about creative ways we communicate? Write the information you would most like to share with the class. Create a group with 3–4 other students who would like to share the same information.

I want the class to know _____.

Step 2 As a group, create a situation to show what you think is most interesting about creative ways to communicate. Where does the situation take place? What people, or characters, are involved? What is the problem? What do the characters do?

The setting is _____.

The characters are _____.

The problem is _____.

The characters' actions are _____.

Step 3 Choose a character. Think about what he or she might say in the situation your group created.

My character is _____.

My character says, " _____."

Step 4 Present the situation to the class.

Home Activity Your child learned how to create a dramatization based on research results. Together find and read a newspaper, magazine, or Internet article. Plan and present a dramatization of the events in the article.

© Pearson Education, Inc., 2

Name _____

Vowel Patterns *o, oa, ow*

Read Carrie's letter. **Circle** three spelling mistakes and one word with a capitalization error. **Write** the words correctly.

Spelling Words	
goat	toast
hold	ago
show	open
most	told
bowl	toad
float	slow

Dear Sir:

    My family tried Corny Puffs a few days ago. We got the box opin, but most of the Corny Puffs were gone. we only could fill one bowl. I had to eat tost.
    I no you will want to send us a new, full box.

          Thank you,
          Carrie

Frequently Misspelled Words

Halloween

know

1. _____

2. _____

3. _____

4. _____

Circle the correct word. **Write** it.

5. gowt   goat   _____

6. hoald   hold   _____

7. slow   slo   _____

8. flowt   float   _____

9. bowl   bowal   _____

10. show   sho   _____

School + Home   **Home Activity** Your child identified misspelled words with long *o* spelled *o, oa,* and *ow*. Have your child underline these letter combinations in the list words.

© Pearson Education, Inc., 2

Name _____

Pick a word from the box to match each clue.
Write the word on the line.

> answer   company   faraway   parents
> persimmons   picture   school
> smudged   wash

1. a long way from something _____

2. ask a question and get this _____

3. where kids learn _____

4. a place where people work _____

5. a photograph or drawing _____

6. to get clean _____

7. mom and dad _____

8. made a dirty mark on an envelope _____

9. a kind of fruit _____

© Pearson Education, Inc., 2

Home Activity Your child matched clues with high-frequency and selection words learned this week. Challenge your child to write a story about a family moving to a new place, using some of these words.

Name _____

Verbs with Singular and Plural Nouns

Mark the letter of the verb that completes each sentence.

1. My cousins _____ letters.
   - ○ **A** write
   - ○ **B** sit
   - ○ **C** writes

2. My grandma _____ e-mails.
   - ○ **A** run
   - ○ **B** sends
   - ○ **C** send

3. My sister _____ on the phone.
   - ○ **A** call
   - ○ **B** calls
   - ○ **C** eat

4. My mom _____ the neighbors.
   - ○ **A** sing
   - ○ **B** visit
   - ○ **C** visits

5. My brother and dad _____ .
   - ○ **A** talk
   - ○ **B** talks
   - ○ **C** fix

6. The dogs _____ at us.
   - ○ **A** barks
   - ○ **B** bark
   - ○ **C** boil

© Pearson Education, Inc., 2

Home Activity Your child prepared to take tests on verbs with singular and plural nouns. Say this sentence starter: *Dad ___.* Have your child complete the sentence with an appropriate verb: *Dad reads.* Continue with this sentence starter: *Grandma and Grandpa ___. (Grandma and Grandpa walk.)*

Name _____

Say the word for each picture.
Use two words to make a compound word that names the picture.
Write the compound word on the line.

river + bank = riverbank

1.

spoon   pot   table   tea

_____

_____

2.

coats   drops   rain   shoes

_____

3.

air   box   mail   plane

_____

_____

4.

shoe   tie   lace   neck

_____

Find the word that you can put together with *meal* to make a compound word.
Mark the space to show your answer.

5. _____meal
   ○ dinner
   ○ oat
   ○ book

6. meal_____
   ○ time
   ○ spoon
   ○ napkin

© Pearson Education, Inc., 2

School + Home **Home Activity** Your child wrote compound words—words that are made up of two smaller words, such as *riverbank*. Work with your child to use the words listed above to make up other compound words, such as *teaspoon, raincoats, airplane,* and *necktie.*

Phonics Compound Words   **217**

Name _____

Pick a word from the box to finish each sentence.
Write the word on the line.

been   believe   caught   finally
today   tomorrow   whatever

_____

1. Spider said, "I _____ I can catch many flies."

_____

2. Spider waited a long time. _____ , he saw
a bug.

_____

3. He _____ one little fly in his web.

_____

4. Lizard has _____ waiting by the mouse's hole.

_____

5. He hopes that _____ will be the day he catches
a fat mouse.

_____

6. Snake said, "I will wait until _____ to hunt
for food."

_____

7. Snake moves fast, so he can catch _____
comes by him.

School + Home **Home Activity** This week your child is learning to read the words *been, believe, caught, finally, today, tomorrow,* and *whatever*. Find a book of Anansi folktales in your library. As you read together, ask your child to look for these high-frequency words.

© Pearson Education, Inc., 2

Name _____

Read the folk tale below, and review the fairy tale on p. 135.
Circle the correct word or words to finish each sentence.
Answer the question on paper.

What Happened When the Sky Fell Down

For thousands of years, people in China have told a folk tale about the day the sky fell down. Children see the sky falling and run to tell Wise Woman. Wise Woman asks the children to pick up the pieces of sky and bring them to her. The children do this, but some pieces are missing. The night sky in China had always been black, but the next night the sky was dotted with little bright lights! Wise Woman had sewn the sky pieces together and put patches of twinkling lights in place of the missing pieces.

1. A folk tale is _____.

   fiction   nonfiction

2. The events in "One Morning in Dragonville" and the events in this folk tale are alike because they could _____ .

   always happen   never happen

3. The character trait that describes Wise Woman and Spots the Dragon is _____.

   kind   mean

4. How is the problem for Spots in "One Morning in Dragonville" different from Wise Woman's problem in this folk tale?

_____

- -

_____

© Pearson Education, Inc., 2

School + Home **Home Activity** Your child made inferences about events in a folk tale. Discuss why this story is fiction, asking your child to name the story events that could not happen in real life. Reread the fairy tale on page 135 and help your child and compare and contrast the characters and events.

Name _____

Writing • Narrative Poem

Silver Snake's Journey

Silver Snake journeyed to visit a friend.
Something stopped him before the end.
A big blue lake was in front of him.
Silver found what he needed to swim.
First he tied a red balloon on his tail.
Then he bit a stick with a bag for a sail.
Soon Silver felt happy swimming away.
He and his friend would have a good day.

Key Features of a Narrative Poem

- has well-chosen words arranged in lines

- tells a brief story

- may have rhyming words

© Pearson Education, Inc., 2

Name _____

Compound Words

Spelling Words					
basketball	someone	weekend	something	birthday	riverbank
bathtub	backyard	driveway	bedtime	raindrop	mailbox

Write a list word to name each picture.

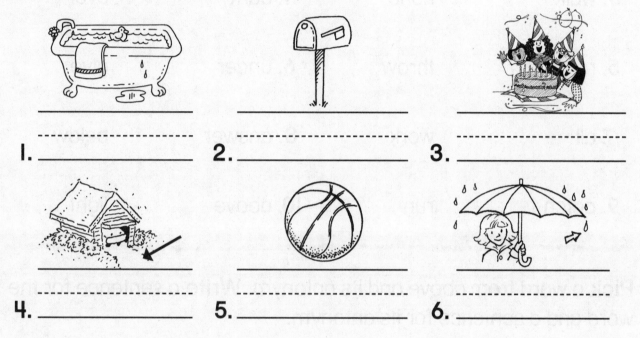

1. _____

2. _____

3. _____

4. _____

5. _____

6. _____

Write the list word that can be made by joining the two words together.

week + end

7. _____

some + one

8. _____

back + yard

9. _____

river + bank

10. _____

bed + time

11. _____

some + thing

12. _____

School + Home **Home Activity** Your child spelled compound words. Ask your child to name the two smaller words in each compound word.

© Pearson Education, Inc., 2

Name _____

Draw lines to match the words to their antonyms.

WORD	ANTONYM	WORD	ANTONYM
I. play	sun	2. take	question
3. walk	none	4. dark	over
5. rain	throw	6. under	give
7. all	work	8. answer	below
9. catch	run	10. above	light

Pick a word from above and its antonym. **Write** a sentence for the word and a sentence for its antonym.

II. _____

12. _____

Home Activity Your child identified and used antonyms. Point different directions and say the appropriate word such as *up, down, left,* and *right.* Have your child say and point the opposite direction.

© Pearson Education, Inc., 2

Verbs for Present, Past, and Future

Today Turtle **rests**.

The verb **rests** tells about now. It ends with **-s**.

Yesterday Turtle **rested**.

The verb **rested** tells about the past. It ends with **-ed**.

Tomorrow Turtle **will rest**.

The verb **will rest** tells about the future. It begins with **will**.

Circle the verb in each sentence. **Write** *N* if the verb tells about now. **Write** *P* if the verb tells about the past. **Write** *F* if the verb tells about the future.

1. Today the spider asks a question. _____

2. Tomorrow the turtle will answer. _____

3. Now the turtle takes a nap. _____

4. Yesterday the spider fished in the river. _____

5. The turtle walked home. _____

© Pearson Education, Inc., 2

Home Activity Your child learned about verbs for present, past, and future. Read a book together. Have your child point out the verbs in simple sentences. Ask your child to tell you if the verbs tell about the present, the past, or the future.

Conventions Verbs for Present, Past, and Future **223**

Name _____

Narrative Poem Chart

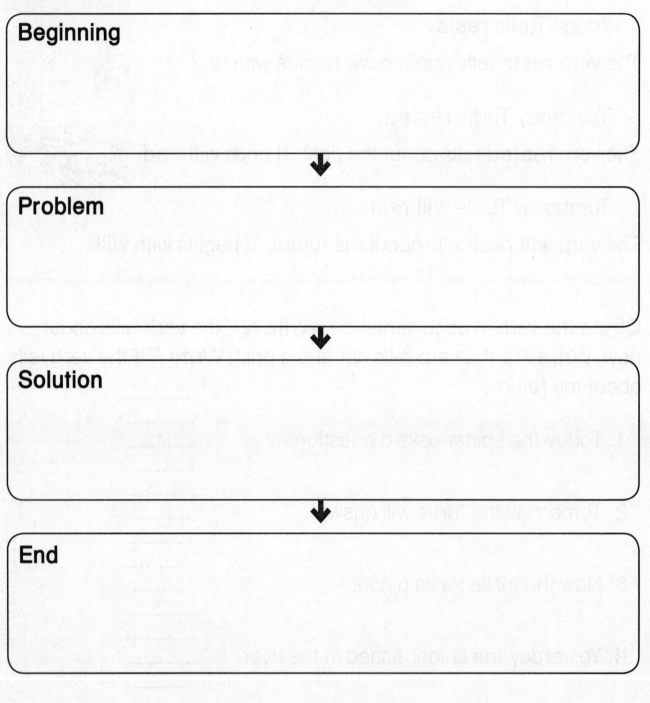

Beginning

Problem

Solution

End

© Pearson Education, Inc., 2

 Home Activity Your child is learning to write stories, poems, brief reports, nonfiction paragraphs, letters, and other products this year. Ask what your child is writing this week

Name _____

Today, you will decide which sources of information might be relevant to answer your questions about the Question of the Week, *How can creative thinking solve a problem?* Use the following steps to help you choose a relevant source to answer your questions.

Step 1- Make sure it is clear what you want to learn about your topic. Write some of your inquiry questions below.

_____   _____
_____   _____
_____   _____
_____   _____

Step 2- Review the many sources of information that you have learned about this year. Write down four sources.

_____   _____
_____   _____
_____   _____
_____   _____

Step 3- Circle the sources that you think will help you answer your inquiry questions. Find these sources and use them to answer your inquiry questions.

Step 4- Are you able to find answers to all of your inquiry questions? If not, work with a partner to think about other sources you might use. Or, think about how a source might be more focused to answer your questions. For example, if you chose an interview, does the person you interviewed have experience solving problems creatively?

© Pearson Education, Inc., 2

Home Activity Your child learned how to decide what sources of information might be relevant to answer his or her inquiry questions. Visit a Media Center or Library and discuss the various information sources that are available. Discuss with your child why some sources might be better than others.

Name _____

Compound Words

Read the journal entry. **Circle** three spelling mistakes. **Write** the words correctly. Then write the second sentence, using the correct verb.

> Here's what happened on my birth day. Dad says to go owtside. I might find something in the driveway. It was a basketbal hoop! I played ball until bedtime.

Spelling Words

basketball	bathtub
someone	backyard
weekend	driveway
something	bedtime
birthday	raindrop
riverbank	mailbox

1. _____

2. _____

3. _____

4. _____

Frequently Misspelled Words

outside

everybody

sometimes

baseball

Circle and **write** the list word that is spelled correctly.

5. You need to hop in the   bath tub
                               bathtub   _____

6. We sat on the   riverbank
                    rivorbank   _____

7. I found a postcard in the   mailbox
                                malebox   _____

8. We will play in the   bakyard
                         backyard   _____

School + Home **Home Activity** Your child identified misspelled compound words. Have your child spell the parts of each compound word separately.

© Pearson Education, Inc., 2

Name _____

Pick a word from the box to match each clue.
Write the word on the line.

> been   believe   caught   delicious
> finally   today   tomorrow   whatever

1. to hope something is true

_____

- -

_____

2. got the ball

_____

- -

_____

3. this day

_____

- -

_____

4. at last

_____

- -

_____

5. the day after this day

_____

- -

_____

6. great-tasting

_____

- -

_____

Circle a word to finish each sentence.
Write the word on the line.

weave   whatever

_____

- -

7. The spider web will catch _____ bug flies by.

been   justice

_____

- -

8. The lazy bat has not _____ flying all night.

Home Activity Your child matched clues and completed sentences with words learned this week. Assist your child in adding these words to a "Word Box" by providing scraps of paper or index cards on which he or she can write the words and definitions.

© Pearson Education, Inc., 2

High-Frequency Words/Story Words 227

Verbs for Present, Past, and Future

Mark the letter that tells the time of the verb in each sentence.
Then **say** a sentence using one verb.

1. The turtle tricked the spider.
   - ○ **A** now
   - ○ **B** past
   - ○ **C** future

2. The spider will work tomorrow.
   - ○ **A** now
   - ○ **B** past
   - ○ **C** future

3. The turtle naps in the sun.
   - ○ **A** now
   - ○ **B** past
   - ○ **C** future

4. The spider spins a web.
   - ○ **A** now
   - ○ **B** past
   - ○ **C** future

5. The turtle will eat the fish later.
   - ○ **A** now
   - ○ **B** past
   - ○ **C** future

6. The spider waved goodbye.
   - ○ **A** now
   - ○ **B** past
   - ○ **C** future

Home Activity Your child prepared to take tests on verbs for present, past, and future. Write these verbs on paper: *walk, talk, jump, climb.* Have your child use the verbs to write sentences that tell about the present, past, and future.

© Pearson Education, Inc., 2

Name _____

child   night   cry   tie

Circle a word to finish each sentence. **Write** the word on the line.

_____
- - - - - - - - - - - - - - -

1. Things seem darker after you look at something _____.

   bite   bring   bright

   _____
   - - - - - - - - - - - -

2. You can _____ out for yourself.

   fin   find   fight

                    _____
                    - - - - - - - - - - - -

3. Put some gray paper _____ some black paper.

   bit   by   bite

   _____
   - - - - - - - - - - - -

4. Put it _____ next to white paper to seem darker.

   rid   right   rye

Read the first word. Then **circle** the word in each row with the same vowel sound.

5. spider   tiger   trigger   ticket

6. pie   undo   unlock   untie

7. light   finger   finish   fright

8. fly   shy   ship   shin

Home Activity Your child identified words with the long *i* sound spelled *i (child), igh (night), ie (cry)* or *y (tie)*. Have your child use the circled words in his or her own sentences.

© Pearson Education, Inc., 2

Name _____

Pick a word from the box to match each clue.
Write the word on the line.

┌───┐
│   alone   buy   daughters   half   │
│   many   their   youngest   │
└───┘

1. a lot

_____

- -

2. the last one born

_____

- -

3. by yourself

_____

- -

4. girl children

_____

- -

Write sentences on the lines below for each word in the box you did not use.

_____

- -

5. _____

_____

- -

6. _____

_____

- -

7. _____

© Pearson Education, Inc., 2

Home Activity This week your child learned to read the words *alone, buy, daughters, half, many, their,* and *youngest.* Have your child make a poster with each high-frequency word and a picture. Then have him or her practice reading the words.

Name _____

Read the story.
Follow the directions.

Poor Sadie

John wondered why his dog Sadie was barking. He looked for Sadie in the yard. Oh, no, Sadie was barking at a skunk! The skunk became frightened and sprayed Sadie. First Sadie howled! Then she rolled in the grass and tried to rub off the spray. John had to wash Sadie because she smelled awful. After her bath, Sadie was happy and wagged her tail.

---

1. What happens to the dog in the story that could happen in real life?

_____

- -

_____

2. Write the numbers 1, 2, 3 to show the correct order of story events.

_____

- - - - - -

_____   Sadie rolled in the grass.

_____

- - - - - -

_____   Sadie howled.

_____

- - - - - -

_____   Sadie wagged her tail.

© Pearson Education, Inc., 2

Home Activity Your child read a story that is realistic fiction. Reread the story together identifying the order of events (sequence). Discuss things Sadie does that most dogs do in real life.

Name _____

Writing • Realistic Story

The Seed Surprise

Writing Prompt: Write a realistic story about someone who gets a good surprise.

Gram walked to Anna's house. She gave Anna some flat seeds. "What are these?" asked Anna.

Gram grinned. "You can plant them and wait to see."

So Anna did. Soon she watered tiny plants. First the plants became vines with fuzzy leaves. Then Anna saw small green balls growing on the vines.

Now Anna has her surprise. She picks huge pumpkins!

© Pearson Education, Inc., 2

Vowel Patterns *i, igh, y*

Spelling Words					
find	child	sky	bright	wild	fly
right	flight	spider	cry	blind	myself

Write a list word to finish the comparison.

1. hear and deaf, _____

   see and _____

2. moon and dim, _____

   sun and _____

3. six legs and ant, _____

   eight legs and _____

4. bad and good, _____

   wrong and _____

5. happy and laugh, _____

   sad and _____

6. dog and run, _____

   bird and _____

7. old and grandparent, _____

   young and _____

8. dog and tame, _____

   tiger and _____

Write a list word to finish each phrase.

9. me, _____, and I

10. _____ the treasure

11. take _____

12. blue _____

© Pearson Education, Inc., 2

School + Home

Home Activity Your child spelled words with long *i*: *i, igh,* and *y*. Have your child choose a number between 1 and 12. Ask your child to spell the word with that item number on this page.

Name _____

Look at the Spanish words and their meanings in the box.
Pick the correct Spanish word to complete each sentence.

Word	Meaning
chiles	hot peppers
vaya	an expression of surprise
amigos	friends
gracias	thanks
por favor	please
aqui	here

1. Do not walk on the grass, _____.

2. I went to the park with my _____.

3. These _____ are too spicy for me to eat.

4. ¡_____! It is so wonderful to see you again.

5. _____ for letting me play with your new game.

6. Come _____ this minute.

Home Activity Your child learned some words in another language. Ask your child to make up his or her own sentences using some of the Spanish words from the chart in place of words in English.

Name _____

More About Verbs

Use the correct verb in each sentence to show something happening now, in the past, or in the future.

Today Blanca **fills** a basket. (now)

Yesterday Blanca **filled** a basket. (in the past)

Tomorrow Blanca **will fill** a basket. (in the future)

Choose the correct verb in ( ). **Write** the verb on the line.

1. Last week Carmen (plants, planted) a garden.

   _____
   _____

2. Yesterday the birds (picks, picked) out the seeds.

   _____
   _____

3. Right now Carmen (visits, visited) a store.

   _____
   _____

4. Soon Carmen (buys, will buy) a scarecrow.

   _____
   _____

5. Tomorrow Carmen (sees, will see) no more birds!

   _____
   _____

© Pearson Education, Inc., 2

School + Home **Home Activity** Your child learned about verbs for present, past, and future. Look through a familiar storybook with your child. Have your child point out some verbs in the sentences and identify whether they tell about now, the past, or the future.

Scoring Rubric: Realistic Fiction

	4	3	2	1
Focus/Ideas	Many details about characters and events make them seem real.	Some details about characters and events make them seem real.	Some details about characters **or** events make them seem real.	The characters **and** events don't seem real.
Organization	The story has a clear beginning, middle, and end.	The beginning, middle, and end are almost clear.	Some of the story events are out of order.	The events are not in any order.
Voice	The writer shows interest in telling the whole story for readers.	The writer shows interest in telling most of the story for readers.	The writer shows interest in telling one part of the story for readers.	The writer shows no interest in telling the story.
Word Choice	Many exact and descriptive words are in the story.	Some exact and descriptive words are in the story.	Some exact **or** descriptive words are in the story.	Words are dull.
Sentences	The sentences are clear and complete.	Most sentences are clear and complete.	Some sentences are clear and complete.	Few sentences are clear and complete.
Conventions	All verbs match when the actions happen.	Most verbs match when the actions happen.	Several verbs match when the actions happen.	Few verbs match when the actions happen.

Home Activity Your child learned to write a realistic story. Ask your child to describe the characters, setting, and events in a story he or she is writing. Your child's writing will be evaluated based on this four-point scoring rubric.

© Pearson Education, Inc., 2

Name _____

Look at the index and picture dictionary. **Follow** the directions to answer the questions.

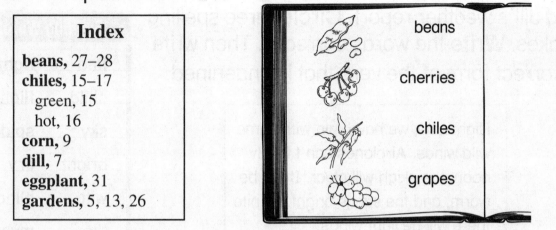

Index

beans, 27–28
chiles, 15–17
  green, 15
  hot, 16
corn, 9
dill, 7
eggplant, 31
gardens, 5, 13, 26

beans

cherries

chiles

grapes

1. How are the topics arranged in the index, ABC order or number order?

   _____

2. If the index had information on cherries, where would it be?

   _____

   _____

3. Which page has information about dill?

   _____

4. Look at the picture dictionary. What does 🍇 stand for?

   _____

5. Think of a fruit or vegetable that is not in the index. Write the name of the fruit or vegetable and tell where it would be in the index. Then draw a picture of it and label it for the picture dictionary.

   _____

   _____

   _____

Home Activity Your child learned how to use an index and a picture dictionary. With your child, look at a nonfiction book with an index. Ask your child to find the locations of specific topics in the book.

© Pearson Education, Inc., 2

Name _____

Vowel Patterns *i, igh, y*

Read Jill's weather report. **Circle** three spelling mistakes. **Write** the words correctly. Then write the correct form of the verb that is underlined.

> Right now, we have rain with some wild winds. Airplanes can't fli. By noon, the skigh will clear. It will be warm, and the sun is bright. At nite there will be light winds.

Spelling Words

find	right
child	flight
sky	spider
bright	cry
wild	blind
fly	myself

1. _____   2. _____

3. _____   4. _____

Frequently Misspelled Words

night

I

Fill in the circle to show the correct word. **Write** the word.

5. His dog is almost ◯ bline ◯ blind.   _____

6. Hit the ball with your ◯ right ◯ rite hand.   _____

7. I can plant the seeds ◯ myself ◯ mighself.   _____

8. There's a ◯ spyder ◯ spider in the corner.   _____

Home Activity Your child has been spelling words with long *i*: *i*, *igh*, and *y*. Ask your child to find examples of list words with these letter combinations.

© Pearson Education, Inc., 2

Name _____

Pick a word from the box to finish each sentence.

> alone   buy   chiles   daughters   half
> luckiest   many   their   youngest

1. At harvest time, _____ friends come.

2. We roast _____ and make tortillas.

3. Most of the time, I live _____ .

4. On our feast day, my _____ help me.

5. Some people _____ food to eat.

6. People bring _____ children.

7. It takes _____ a day to get ready.

8. Even the _____ child has fun!

9. I think I am the _____ person at the party.

Home Activity Your child completed sentences using words learned this week. Together write a letter to a family member or friend and invite him or her to come for a meal using some of the words.

© Pearson Education, Inc., 2

Name _____

More About Verbs

Mark the letter of the verb that completes each sentence.
Say a sentence using one of the verbs.

1. Rosa _____ tomatoes yesterday.
   - ○ **A** picks
   - ○ **B** picked
   - ○ **C** will pick

2. Blanca _____ a basket now.
   - ○ **A** fills
   - ○ **B** filled
   - ○ **C** will fill

3. Rosa _____ at her garden tomorrow.
   - ○ **A** will look
   - ○ **B** looks
   - ○ **C** looked

4. Blanca _____ to her house now.
   - ○ **A** walked
   - ○ **B** walk
   - ○ **C** walks

5. Rosa _____ on the door last night.
   - ○ **A** knocks
   - ○ **B** knocked
   - ○ **C** will knock

6. Blanca _____ the vegetables now.
   - ○ **A** wanted
   - ○ **B** want
   - ○ **C** wants

PEAS

© Pearson Education, Inc., 2

Home Activity Your child prepared to take tests on verbs for present, past, and future. Have your child tell you about activities he or she does each day, has done in the past, or will do in the future, using verbs for present, past, and future.

Name _____

Circle a word to finish each sentence.
Write the word on the line.

Spot is **big**.
Rover is **bigger**.
Spike is **biggest**.

smaller   smallest
_____
- - - - - - - - - - - - - - - - -

1. The spotted one is the _____ .

taller   tallest
_____
- - - - - - - - - - - - - - - - -

2. Jack is _____ than Nate.

happier   happiest
_____
- - - - - - - - - - - - - - - - -

3. Ben is _____ than Josh.

wetter   wettest
_____
- - - - - - - - - - - - - - - - -

4. Jill is the _____ of all.

fatter   fattest
_____
- - - - - - - - - - - - - - - - -

5. This clown is _____ than that one.

School + Home **Home Activity** Your child wrote words that end in *-er (hotter)* and *-est (hottest)* to make comparisons. Ask your child to create an advertisement for a product, real or imaginary, using words such as *bigger* or *brightest*.

© Pearson Education, Inc., 2

Name _____

Pick a word from the box to finish each sentence.
Write the word on the line.

```
        clothes    hours    money
neighbor    only    question    taught
```

1. My _____ is a nice lady.

2. She _____ me how to plant a garden.

3. After school, I put on some old _____ .

4. Every day, I work for two _____ digging and planting.

5. My mom asked me a _____ about why I work so hard.

6. "I am _____ doing it for fun," I said.

7. "You could sell the flowers for _____ ," Mom said. What a great idea!

© Pearson Education, Inc., 2

School + Home

Home Activity This week your child learned to read the words *clothes, hours, money, neighbor, only, question,* and *taught.* Work with your child to write a story about your neighborhood using these words.

Name _____

Read the story.
Circle or **write** the answer to each question.

Mary Anderson

The inventor of the first window wipers for a car was Mary
Anderson. In the 1880s, Mary visited New York City and took
a ride on a streetcar during stormy weather. She noticed that
the driver had to get off the streetcar to clean his window. That
must have made the driver angry. It gave Mary the idea for her
invention. She designed wipers that a driver could control from
inside a car. Mary Anderson got the rights to her invention in 1905.

1. How do you know this story is nonfiction?

   The story is about a real person.

   The story is about an interesting subject.

2. What fact tells you Mary Anderson really invented wipers
   for cars?

   _____

   -

   _____

3. Which sentence in the story is an opinion?

   _____

   -

   _____

© Pearson Education, Inc., 2

Home Activity Your child read a biography and answered questions about it. Reread the story together.
Invite your child to give his or her opinion about Mary Anderson.

Name _____

Writing • Review

Read Together

Review of *Anansi Goes Fishing*

I think Turtle was the most interesting animal in this good story. Turtle knew that Anansi would try to trick him. He stayed nice instead of getting angry. Turtle was very smart. He made Anansi think working was a good idea. Then Turtle was funny when he rested. I am sure many people will enjoy Turtle and this story as much as I did.

Key Features of a Review

- explains what you liked or did not like in a selection

- tells your opinion about what you have read

© Pearson Education, Inc., 2

Name _____

Comparative Endings -er, -est

Spelling Words					
sooner	soonest	hotter	hottest	busier	busiest
happier	happiest	smaller	smallest	fatter	fattest

Draw a line to connect the rule for adding **-er** and **-est** to the base word. **Write** the **-er** and **-est** words.

Double the final consonant.

Change y to i.

Do nothing to the base word.

soon   1. _____ 2. _____

fat   3. _____ 4. _____

busy   5. _____ 6. _____

Add -er or **-est** to the underlined word. **Write** the word.

7. Today is <u>hot</u> than Tuesday.   _____

8. This child is the <u>happy</u> one in the group.   _____

9. These are the <u>small</u> caps I've ever seen.   _____

10. She is <u>happy</u> than she used to be.   _____

11. This is the <u>hot</u> day of the year.   _____

12. My cat is <u>small</u> than your cat.   _____

School + Home **Home Activity** Your child spelled words with -er and -est. Ask your child to name other list words that follow each rule.

© Pearson Education, Inc., 2

Name _____

Rewrite each sentence. **Replace** each
underlined word with a synonym from the box.

> huge   begged   ruined   full   lady   similar   silly

1. The <u>woman</u> left a <u>gigantic</u> box.

_____

- -

_____

2. The twins look <u>alike</u>.

_____

- -

_____

3. Most clowns like to act <u>foolish</u>.

_____

- -

_____

4. Billy <u>pleaded</u> for a new toy.

_____

- -

_____

5. The cup was <u>filled</u>.

_____

- -

_____

6. The vase was <u>destroyed</u>.

_____

- -

_____

School + Home **Home Activity** Your child identified and used synonyms in sentences. Ask your child to read some sentences from a favorite book. Then help your child replace some of the words in the sentences with synonyms.

© Pearson Education, Inc., 2

Verbs: *Am, Is, Are, Was, Were*

The verbs **am**, **is**, **are**, **was**, and **were** do not show action.
They show what someone or something is or was.
These verbs are forms of the verb *to be.*

The verbs **am, is,** and **are** tell about now.
　I **am** a teacher.
　Juan **is** a teacher.
　Kit and Mack **are** teachers.

The verbs **was** and **were** tell about the past.
　I **was** a teacher.
　Rachel and Sara **were** teachers.

Use **am, is,** and **was** to tell about one person, place, or thing.
Use **are** and **were** to tell about more than one person, place, or thing.

Choose the correct verb in ( ). **Write** the sentence.
Say sentences for each verb.

1. The plants (was, were) healthy.

_____

- -

_____

2. Dr. Carver (is, are) a hero to me.

_____

- -

_____

Home Activity Your child learned about *am, is, are, was,* and *were.* Read a book together. Have your child find the verbs *am, is, are, was,* and *were,* read aloud the sentences in which the verbs appear, and identify the subjects.

© Pearson Education, Inc., 2

Review of A Weed Is a Flower

Main Idea

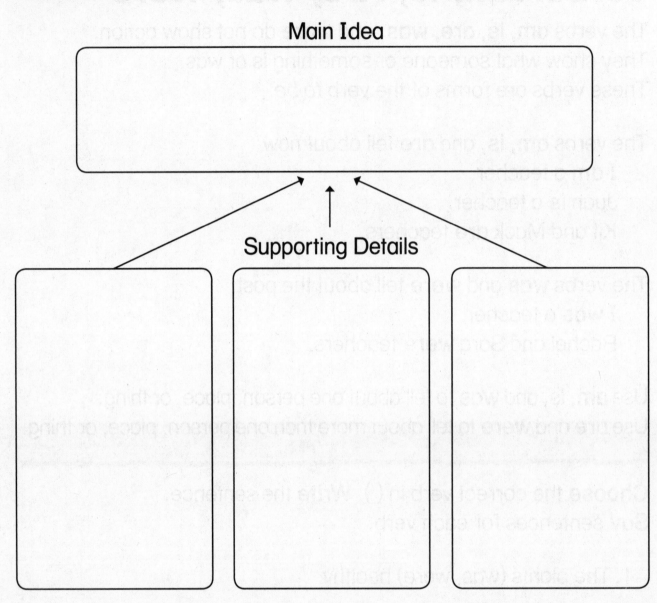

Supporting Details

 School + Home **Home Activity** Your child is learning to write stories, poems, brief reports, nonfiction paragraphs, letters, and other products this year. Ask what your child is writing this week.

248 **Writing** Plan

© Pearson Education, Inc., 2

Name _____

You will be presenting a dramatization answering the Question of the Week, *Where do creative ideas come from?* Use the following steps to help you plan your dramatization.

Step 1 What did you learn that interests you most about where creative ideas come from? Write the information you would most like to share with the class. Create a group with 3–4 other students who would like to share the same information.

I want the class to know _____.

Step 2 As a group, create a situation to show what you think is most interesting about where creative ideas come from. Where does the situation take place? What people, or characters, are involved? What is the problem? What do the characters do?

The setting is _____.

The characters are _____.

The problem is _____.

The characters' actions are _____.

Step 3 Choose a character. Think about what he or she might say in the situation your group created.

My character is _____.

My character says, "_____."

Step 4 Present the situation to the class.

Home Activity Your child learned how to create a dramatization based on research results. Together find and read a newspaper, magazine, or Internet article. Plan and present a dramatization of the events in the article.

© Pearson Education, Inc., 2

Comparative Endings -er, -est

Read Sara's travel tips. **Circle** three spelling mistakes. **Circle** the word with a capitalization mistake. **Write** the words correctly.

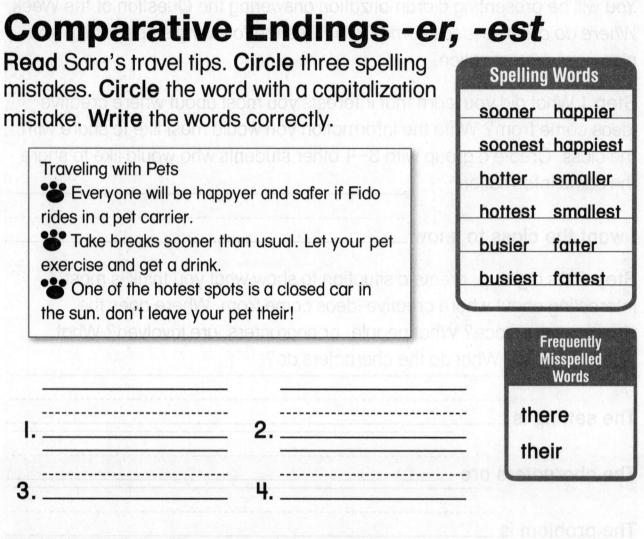

Traveling with Pets

🐾 Everyone will be happyer and safer if Fido rides in a pet carrier.

🐾 Take breaks sooner than usual. Let your pet exercise and get a drink.

🐾 One of the hotest spots is a closed car in the sun. don't leave your pet their!

Spelling Words	
sooner	happier
soonest	happiest
hotter	smaller
hottest	smallest
busier	fatter
busiest	fattest

Frequently Misspelled Words

there

their

1. _____

2. _____

3. _____

4. _____

Circle the correctly spelled word. Write it.

5. busyiest
   busiest
   _____

6. fatest
   fattest
   _____

7. smaller
   smallier
   _____

8. sonnest
   soonest
   _____

9. fatter
   fater
   _____

10. busier
    busyer
    _____

School + Home

Home Activity Your child identified misspelled words with -er and -est. Pronounce a list word with -er. Ask your child to spell the -est word.

© Pearson Education, Inc., 2

Name _____

Pick a word from the box to
match each clue.
Write the word on the line.

| agriculture   clothes   greenhouse   hours   laboratory |
| money   neighbor   only   question   taught |

1. lives next door
_____
- - - - - - - - - - - - - - - - -
_____

2. pants and shirt
_____
- - - - - - - - - - - - - - - - -
_____

3. 24 in a day
_____
- - - - - - - - - - - - - - - - -
_____

4. gave lessons at college
_____
- - - - - - - - - - - - - - - - -
_____

5. coins and dollars
_____
- - - - - - - - - - - - - - - - -
_____

6. science of growing crops
_____
- - - - - - - - - - - - - - - - -
_____

7. just
_____
- - - - - - - - - - - - - - - - -
_____

8. indoor plants grow there
_____
- - - - - - - - - - - - - - - - -
_____

9. science testing room
_____
- - - - - - - - - - - - - - - - -
_____

10. what you ask
_____
- - - - - - - - - - - - - - - - -
_____

© Pearson Education, Inc., 2

Home Activity Your child matched high-frequency and selection words with word clues. Work with your child to include these words in a "Word Box." Have your child write the words on slips of paper or index cards that include the word, its definition, and a picture, if appropriate.

School + Home

Name _____

Verbs: *Am, Is, Are, Was, Were*

Mark the letter of the verb that completes each sentence.

1. Carver _____ a great man.
   - ○ **A** were
   - ○ **B** am
   - ○ **C** was

2. Peanuts _____ valuable for many reasons.
   - ○ **A** are
   - ○ **B** is
   - ○ **C** am

3. Inventors _____ hard workers.
   - ○ **A** am
   - ○ **B** are
   - ○ **C** is

4. I _____ an inventor.
   - ○ **A** were
   - ○ **B** am
   - ○ **C** is

5. This invention _____ useful.
   - ○ **A** is
   - ○ **B** am
   - ○ **C** are

6. Cars _____ a good invention.
   - ○ **A** was
   - ○ **B** am
   - ○ **C** were

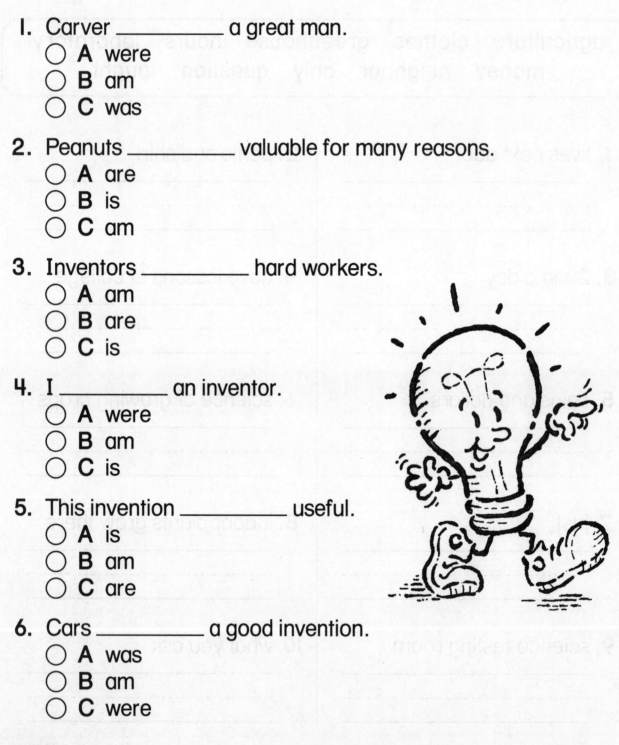

© Pearson Education, Inc., 2

School + Home

Home Activity Your child prepared to take tests on *am, is, are, was,* and *were*. Write the verbs *am, is, are, was,* and *were* on paper. With your child, listen to an ad on TV. Try to count how many times each verb is used.

Name _____

Pick a word from the box to match each clue.
Write the word on the line.
Underline the letters of the word that make the long **e** sound.

> beak   bake   sheep   ship   kitty   be   bee

1. a cat

_____

- - - - - - - - - - -

2. a bird's bill

_____

- - - - - - - - - - -

3. wooly animals

_____

- - - - - - - - - - -

4. a buzzing bug

_____

- - - - - - - - - - -

Read the story.

Dad took Bree and me to the beach. We rode in the jeep along the seashore. We parked in the lot and went to the sand. We could feel the heat of the sand on our feet. There was a lot of seaweed on the sand. At the snack bar, I got bean and cheese wraps for Bree and me. I got an iced tea for Dad. He wanted to read his book. Bree wanted to feed her beans to the seagulls. She dropped one on the sand, and a seagull snatched it in his beak. The seagulls were glad we came. So were we.

© Pearson Education, Inc., 2

Home Activity Your child reviewed words with the long e sound spelled e as in *she*, ee as in *beet*, ea as in *wheat*, and y as in *bunny*. Ask your child to circle the long e words in the story above and write a poem or story using some of these long e words. Have your child read aloud his or her writing.

Name _____

Vowel Patterns *ee, ea, y*

Spelling Words

read	feet	easy	deep	seat	party
wheel	leave	windy	sleep	teeth	team

Write the list word that means almost the same as the phrase.

1. to say the written words
_____
- -
_____

2. a place to sit
_____
- -
_____

3. people playing together
_____
- -
_____

4. to go away
_____
- -
_____

5. not hard to do
_____
- -
_____

6. a good-time event
_____
- -
_____

7. not shallow
_____
- -
_____

8. lots of air moving
_____
- -
_____

9. you walk on these
_____
- -
_____

10. the round part of a bicycle
_____
- -
_____

Unscramble the list word. **Write** it.
_____

11. h e t t e _____
- - - - - - - - - - - - - - - - -

12. e p l s e _____
- - - - - - - - - - - - - - - - -

School + Home **Home Activity** Your child learned to spell words with long e spelled *ee, ea,* and *y*. Look through a book, magazine, or newspaper with your child. Have your child identify and point to words with these letter combinations.

© Pearson Education, Inc., 2

Name _____

Pick a word from the box to match each clue.
Write the letters of each word in the puzzle.
Read the letters in the gray squares to find two hidden words.

> guess   pretty   science   shoe
> village   watch   won

1. a small town

2. to suppose

3. good-looking

4. opposite of **lost**

5. a school subject

6. time teller

7. a sneaker

Hidden Words: _____
_ _

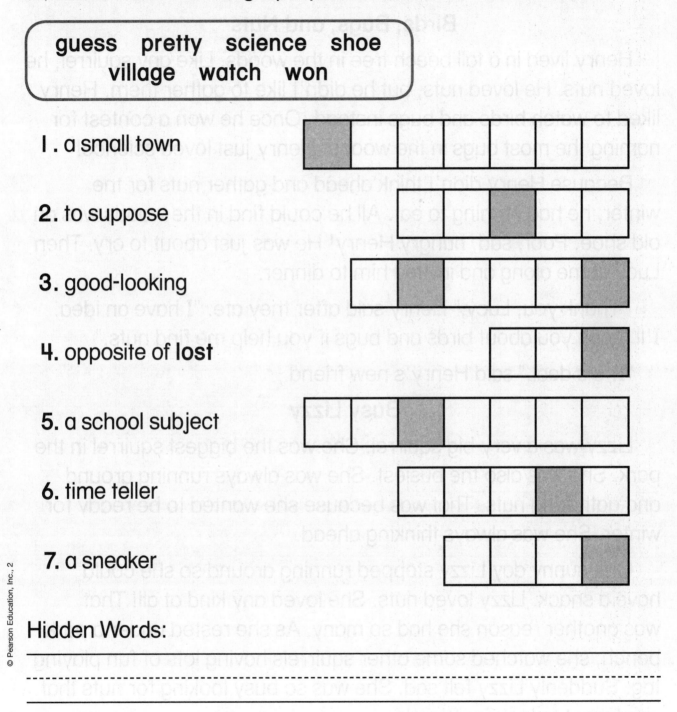

School + Home   **Home Activity** Your child solved a puzzle by matching clues with words learned in this unit. Write each word on an index card or slip of paper. Then have your child pick a card, read the word aloud, and use it in a sentence.

© Pearson Education, Inc., 2

Name _____

Read the story.
Answer the questions.

Birds, Bugs, and Nuts

Henry lived in a tall beech tree in the woods. Like any squirrel, he loved nuts. He loved nuts, but he didn't like to gather them. Henry liked to watch birds and bugs instead. Once he won a contest for naming the most bugs in the woods. Henry just loved science!

Because Henry didn't think ahead and gather nuts for the winter, he had nothing to eat. All he could find in the woods was an old shoe. Poor, sad, hungry Henry! He was just about to cry. Then Lucy came along and invited him to dinner.

"Thank you, Lucy," Henry said after they ate. "I have an idea. I'll teach you about birds and bugs if you help me find nuts."

"It's a deal," said Henry's new friend.

Busy Lizzy

Lizzy was a very big squirrel. She was the biggest squirrel in the park. She was also the busiest. She was always running around and gathering nuts. That was because she wanted to be ready for winter. She was always thinking ahead.

One sunny day Lizzy stopped running around so she could have a snack. Lizzy loved nuts. She loved any kind at all! That was another reason she had so many. As she rested under a park bench, she watched some other squirrels having lots of fun playing tag. Suddenly Lizzy felt sad. She was so busy looking for nuts that she forgot to look for friends.

© Pearson Education, Inc., 2

School + Home **Home Activity** Your child identified the author's purpose. Have your child tell you what lessons the author wanted to teach in these two stories.

Name _____

That night Lizzy had an idea. She scampered over to Neal's house, which was in the tree next door.

"Neal," said Lizzy, "I have lots of yummy nuts. Can you come for dinner?"

Neal and Lizzy had dinner the next day. And guess what? After dinner they played tag.

1. What lesson do you think the author wants you to learn in "Birds, Bugs, and Nuts"?

_____
- -
_____
_____
- -
_____

2. What lesson does the author want you to learn in "Busy Lizzy"?

_____
- -
_____
_____
- -
_____

3. After reading these two stories by the same author, what do you think is most important to this author?

_____
- -
_____
_____
- -
_____

© Pearson Education, Inc., 2

Name _____

Verbs

Underline the verb in each sentence.

1. The children talk about the fair.

2. The girl works hard at school.

3. The two friends make a robot.

4. Pearl draws eyes on the robot.

___

Write the verb in each sentence.

5. The children wait for the judge. _____

6. The judge looks at the robot. _____

7. The robot winks at the judge. _____

8. The judge laughs. _____

© Pearson Education, Inc., 2

Name _____

Day 1 Unit 3 Week 1   **Pearl and Wagner**

Copy the sentences. Make sure you use correct spacing between the words.

Zeb sees a zebra at the zoo.

_____

_____

Zeke lives on X Street.

_____

_____

Day 2 Unit 3 Week 2   **Dear Juno**

Copy the numbers and then the sentence. Make sure you form your numbers correctly.

1 2 3 4 5 6 7 8 9 10

_____

_____

Tony's number is 890-1743.

_____

_____

© Pearson Education, Inc., 2

Name _____

Day 3 Unit 3 Week 3   Anansi

Copy the letters. Make sure you form the letters correctly.

l h k t I u e

_____

- -

_____

━━━━━━━━━━━━━━━━━━━━━━━━━━━━━━━━━━━━━━

Day 4 Unit 3 Week 4   Rosa and Blanca

Copy the letters. Make sure you form the letters correctly.

a d c n m x

_____

- -

_____

━━━━━━━━━━━━━━━━━━━━━━━━━━━━━━━━━━━━━━

Day 5 Unit 3 Week 5   A Weed Is a Flower

Copy the letters. Make sure you form the letters correctly.

o w b v z s r f

_____

- -

_____

Home Activity Your child practiced writing letters *Zz, Xx* and *l, h, k, t, l, u, e, a, d, c, n, m, x, o, w, b, v, z, s, r,* and *f.* He or she also wrote numbers 1, 2, 3, 4, 5, 6, 7, 8, 9, 10. Have your child write and complete this sentence: My phone number is _____.

© Pearson Education, Inc., 2

Name _____

Read the words.

Circle the word with the long **o** sound.

1.
hold   mop

2.
hop   snow

3.
float   pond

4.
open   box

Read the story.

Joan was new in the city, so Toby was showing her around. They went to the park. It was cold, so they wore coats. A toad hopped over the grass. A crow was flying over the pond. It landed on a post. Some little boats floated in the pond. Joan told Toby she liked the park. Then they went home on a path beside the road.

© Pearson Education, Inc., 2

School + Home **Home Activity** Your child reviewed words with the long *o* sound spelled *o* as in *polar*, *oa* as in *boat*, and *ow* as in *bow*. Say each of these words one at a time. Have your child repeat the word and then spell it aloud or write it.

Name _____

Vowel Patterns *o, oa, ow*

Spelling Words					
goat	hold	slow	most	bowl	float
toast	ago	open	told	toad	show

Circle the hidden list word. **Write** the word.

1. d a g o e x l p

_____

- - - - - - - - - - - - - - - - -

2. f v e s h o w k a q

_____

- - - - - - - - - - - - - - - - -

3. y g h n m o s t

_____

- - - - - - - - - - - - - - - - -

4. h w o p e n m i s d

_____

- - - - - - - - - - - - - - - - -

Circle the hidden list words. Look across and down.

j	g	t	r	g	o	o	s
y	h	o	l	d	s	a	l
d	e	l	v	b	c	l	o
n	e	o	d	m	x	f	w
q	h	y	f	p	l	i	c
a	o	o	g	g	o	a	t
s	n	b	x	c	a	k	o
w	t	o	a	s	t	z	a
a	i	w	j	k	b	r	d
o	r	l	l	p	f	e	o

goat
hold
bowl
float
toast
told
toad
slow

© Pearson Education, Inc., 2

Home Activity Your child learned to spell words with long *o* spelled *o*, *oa*, and *ow*. Have your child identify and spell the four words from the list that he or she has the most difficulty spelling.

262 Spelling

Name _____

Pick a word from the box to answer each question.
Write the word on the line.

> answer   company   faraway
> parents   picture   school   wash

1. Where do you learn things? _____

2. What do you do to get your hands clean? _____

3. What do you draw? _____

4. When you add 10 + 2, what is 12? _____

5. Where is the moon? _____

6. Who are a baby's mother and father? _____

7. What is a business firm? _____

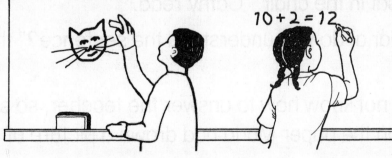

Home Activity Your child used high-frequency words learned in this unit to answer questions. Challenge your child to write a letter to a friend or family member using as many of these words as he or she can.

© Pearson Education, Inc., 2

Name _____

Read the story. **Answer** the questions.

Every Picture Tells a Story

Today is Maria's first day of school in the United States. Maria and her parents are from Mexico. Maria speaks very little English. She is afraid that no one will understand her.

"I want everyone to welcome Maria to class," the teacher said.

"Welcome, Maria," the class said.

The teacher started the class with adding numbers. It was easy for Maria to follow what the teacher was saying. She was very good with numbers.

The teacher wrote words on the board that Maria did not know.

"Say these words after me," said the teacher.

"Chair, table, plate, glass, fork, knife," she said slowly.

Maria followed what the class was saying. As the teacher called out a word, a child came up and drew a picture next to the word. Once Maria saw the picture, she knew the meaning of the word.

"Now, write a sentence for the first word," the teacher said. Maria did not know what to do. Then she had an idea.

"Cathy, read your sentence aloud, please," the teacher said.

"The girl sat in the chair," Cathy read.

"Good. Maria, do you understand the sentence?" the teacher asked.

Maria did not know how to answer the teacher, so she held up her paper. On the paper Maria had drawn a picture of a beautiful

© Pearson Education, Inc., 2

chair. A girl was sitting in the chair. She was reading a book.

"What a wonderful picture!" the teacher exclaimed. "Let's write sentences about this picture."

As the teacher pointed to the chair, she said, "This is a beautiful chair." Then she wrote the sentence on the board. Maria wrote each sentence in her book that the teacher wrote on the board.

Drawing is Maria's favorite activity. The next day she brought more of her drawings to school. The teacher was very excited.

"Let's write a story for each picture," the teacher said.

The class had fun making up stories. Maria was happy. She learned English quickly with the help of her teacher and the class.

_____

1. Why was it easy for Maria to understand adding numbers?

_____

- -

_____

2. Why did the teacher ask children to draw pictures for the words?

_____

- -

_____

3. How did pictures help Maria learn English?

_____

- -

_____

_____

- -

_____

© Pearson Education, Inc., 2

Home Activity Your child drew conclusions to answer questions about a story. Look through a picture book with your child. Have your child tell what the story is about by looking only at the pictures.

Name _____

Verbs with Singular and Plural Nouns

Circle the verb in ( ) that completes each sentence.

1. Juno (wonder, wonders) about the planes.

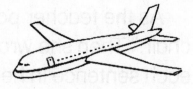

2. Grandma (live, lives) near Seoul.

3. His parents (read, reads) the letter to him.

4. They (smell, smells) the flower.

Write the verb in ( ) that completes each sentence.

5. Grandma (like, likes) letters.

_____

_____

6. My pictures (tell, tells) a story.

_____

_____

7. We (mail, mails) the letter.

_____

_____

8. Grandma (smiles, smile) at the letter.

_____

© Pearson Education, Inc., 2

Name _____

Say the word for each picture.
Use two words to make a compound word that names the picture.
Write the compound word on the line.

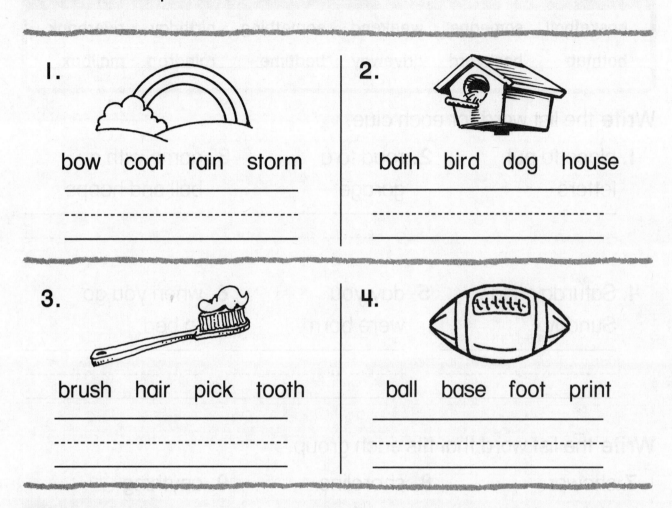

I.

bow   coat   rain   storm

_____

_____

2.

bath   bird   dog   house

_____

_____

3.

brush   hair   pick   tooth

_____

_____

4.

ball   base   foot   print

_____

_____

Read the story.

Reiko was doing her homework by the fireplace. Her eyesight was bad, so she had her eyeglasses on. She heard a footstep outside the window. She picked up her flashlight and went outside to look. Someone had left footprints in the backyard. Reiko went inside. She would be able to see the footprints better in daylight. Then she saw a man in the moonlight. It was her dad. He had made the footprints. Everything was okay.

School + Home **Home Activity** Your child wrote compound words, words made up of two smaller words, such as *waterfall*. Work with your child to use the words above to write other compound words, such as *raincoat, doghouse, toothpick, baseball, lighthouse,* and *eyelashes.*

© Pearson Education, Inc., 2

Name _____

Compound Words

Spelling Words					
basketball	someone	weekend	something	birthday	riverbank
bathtub	backyard	driveway	bedtime	raindrop	mailbox

Write the list word for each clue.

1. place to put
   letters
   _____
   ----

2. road to a
   garage
   _____
   ----

3. game with a
   ball and hoops
   _____
   ----

4. Saturday and
   Sunday
   _____
   ----

5. day you
   were born
   _____
   ----

6. when you go
   to bed
   _____

Write the list word that fits each group.

7. shower
   sink
   _____
   ----

8. shoreline
   beach
   _____
   ----

9. anything
   everything
   _____
   ----

10. cloud
    storm
    _____
    ----

11. anyone
    everyone
    _____
    ----

12. lawn
    fence
    _____

Home Activity Your child learned to spell compound words. Take a walk with your child around your home or your neighborhood. Identify objects whose names are compound words such as *highway, birdbath, sunglasses,* or *railroad.* Have your child identify the two smaller words in each compound word.

© Pearson Education, Inc., 2

Name _____

Pick a word from the box to answer each sentence.
Write the word on the line.

> been   believe   caught   finally
> today   tomorrow   whatever

_____

1. Emma has _____ playing catch with her brother all week.

_____

2. Her brother said, "I _____ you are a great catcher."

_____

3. Emma will play in her first baseball game _____ morning.

_____

4. She was glad when the day of the game _____ came.

_____

5. Her brother said, "Just have fun, _____ happens."

_____

6. During the game, Emma _____ every ball that came near her.

_____

7. After the game, Emma said, "Wow, _____ was a great day!"

Home Activity Your child learned to read the high-frequency words *been, believe, caught, finally, today, tomorrow,* and *whatever.* Ask your child to choose books to read together. As you read aloud, have your child look for these words.

© Pearson Education, Inc., 2

Name _____

Read the story. **Answer** the questions.

The Ant Story

Once upon a time there were two young ants. Their names were Andy and Annie. Like all ants, Andy and Annie were always busy. Today they were busy helping to dig holes.

"Why do we have to dig so deep?" Andy said.

"Mother said that deep holes will make our home safe," Annie explained.

"This is a waste of time," Andy said.

"This is our job so we must do it," Annie answered.

"Why are we the only ones working?" asked Andy.

"Everyone has a job," Annie said.

"I hope we have a different job tomorrow," Andy said.

The next day Andy and Annie were told to bring food through the hole.

"Why do we have to bring food through the hole?" Andy asked.

"It is our job for today," answered Annie.

"We can eat outside of the hole," Andy said.

"It is not hard to carry the food," Annie answered.

"This is a waste of time," Andy said. "We should be building our home."

"We are," Annie said.

"I don't see how we are helping," Andy said.

The next day all the ants gathered in their new home. Andy was surprised to see a beautiful large room.

© Pearson Education, Inc., 2

"Who built this?" asked Andy.

"We all did," his mother answered.

"I don't remember helping," Andy said.

"Every ant had a job," his mother explained. "Your job was to build a hole that would bring us to this room."

Then the Great Ant walked into the room. He went to the front of the room and waved to all the ants.

"This is a great day for us," the Great Ant exclaimed.

"We all worked very hard to build this home. Every ant should be proud," he said. "Now let us enjoy a wonderful meal together."

There were tables filled with different kinds of food. "This is the best meal I have ever had," Andy exclaimed.

Andy was proud that he helped build the home. Now he could see how every job was important.

I. How are Andy and Annie alike?

_____

_____

2. How are Andy and Annie different?

_____

_____

Home Activity Your child made inferences about how two characters in a story are alike and different. Have your child give a speech comparing and contrasting himself or herself with one of the characters in the story.

Comprehension 271

Name _____

Verbs for Present, Past, and Future

Underline the verb in each sentence. **Write** *N* if the verb tells about now. **Write** *P* if the verb tells about the past. **Write** *F* if the verb tells about the future.

1. Anansi will come tomorrow.   _____

2. He fished last night.   _____

3. Anansi feels full now.   _____

4. He will sleep soon.   _____

Circle the correct verb in ( ) to complete the sentence.

5. Yesterday Anansi (works, worked) hard.

6. Yesterday Turtle (will rest, rested) by the river.

7. Now Anansi (will complain, complains) about Turtle.

8. Tomorrow Warthog (frowned, will frown) at Anansi.

© Pearson Education, Inc., 2

Name _____

Circle the word in each row with the long **i** sound.
Write the word on the line.

_____

1. ticket   timber   tiger   _____

_____

2. drift   drip   dry   _____

_____

3. rich   right   river   _____

_____

4. tries   tricks   trip   _____

_____

5. grill   grinning   grind   _____

Read the story.

Ty and his sister ate dinner in the yard last night.
The moon was bright and high in the sky. They sat
by an outside light. Mom had fried some ham, and Dad had baked
a pie. They untied their aprons and came outside to eat. Everything
tasted just right. After they finished the pie, Ty went in and dried
the dishes.

Home Activity Your child identified words in which long *i* is spelled *i, ie, igh,* or *y*. Write the word endings
-ind and *-ild* as headings on a sheet of paper. Have your child add beginning letters to each ending to form
long *i* words. Have him or her use each word in a sentence.

© Pearson Education, Inc., 2

Name _____

Vowel Patterns *i, igh, y*

Spelling Words					
find	child	sky	bright	wild	fly
right	flight	spider	cry	blind	myself

Follow the words with the long *i* sound.
Write each list word that you pass.

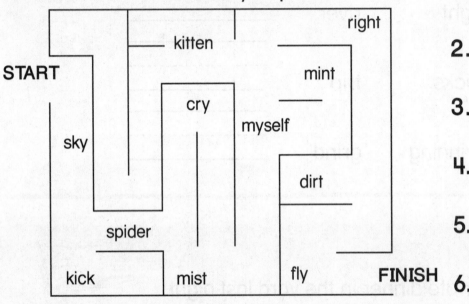

1. _____
2. _____
3. _____
4. _____
5. _____
6. _____

Write the list words that rhyme with each word.

7. mild   _____   _____

8. night   _____   _____   _____

9. try   _____   _____   _____

10. kind   _____   _____

Home Activity Your child has been learning to spell words with long i spelled *i*, *igh*, and *y*. Brainstorm more words that rhyme with the words in items 7–10 with your child.

© Pearson Education, Inc., 2

Name _____

Pick a word from the box to finish each sentence.
Write the word on the line.

| alone buy daughters half |
| many their youngest |

1. The woman only has sons. She has no _____ .

2. The man cut the paper into two parts that are the same size.
   _____

   He cut it in _____ .

3. My sister is eleven. My brother is nine. I am seven. I am the
   _____

   _____ .

4. I picked three baskets of apples. I picked _____
   apples!

5. I am with my friends. I am not _____ .

6. We need milk. Dad will _____ it at the store
   today.

7. That dog belongs to my friends. It is _____ dog.

Home Activity Your child reviewed the high-frequency words *alone, buy, daughters, half, many, their,* and *youngest.* Ask your child questions that contain these words. Have your child point to the word and then use it in his or her answer. *(Are you* alone *now? No, I am not* alone.*)*

© Pearson Education, Inc., 2

High-Frequency Words 275

Name _____

Read the story. Then follow the directions and answer the questions.

The Pie Contest

Tanya looked at the pies cooling on the table. "My peach pie will win first prize at the state fair!" she declared.

"Oh yeah?" said Wanda. "Well, I think mine will win!"

They were best friends, but not when it came to pie contests. Each one wanted to win.

Wanda and Tanya waited for the peach pie contest to start. There were three judges and nine pies entered. Each judge would taste all the pies and then decide.

Tanya and Wanda watched closely as the judges ate. The first judge seemed unhappy with the pies. Then he got to Tanya's pie. He started to smile. "This pie is delicious!" he sighed.

The second judge liked Wanda's pie. She ate every last bite of her piece. Then she put that plate aside, away from the others.

The third judge couldn't decide. She took a bite of Tanya's pie. Then she took a bite of Wanda's pie. Then she took a bite of Tanya's pie. She did that until both pieces were gone.

Tanya and Wanda looked at each other. Who was going to win?

The judges began whispering together. They whispered for a long time.

Finally, the judges decided. The first judge put a white ribbon on Minnie's pie. She won third place. The second judge put a red ribbon on Raymond's pie. He won second place. Now Tanya and Wanda held their breath. Who would get first place?

© Pearson Education, Inc., 2

Name _____

The third judge said, "This year, we have a tie for first place." She put blue ribbons on two pies. Tanya and Wanda couldn't believe it. Both their pies had won!

1. What event in this story could happen in real life?

_____

- -

_____

2. Write the most important events from the story to show the correct order.

First

_____

- -

_____

Next

_____

- -

_____

Finally

_____

- -

_____

© Pearson Education, Inc., 2

Home Activity Your child read a story that is realistic fiction. Have your child tell what happened in the beginning, middle, and end.

Name _____

More About Verbs

Circle the correct verb in ( ).

1. Right now Blanca (needs, will need) flour.

2. Later Rosa (walked, will walk) to the store.

3. Yesterday Rosa (cleans, cleaned) the sidewalk.

4. Now Blanca (helps, helped) Rosa.

Write the correct verb in each sentence.

5. Last night Rosa (picks, picked) up the baby.

_____
- -
_____

6. Today Rosa (rocks, rocked) the baby.

_____
- -
_____

7. Tomorrow the sisters (hugged, will hug) each other.

_____
- -
_____

8. Now their mother (smiles, smiled) at them.

_____
- -
_____

© Pearson Education, Inc., 2

Name _____

Look at the circled picture. **Pick** the word that matches the circled picture. **Write** the word on the line.

1. bigger   biggest   _____

2. faster   fastest   _____

3. darker   darkest   _____

4. dirtier   dirtiest   _____

Read the story.

Ray and I went to the zoo with Mom. It was the hottest day of the summer. We went to see the tigers first. They were scary, but the sharks were even scarier. Then we went to see the elephants. Mom said elephants can run faster than people. The largest elephant had a baby beside her. Ray told me the cutest animals were the baby pandas. But I said the baby elephant was cuter than the panda. I think the chimps were the smartest animals. We rode home on the slowest bus ever, but we had fun seeing the sights.

Home Activity Your child wrote words that end in *-er* as in *taller* and *-est* as in *tallest* to make comparisons. Ask your child to draw pictures of groups of animals (two animals, four animals). Have your child write a sentence for each picture, using words such as *longer/longest, heavier/heaviest,* and *tamer/tamest.*

© Pearson Education, Inc., 2

Name _____

Comparative Endings *-er, -est*

Spelling Words

sooner	soonest	hotter	hottest	busier	busiest
happier	happiest	smaller	smallest	fatter	fattest

Circle the list word that best fits the sentence.

1. Marco is **smaller smallest** than his brother.

2. That is the **fatter fattest** pumpkin I have ever seen!

3. The weather in July is **hotter hottest** than in December.

4. Fall is the **busier busiest** season for farmers.

5. Carl was the **happier happiest** kid on the team when he won the race.

6. The train will arrive **sooner soonest** than the bus.

Write the list word that means the opposite of each word.

7. coldest _____

8. biggest _____

9. sadder _____

10. thinner _____

11. latest _____

12. lazier _____

© Pearson Education, Inc., 2

Home Activity Your child learned to spell words with *-er* and *-est*. Take turns with your child naming base words and adding endings.

280 **Spelling**

Name _____

Pick a word from the box to match each clue.
Write the words in the puzzle.

> clothes   hours   money
> neighbor   only   question   taught

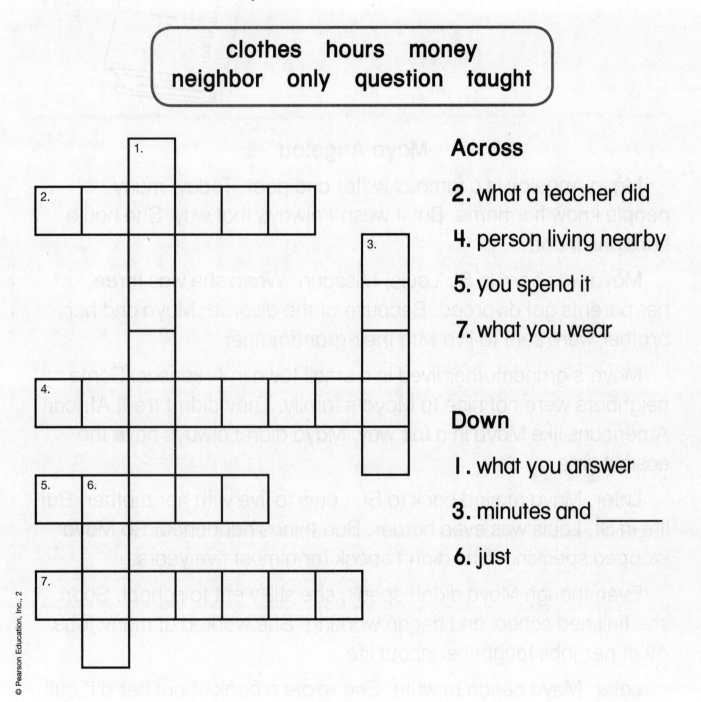

Across

2. what a teacher did

4. person living nearby

5. you spend it

7. what you wear

Down

1. what you answer

3. minutes and _____

6. just

© Pearson Education, Inc., 2

Home Activity Your child completed a crossword puzzle using high-frequency words learned in this unit. Help your child write a story about shopping using some of these words.

Name _____

Read the story. Then **follow** the directions and **answer** the questions.

Maya Angelou

Maya Angelou is a famous writer and poet. Today, many people know her name. But it wasn't always that way. She had a hard childhood.

Maya was born in St. Louis, Missouri. When she was three, her parents got divorced. Because of the divorce, Maya and her brother were sent to live with their grandmother.

Maya's grandmother lived in a small town in Arkansas. Some neighbors were not nice to Maya's family. They didn't treat African Americans like Maya in a fair way. Maya didn't always have the easiest time.

Later, Maya moved back to St. Louis to live with her mother. But life in St. Louis was even harder. Bad things happened. So Maya stopped speaking. She didn't speak for almost five years.

Even though Maya didn't speak, she still went to school. Soon she finished school and began working. She worked at many jobs. All of her jobs taught her about life.

Later, Maya began to write. She wrote a book about her difficult childhood. It was called *I Know Why the Caged Bird Sings*. The book was a hit when it came out. Maya was very happy.

© Pearson Education, Inc., 2

Name _____

   That was more than 30 years ago. Today, Maya's book is still very popular. It has made her famous. Because of her fame, Maya received a great honor. She was asked to recite a poem for the President of the United States. Only a few poets get to do something so special.

   Maya is still writing books and poems today. She continues to speak out about her life as an African American.

1. How do you know this story is nonfiction?

_____

- -

_____

2. What fact tells you about Maya Angelou does for a living?

_____

- -

_____

3. Look at the second paragraph. Write a fact about Maya Angelou.

_____

- -

_____

4. Write one sentence from the story that is an opinion.

_____

- -

_____

Home Activity Your child read a biography and answered questions about it. Help your child identify one fact and one opinion about Maya Angelou in the biography.

© Pearson Education, Inc., 2

Name _____

Verbs: *Am, Is, Are, Was, Were*

Underline the correct verb in ( ).

1. George Washington Carver (were, was) an inventor.

2. Carver's ideas (was, were) good for farmers.

3. Computers (are, is) a modern invention.

4. I (is, am) happy with my computer.

Choose the correct verb in ( ).
Write the sentence.

5. I (am, is) excited.

----

6. My idea (are, is) a good one.

----

7. This toy (was, were) my first invention.

----

8. Inventions (are, is) important.

© Pearson Education, Inc., 2

Name _____

Compare and Contrast T-Chart

Fill out this chart to help you organize your ideas. **Write** your ideas in sentences.

Introduction _____
_____
_____

Alike	Different

Conclusion _____
_____
_____

© Pearson Education, Inc., 2

Name _____

Use Words That Compare and Contrast

Read each set of sentences.
Write a word from the box to complete the last sentence.
Use each word one time.

> and
> like
> too
> but
> unlike

1. I like art class. My sister does not.

   _____

   I like art class, _____ my sister does not.

2. My sister's ballet lesson is at noon. My lesson is at 1:00.

   _____

   My sister's ballet lesson is at noon, _____ my lesson is at 1:00.

3. I drew purple flowers. Maria drew purple flowers.

   _____

   _____ Maria, I drew purple flowers.

4. Nate made a clay pot. I made a clay plate.

   _____

   _____ Nate, I made a clay plate.

5. Pearl has a robot. Wagner has a robot.

   _____

   Pearl has a robot, and Wagner has a robot _____.

© Pearson Education, Inc., 2

Name _____

Deleting Words, Phrases, or Sentences

When you revise, delete words and phrases to make your writing less wordy and clearer for your readers. Delete sentences that don't tell about your topic.

Follow the directions.

1. Look at the sentences. Which word did the writer delete? Write the word on the lines.

   The artist is working on a great big painting.

   The artist is working on a big painting.

   _____
   _____

2. Look at the sentences. Which phrase did the writer delete? Write the phrase on the lines.

   The colors in the painting are kind of different.

   The colors in the painting are different.

   _____
   _____

3. Look at the sentences. Which sentence did the writer delete? Write the sentence on the lines.

   The judges liked the painting. It won a prize. I liked his pottery too.

   The judges liked the painting. It won a prize.

   _____
   _____
   _____

© Pearson Education, Inc., 2

Name _____

Editing 2

Proofreading Marks	
Delete (Take out)	ℒ
Add	∧
Spelling	⬭
Uppercase letter	≡
Lowercase letter	/

Edit these sentences. **Look** for errors in grammar, punctuation, capitalization, and spelling. **Use** proofreading marks to show the corrections.

1. More than a hundred years ago two men will invented the airplane.

2. There names were Wilbur and orville Wright.

3. The two bruthers worked for many years on ideas for a airplane.

4. Sometimes their ideas did not work but they keep trying.

5. i wanted to read more about the Wrights work.

6. Tomorrow I go to the libary to find more information.

Now you'll edit your compare and contrast essay as your teacher directs you. Then you'll use your draft to make a final copy of your essay. Finally, you'll publish your writing and share it with others.

© Pearson Education, Inc., 2

Name _____

| ankle   bubble   bugle   people   table   turtle |

Say the word for each picture.
Write the word on the line.
Use the words in the box if you need help.

appl<u>e</u>

1. _____

2. _____

3. _____

4. _____

5. _____

6. _____

Circle the word in each sentence that ends with the same sound as *apple*.

7. José took a tumble when he tripped on the branch.

8. I got a new puzzle for my birthday.

9. Can you read the title of this book?

School + Home

Home Activity Your child wrote words that end in *-le* and have more than one syllable, such as *apple*. Have your child make word cards for *-le* words, such as those above. Ask your child to write the word on the front and draw a picture on the back.

© Pearson Education, Inc., 2

Name _____

Read the story. **Pick** a word from the box to complete each sentence. **Write** the word on the line.

> clearing   perfect   traveled   splashing
> pond   crashed   spilling

_____

A few months ago, I _____ to the woods with my mother, father, and sister. We stopped at a falls where water

_____

_____ down from the rocks above. The warm

_____

weather was _____ for a hike, so my family took one. We hiked along a path for a while. Then we stepped

_____

out of the trees into a _____ in the woods. In the middle of a grassy meadow, fish were swimming in a

_____   _____

_____. Frogs were _____

one another in the green water. My sister enjoyed scooping up

_____

water and _____ it on the grass. Then we hiked back, tired but happy.

© Pearson Education, Inc., 2

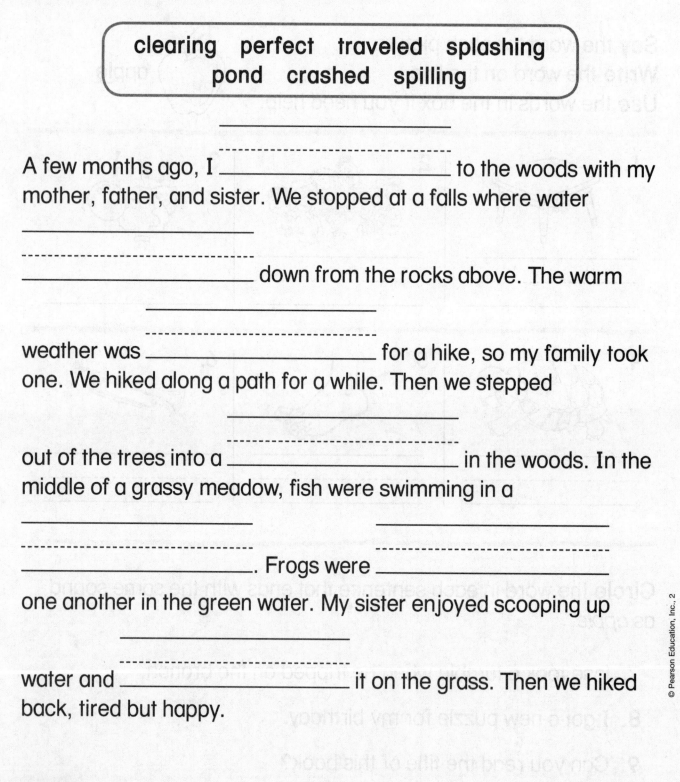

School + Home

Home Activity Your child used lesson vocabulary words to complete a story. Ask your child to use the vocabulary words to make up his or her own sentences.

Name _____

Read the story.
Write a word or words to finish each sentence.

The Wasp and the Mouse

One fall day, a wasp spotted a field mouse lugging a big nut.

"Where are you going with that nut?" the wasp asked.

The mouse replied, "I'm taking it home to my burrow. I'm storing food for the winter."

"Oh, there's plenty of food," the wasp said. "Come play with me."

But the mouse did not stop to play. When winter came, the wasp had no food and was very hungry. It was then that she knew:
Plan ahead.

---

1. The animal characters in a fable _____ and
_____
_____ like people.

2. The wasp thinks the mouse is _____ to store food.

3. In the winter, the mouse probably feels _____.

4. The moral of this fable is _____.

Home Activity Your child read a fable and drew conclusions about the fable. Reread the fable with your child. Ask your child how he or she can tell the story is a fable.

© Pearson Education, Inc., 2

Writing • Friendly Letter

 Janie's Letter

March 5, 2011

Dear Frog,

How would you like to see more of the world? I think you should visit our farm. You will enjoy yourself in the peaceful country.

There are huge fields planted with grass. You can hop around and chomp on sweet bugs. The flowers smell so sweet. On warm days, you will love to jump into the cool water of our pond. It's fun to listen to the loud moos of the cows and soft clucks of the chickens. You will be able to relax and have fun on our farm.

Your friend,
Janie

Key Features of a Friendly Letter

• has the date, a greeting, the body, a closing, and a signature

• the body tells the message

© Pearson Education, Inc., 2

Name _____

Final Syllable -*le*

Spelling Words					
ankle	title	apple	cable	purple	able
bugle	bundle	bubble	giggle	sparkle	tickle

Use a list word to complete each phrase.

1. _____ of my eye   2. burst your _____

3. _____ up   4. strong and _____

5. book _____   6. sprain an _____

Write a list word to answer each riddle.

It rhymes with **wiggle**. It starts like **gate**.	It rhymes with **stable**. It starts like **can**.	It rhymes with **pickle**. It starts like **tent**.
7. _____	8. _____	9. _____

Write the missing word.

10. He plays the _____ .

11. I like the color _____ .

12. The stars in the sky shine and _____ .

© Pearson Education, Inc., 2

School + Home **Home Activity** Your child spelled words that end with -*le*. Ask your child to explain the meanings of the popular sayings on this page.

Spelling Final Syllable -*le*   **293**

Name _____

Read the sentence. **Circle** the correct meaning of the underlined word. **Write** your own sentence for the underlined word. Make sure you include words that will help others figure out the correct meaning of the word.

1. We all took a <u>trip</u> along the path to the pond.

    a. fall   b. journey   c. mistake

_____
- -
_____

2. At the pond we saw frogs <u>dive</u> in and out of the water.

    a. jump   b. rest   c. fall to the ground

_____
- -
_____

3. At the <u>end</u> of the day we went home.

    a. a piece left over   b. stop   c. last part

_____
- -
_____

4. I can't wait to <u>return</u> to the pond tomorrow.

    a. see again   b. go back   c. begin

_____
- -
_____

© Pearson Education, Inc., 2

Home Activity Your child used context clues to figure out the correct meaning of words that have more than one meaning. Ask your child to tell you the clues they used in each sentence to help them choose the correct meaning.

Name _____

Adjectives and Our Senses

An **adjective** describes a person, place, animal, or thing.
An **adjective** can tell how something looks, sounds, tastes, feels, or smells.

> The frog liked the **warm** sun.
> **Warm** describes the way the sun feels.

Find the adjectives that tell how something looks, sounds, tastes, feels, or smells. **Circle** the adjectives.

1. The noisy otters lived near the pond.

2. The soft caterpillar likes change.

3. The tall tree fell in the pond.

Choose an adjective from the box to finish each sentence. **Write** the adjective. **Say** a new sentence with the adjective.

> old   brown   loud

_____

4. I heard _____ noises.

_____

5. I saw the _____ otters.

_____

6. I liked the _____ pond.

Home Activity Your child learned about adjectives that appeal to the senses. Look around the room. Take turns using adjectives to tell how things look, sound, taste, feel, or smell. For example, *I see* <u>green</u> *chairs* or *I hear* <u>loud</u> *music*.

© Pearson Education, Inc., 2

Name _____

Main Idea

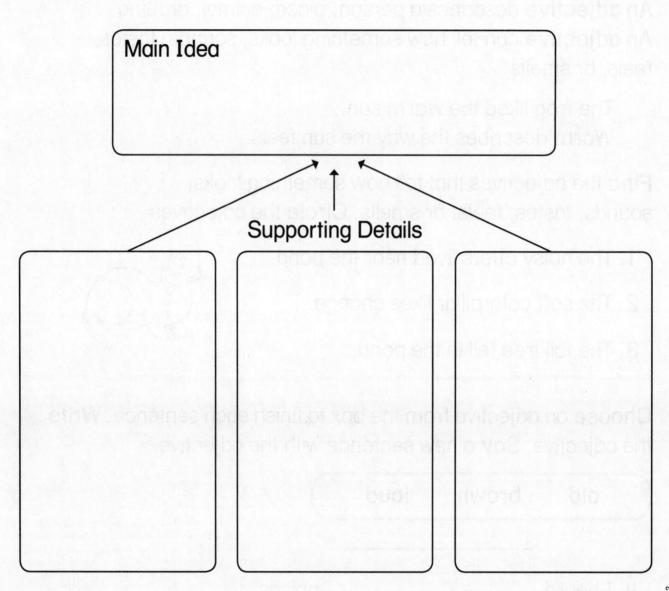

Home Activity Your child is learning to write stories, poems, brief reports, nonfiction paragraphs, letters, and other products this year. Ask what your child is writing this week.

296 **Writing** Plan

© Pearson Education, Inc., 2

Name _____

Today, you will review your topic to check that you have found the answers to your original research topic. Use the following steps to help you review your topic and revise it if necessary.

Step 1- Make sure it is clear what you originally set out to learn about your topic. Write your research topic below.

_____

I want to know _____.

Step 2- Review the list of questions you created about this topic and the answers from your research. Ask yourself the following questions:

• Do I have many unanswered questions?

• Did I learn something surprising that affects what I originally wanted to know?

• Based on what I learned, do I have new questions?

Step 3- Did you answer yes to any of the questions in Step 2? If so, you might want to consider revising your topic.

Step 4- Use your new questions and the surprising information you learned to revise your topic. You might need to just change a few words or you might need to rewrite the entire topic. Write your new topic and go back to Step 2. Can you answer no to all of the questions?

_____

My new topic is _____.

Home Activity Your child learned how to revise a topic if needed. Discuss why it is important to revise a topic as a result of new information.

© Pearson Education, Inc., 2

Name _____

Final Syllable -*le*

Read the directions. **Circle** two spelling mistakes. **Write** the words correctly. **Rewrite** Step 4 as two sentences.

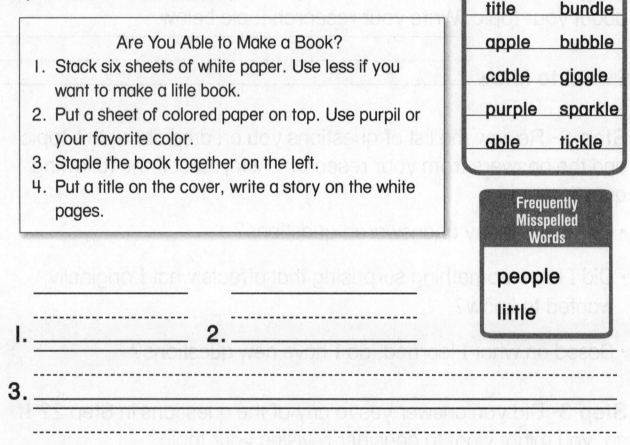

Are You Able to Make a Book?
1. Stack six sheets of white paper. Use less if you want to make a litle book.
2. Put a sheet of colored paper on top. Use purpil or your favorite color.
3. Staple the book together on the left.
4. Put a title on the cover, write a story on the white pages.

Spelling Words	
ankle	bugle
title	bundle
apple	bubble
cable	giggle
purple	sparkle
able	tickle

Frequently Misspelled Words

people

little

1. _____ 2. _____

3. _____

Fill in the circle to show the correctly spelled word.

4. ○ ankel   ○ ankl   ○ ankle
5. ○ giggle   ○ gigle   ○ giggel
6. ○ sparkel   ○ sparkle   ○ sparkal
7. ○ bundal   ○ bundel   ○ bundle
8. ○ bugel   ○ bugl   ○ bugle

Home Activity Your child identified misspelled words that end with -*le*. Your child may enjoy following the directions at the top of the page to assemble and write a book.

© Pearson Education, Inc., 2

Name _____

Read the story. **Write** the answer to each question.

The Hare and the Tortoise

The hare and the tortoise were having a race. The hare was sure he would win.

The race began. The hare ran off quickly. Soon he was so far ahead, he could barely see the tortoise. "I'll just stop and rest for a minute," he said. "The tortoise will never catch up to me."

The hare lay down and stretched out. He fell asleep.

When the hare awoke, it was late afternoon. The tortoise had passed him and was at the finish line. The hare had lost! But he had learned an important lesson. Slow and steady wins the race.

I. Why is the hare sure he will win the race?

_____

- -

_____

2. Why does the hare decide to rest?

_____

- -

_____

3. What is the moral of this fable?

_____

- -

_____

© Pearson Education, Inc., 2

Home Activity Your child read a fable and drew conclusions about the fable. Reread the fable with your child. Ask your child how he or she can tell the story is a fable.

Name _____

Adjectives and Our Senses

Mark the letter of the adjective that completes each sentence.

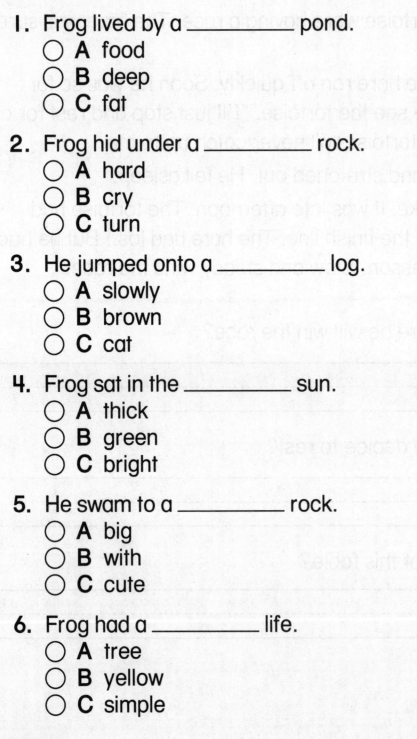

1. Frog lived by a _____ pond.
   - ○ **A** food
   - ○ **B** deep
   - ○ **C** fat

2. Frog hid under a _____ rock.
   - ○ **A** hard
   - ○ **B** cry
   - ○ **C** turn

3. He jumped onto a _____ log.
   - ○ **A** slowly
   - ○ **B** brown
   - ○ **C** cat

4. Frog sat in the _____ sun.
   - ○ **A** thick
   - ○ **B** green
   - ○ **C** bright

5. He swam to a _____ rock.
   - ○ **A** big
   - ○ **B** with
   - ○ **C** cute

6. Frog had a _____ life.
   - ○ **A** tree
   - ○ **B** yellow
   - ○ **C** simple

Home Activity Your child prepared for taking tests on adjectives that appeal to the senses. Take turns naming a food. Use adjectives to tell how it looks, tastes, feels, or smells or how it sounds when eaten.

© Pearson Education, Inc., 2

Name _____

c<u>oo</u>k   b<u>u</u>ll

| full | hood | hook | pull | shook | stood | took | wood |

Write three words from the box that rhyme with **good**.

1. _____ 2. _____ 3. _____

Write three words from the box that rhyme with **look**.

4. _____ 5. _____ 6. _____

Write a word from the box that is the opposite of each word below.

7. push   8. empty

_____   _____

_____   _____

Write a word from the box to finish each sentence.

| brook | put |

_____

9. I _____ a hook on the fishing pole.

_____

10. I pulled a fish from the _____ .

School + Home **Home Activity** Your child wrote words that have the vowel sound in *cook* and spelled *oo* and *u* as in *bull*. Help your child write a rhyming poem using words with the vowel sound in *cook*. The poem can be silly or serious. Encourage your child to illustrate the poem and read it aloud.

© Pearson Education, Inc., 2

Name _____

Read the story. **Pick** a word from the box to finish each sentence. **Write** the word on the line.

| bumpy   fruit   harvest   root   smooth   soil   vine |

The Life of a Pumpkin

Most pumpkins look like sleek, _____, round heads.

Pumpkins begin when the seeds are planted in the _____ _____ . Then they sprout and _____ in the ground. Baby pumpkins will grow on a long _____ .

Soon they are bigger than any _____ . They look like little suns. Their stems are hard and _____ .

Then comes the pumpkin _____ . After the pumpkins are picked, the vines are turned back into the soil. The pumpkin's life will start again next year.

Home Activity Your child completed sentences in a story using vocabulary words learned this week. Together, visit a local pumpkin patch or plant pumpkin seeds in a planter or in your yard. Ask your child to use these vocabulary words to describe the pumpkins on the vine.

© Pearson Education, Inc., 2

Name _____

Read the story. **Follow** the directions.

Footprint Fossils

Fossils are the remains or prints of plants or animals that lived thousands or millions of years ago. Some fossils are footprints. How do footprints become fossils? First, an animal walks across a muddy area and leaves footprints. Next, water with minerals in it fills the shape of each footprint. Then the water seeps out of the prints. The minerals, however, remain in the footprints. Last of all, the minerals turn the mud into rock and form fossils.

1. Circle the words in the story that give clues to the order of events.

2. Write the numbers 1, 2, 3, 4 to show the correct order of events.

   _____ Water with minerals fills the shape of each footprint.

   _____ Minerals turn the mud into rock.

   _____ An animal walks across a muddy area.

   _____ Water seeps out of the prints.

© Pearson Education, Inc., 2

Home Activity Your child identified words that show sequence and placed events in the correct order. Have your child help you make a bed. Talk about what you do first, next, and last.

Name _____

Writing • Expository Nonfiction

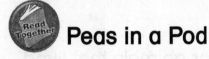 **Peas in a Pod**

Writing Prompt: Write a paragraph explaining how a plant grows and changes.

A pea plant starts from one round seed. After the seed spouts, green stems start to grow. The thin vines often climb on a wire or string fence that a gardener puts next to the plants. The vines can grow up to 6 feet long. The fence holds the vines up. Little flowers bloom, and then the pea pod grows from the flower. The pea pod grows up to 4 inches long. Inside the pods are little round seeds. These seeds, or peas, are what people eat. Snap peas, sugar peas, and snow peas are kinds of peas that have tender pods you can eat.

© Pearson Education, Inc., 2

Name _____

Vowel Patterns *oo, u*

Spelling Words					
put	cook	stood	full	wood	July
shook	push	pull	brook	book	hood

Write a list word that rhymes with the underlined word.

_____

1. Where does Alexa <u>look</u> for stones?
_____

2. What did Bob wear to keep <u>good</u> and dry?
_____

3. Sam <u>took</u> it from the library.
_____

4. Who kept the food in a <u>nook</u>?
_____

Read the word. **Write** a related list word.

5. June: _____   6. empty: _____

7. tug: _____   8. set: _____

9. pull: _____   10. shake: _____

11. sat: _____   12. chair: _____

Home Activity Your child wrote words with the vowel patterns *oo* and *u*. Pronounce a list word. Ask your child if the vowel sound is spelled *oo* or *u*.

© Pearson Education, Inc., 2

Name _____

Write an antonym from the box to complete each sentence correctly. Use the words in the sentence to help.

> tall bumpy same brave easy
> less adult sooner back quiet

1. The gym is noisy, but our classroom is _____.

2. The path is smooth, but the road is _____.

3. My cousin is a child, but my aunt is an _____.

4. The kitten was afraid, but the lion was _____.

5. I think math is hard, but spelling is _____.

6. I have _____ red paint, but more white paint.

7. The pants are the _____ color, but they are different sizes.

8. Mel is in the _____ of the line, but Sam is in the front.

9. I asked Jan to come _____, but she came later.

© Pearson Education, Inc., 2

School + Home **Home Activity** Your child learned about antonyms. Have your child circle the word in each sentence that is the antonym for the word they wrote on the line.

Name _____

Adjectives for Number, Size, and Shape

Words for number, size, and shape are **adjectives**.
The words **a** and **an** are also adjectives.

> **An** apple has **small, round** seeds.
> The word **an** describes how many apples—one.
> **Small** describes the size of the seeds.
> **Round** describes the shape of the seeds.

Circle the adjectives that describe the number, size, or shape of something. **Write** the adjectives in the chart.

1. Watermelons have oval seeds.

2. Peaches have large pits.

3. Cherries have one pit.

4. Pea pods hold round peas.

5. An orange has seeds inside.

Describe Number	Describe Size	Describe Shape

Say sentences for each adjective.

© Pearson Education, Inc., 2

Home Activity Your child learned about adjectives for number, size, and shape. Look at foods together. Have your child use adjectives to describe each food's number (*two* apples), size (*big* potatoes), or shape (*round* oranges).

Name _____

Scoring Rubric: Expository Nonfiction

	4	3	2	1
Focus/Ideas	The writing has facts and excellent details.	The writing has some facts and details.	The writing has facts with no details.	The writing does not have any facts.
Organization	The facts are clear and in a logical order.	The facts are in a logical order.	Not all the facts are in a logical order.	The facts are not in any logical order.
Voice	The writer understands the topic completely.	The writer mostly understands the topic.	The writer understands a little of the topic.	The writer does not understand the topic.
Word Choice	The writer uses exciting words to describe.	The writer uses some exciting words to describe.	The writer uses few exciting words to describe.	The writer's words are dull.
Sentences	The sentences are complete and read smoothly.	Most sentences are complete and read smoothly.	Some sentences are unclear and choppy.	Sentences are confusing or incomplete.
Conventions	There are no mistakes with spelling, capital letters, or ending marks.	There are few mistakes with spelling, capital letters, or ending marks.	There are some mistakes with spelling, capital letters, or ending marks.	Many mistakes make the writing hard to understand.

© Pearson Education, Inc., 2

School + Home

Home Activity Your child is learning to write expository nonfiction. Ask your child to describe his or her writing about something in nature. Your child's writing will be evaluated based on this four-point scoring rubric.

Name _____

Circle the picture or pictures that best answer each question.

I. **Which** source would you use to find the meaning of **harvest**?

2. Where would you most likely find pumpkins growing?

3. Which sources would you use to find facts about plants?

4. Which source would you use to find out about pumpkin picking in your town?

5. Where does this (pumpkin) come from?

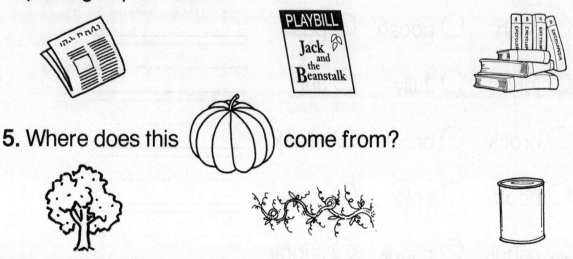

© Pearson Education, Inc., 2

School + Home **Home Activity** Your child learned how to gather evidence from personal sources. Together with your child, make a list of food items you have in your home. Ask your child what sources he or she could use to gather information about these items.

Research Personal Sources   **309**

Name _____

Vowel Patterns *oo, u*

Circle two spelling mistakes. **Circle** the word with the capitalization mistake.
Write the words correctly.

Spelling Words	
put	shook
cook	push
stood	pull
full	brook
wood	hook
July	hood

Helper Wanted

Have you cooked out alot?

Can you cook on a wud fire?

Help younger campers cook.

camp begins on July 7.

1. _____
2. _____
3. _____

Frequently Misspelled Words

took

a lot

Fill in the circle to show the correctly spelled word.
Write the word.

4. ○ stede   ○ stude   ○ stood   _____

5. ○ hud   ○ hood   ○ hude   _____

6. ○ push   ○ poosh   ○ pash   _____

7. ○ july   ○ Jully   ○ July   _____

8. ○ brock   ○ brook   ○ bruck   _____

9. ○ book   ○ bokk   ○ bock   _____

10. ○ oshuk   ○ osook   ○ shook   _____

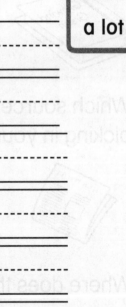

© Pearson Education, Inc., 2

School + Home **Home Activity** Your child identified misspelled words with the vowel patterns *oo* and *u*. Have your child underline *oo* and *u* in the list words.

Name _____

Read the story. **Follow** the directions and **answer** the question.

Raisins

Dark, chewy, sweet raisins are a popular snack. Did you know that all raisins start out as grapes? Here's how they make the journey from grape to raisin. First, bunches of ripe grapes are cut from their vines. Next, the grapes are laid on paper trays to dry in the sun. They usually dry for two to three weeks. After that, the raisins are sent across a shaker that gets rid of dirt and rocks. Finally, the raisins are washed and put into boxes or bags.

1. Circle the words in the story that give clues to the order of events.

2. Write the numbers **1, 2, 3, 4** to show the order of events.

_____ The raisins are sent across a shaker to get rid of dirt and rocks.

_____ Bunches of grapes are cut from their vines.

_____ The raisins are washed and put into boxes or bags.

_____ The grapes are laid on paper trays to dry in the sun.

3. What are raisins?

_____

_____

_____

© Pearson Education, Inc., 2

School + Home **Home Activity** Your child identified words that show sequence and placed events in the correct order. Have your child help you make dinner or set the table. Talk about what you do first, next, and last.

Adjectives for Number, Size, and Shape

Mark the letter of the adjective for number, size, or shape that is in each sentence. **Say** a sentence using an adjective.

1. Oval bean seeds were planted.
   - ○ **A** Oval
   - ○ **B** seeds
   - ○ **C** planted

2. Six seeds grew slowly.
   - ○ **A** seeds
   - ○ **B** Six
   - ○ **C** grew

3. Tiny leaves soon pushed up.
   - ○ **A** Tiny
   - ○ **B** leaves
   - ○ **C** up

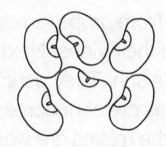

4. There were five plants left.
   - ○ **A** There
   - ○ **B** were
   - ○ **C** five

5. Then long beans appeared.
   - ○ **A** beans
   - ○ **B** long
   - ○ **C** appeared

6. I saw small seeds inside.
   - ○ **A** I
   - ○ **B** saw
   - ○ **C** small

Home Activity Your child prepared for taking tests on adjectives for number, size, and shape. Read a book together. Then go back and have your child look for adjectives that describe number, size, and shape.

© Pearson Education, Inc., 2

Name _____

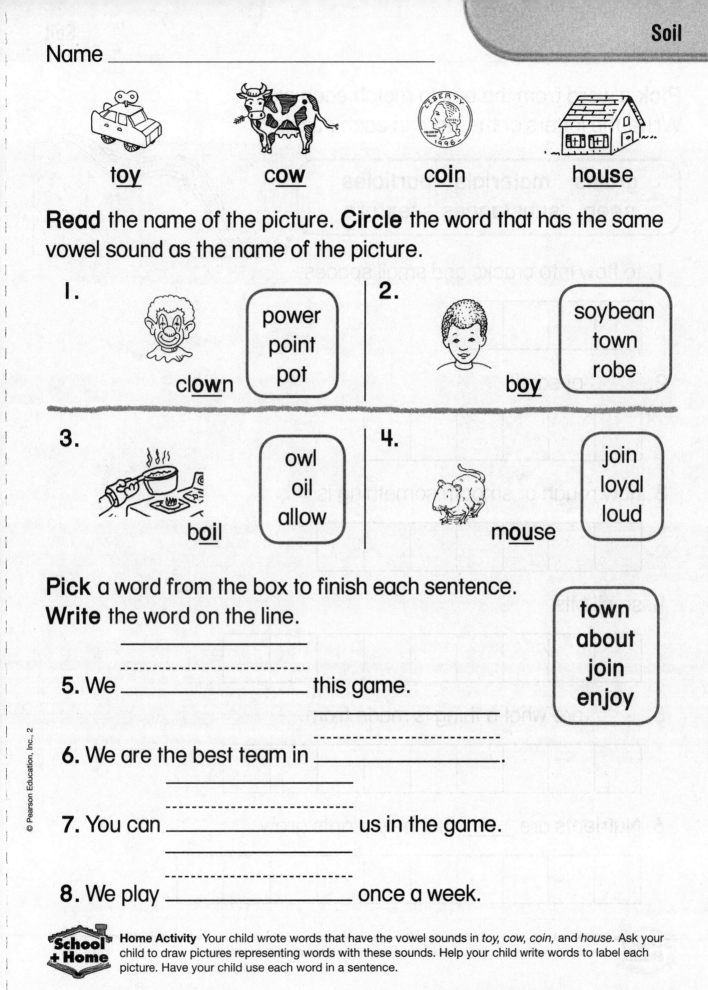

toy   cow   coin   house

Read the name of the picture. **Circle** the word that has the same vowel sound as the name of the picture.

1.

clown

power
point
pot

2.

boy

soybean
town
robe

3.

boil

owl
oil
allow

4.

mouse

join
loyal
loud

Pick a word from the box to finish each sentence.
Write the word on the line.

town
about
join
enjoy

5. We _____ this game.

6. We are the best team in _____.

7. You can _____ us in the game.

8. We play _____ once a week.

School + Home **Home Activity** Your child wrote words that have the vowel sounds in *toy, cow, coin,* and *house.* Ask your child to draw pictures representing words with these sounds. Help your child write words to label each picture. Have your child use each word in a sentence.

© Pearson Education, Inc., 2

Name _____

Pick a word from the box to match each clue.
Write the letters of the word in each puzzle.

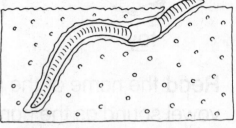

> grains   materials   particles
> seep   substances   texture

1. to flow into cracks and small spaces

2. _____ of sand

3. how rough or smooth something is

4. small bits

5. _____ are what a thing is made from.

6. Nutrients are _____ that help plants grow.

School + Home

Home Activity Your child used clues to write vocabulary words learned this week. Work with your child to use some of this week's vocabulary words to describe soil and how it is formed.

314 **Vocabulary**

© Pearson Education, Inc., 2

Name _____

Read the story.
Write the answer to each question.

An Indoor Sport

James Naismith invented the game of basketball. He was a Physical Education teacher from Canada who went to Springfield, Massachusetts, in 1890 to teach at a college there. James Naismith wanted his students to have an indoor sport to play during the winter. By 1891, he had invented basketball. In his early game, players bounced a soccer ball and tried to throw it into a peach basket. Unlike the baskets used today, the peach basket was not open at the bottom. Basketball was first played in the Olympics in 1936. James Naismith was thrilled to be there to watch the game he invented.

1. Where did James Naismith teach?

_____

_____

2. When did James Naismith invent basketball?

_____

_____

3. Why did Naismith invent a game?

_____

_____

© Pearson Education, Inc., 2

Home Activity Your child read a story with facts in it. Help your child write sentences with facts about himself/herself, for example: age, name of town where you live, name of school he or she attends, and so on.

Name _____

Writing • Expository Report

Soil in My Neighborhood

I live near a river. The soil next to my house is brown. When I add a little water to the soil, the water doesn't run through it too fast. The soil must have some clay in it, but it also must have some sand in it. Near the river, the soil is darker and smoother than the soil by my house. It has silt in it. The soil under the trees next to the river has lots of dead leaves in it. It is the darkest soil in the area.

Key Features of an Expository Report

• tells what you have learned about a topic

• includes facts and ideas about that topic

• sometimes uses graphic features such as pictures

© Pearson Education, Inc., 2

Name _____

Diphthongs *ou, ow, oi, oy*

Spelling Words					
around	out	gown	sound	flower	howl
toy	noise	royal	moist	coil	cow

Write a list word to complete each phrase.

1. _____ the corner   2. a dairy _____

3. the _____ throne   4. _____ of town

5. a _____ pot   6. a very loud _____

Read the clue. **Write** the list word.

7. the same as damp   _____

8. something to play with   _____

9. to curl   _____

10. the opposite of silence   _____

11. the same as to yell   _____

12. the same as dress   _____

Home Activity Your child wrote words with the vowel sounds in *gown* and *toy*. Have your child circle *ou*, *ow*, *oi*, and *oy* in the list words.

© Pearson Education, Inc., 2

Name _____

Circle the suffix in each word. **Underline** the correct meaning.
Write a sentence using the word.

1. fearful

a. having no fear   b. full of fear   c. full of anger

_____
- -
_____

2. useless

a. a person who has use   b. full of use   c. without use

_____
- -
_____

3. beautiful

a. full of beauty   b. full of happiness   c. without beauty

_____
- -
_____

4. cheerful

a. without cheer   b. full of cheer   c. a person with cheer

_____
- -
_____

5. teacher

a. a person who teaches   b. to teach well   c. not to teach

_____
- -
_____

© Pearson Education, Inc., 2

School + Home

Home Activity Your child learned about words with suffixes. Challenge your child to name other words that end with the suffixes he or she circled on this page and then tell what the words mean.

Comparative and Superlative Adjectives

Add *-er* to an adjective to compare two persons, places, or things.
Add *-est* to an adjective to compare three or more persons, places, or things.

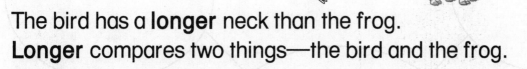

The bird has a **longer** neck than the frog.
Longer compares two things—the bird and the frog.

The giraffe has the **longest** neck of the three animals.
Longest compares three things—the frog, the bird, and the giraffe.

Circle adjectives that compare two things. **Underline** adjectives that compare three or more things.

1. Clay particles are smaller than silt particles.

2. Clay particles are the smallest particles in soil.

3. Humus is a darker color than sand.

Add *-er* or *-est* to the word in ( ) to complete each sentence. **Write** the word. **Say** other sentences using the words you wrote.

_____

4. Some soil has _____ air spaces than others. (small)

5. The _____ air spaces are between minerals and humus.

© Pearson Education, Inc., 2

School + Home **Home Activity** Your child learned about adjectives that compare. With your child, use the *-er* and *-est* endings to compare things in the room. For example, say *The chair is bigger than the lamp. The sofa is biggest of all.*

Name _____

Web

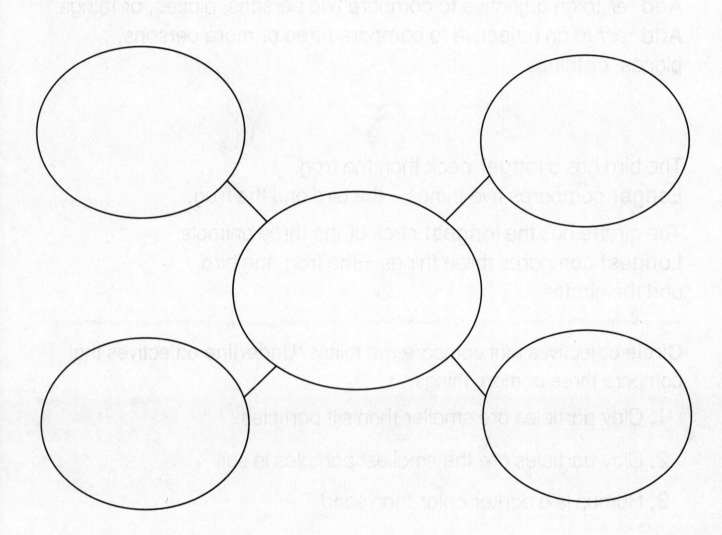

Home Activity Your child is learning to write stories, poems, brief reports, nonfiction paragraphs, letters, and other products this year. Ask what your child is writing this week.

320 Writing Plan

Name _____

Use the diagram to answer the questions.

Goldfish

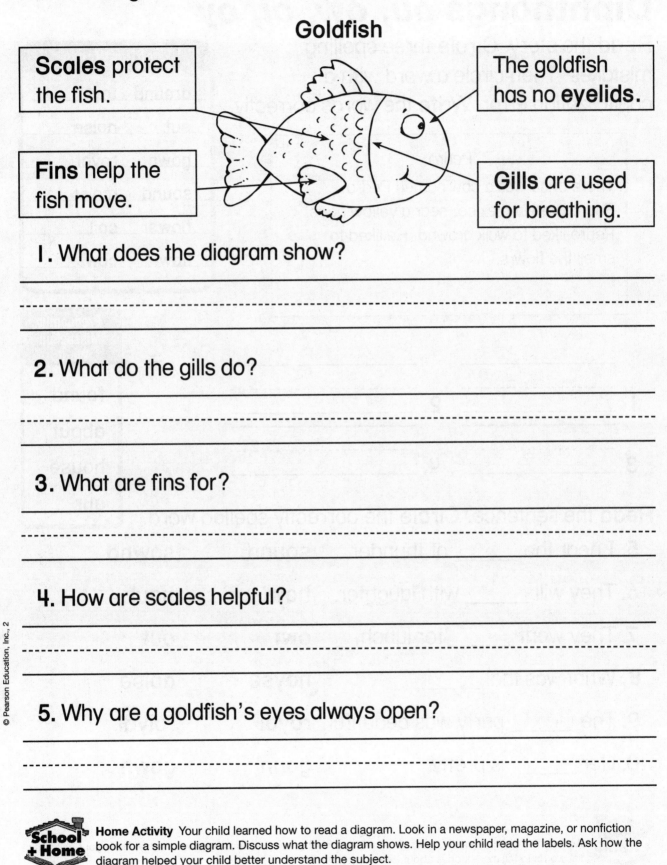

Scales protect the fish.

Fins help the fish move.

The goldfish has no **eyelids**.

Gills are used for breathing.

1. What does the diagram show?

_____

_____

_____

2. What do the gills do?

_____

_____

_____

3. What are fins for?

_____

_____

_____

4. How are scales helpful?

_____

_____

_____

5. Why are a goldfish's eyes always open?

_____

_____

_____

© Pearson Education, Inc., 2

School + Home **Home Activity** Your child learned how to read a diagram. Look in a newspaper, magazine, or nonfiction book for a simple diagram. Discuss what the diagram shows. Help your child read the labels. Ask how the diagram helped your child better understand the subject.

Name _____

Diphthongs *ou, ow, oi, oy*

Read the story. **Circle** three spelling
mistakes. Then circle a word with a
capitalization error. **Write** the words correctly.

Spelling Words	
around	toy
out	noise
gown	royal
sound	moist
flower	coil
howl	cow

Pedro

There once was a cow named Pedro.
Pedro lived in mexico, near a yellow hous.
Pedro liked to walk arownd. He liked to
smell the flowrs.

1. _____   2. _____

3. _____   4. _____

**Frequently
Misspelled
Words**

found

about

house

our

Read the sentence. **Circle** the correctly spelled word.

5. I hear the _____ of thunder.   **sound**   **sownd**

6. They will _____ with laughter.   **howl**   **houl**

7. They went _____ for lunch.   **owt**   **out**

8. What was that _____?   **noyse**   **noise**

9. The _____ party was beautiful.   **royal**   **roiyal**

10. Her _____ is pretty.   **goun**   **gown**

Activity Your child identified misspelled words with the vowel sounds in *gown* and *toy*. Have your child use list words to tell more stories about Pedro the cow.

© Pearson Education, Inc., 2

Name _____

Read the story. **Follow** the directions.

A Beautiful Place

The prettiest national park in the country is Zion National Park. Zion became a national park almost a hundred years ago, in 1919. Today, the park covers an area of 229 square miles. Inside the park are beautiful cliffs and breathtaking Zion canyon. Coyotes, mountain lions, deer, and bighorn sheep roam the area. The park also has the world's largest stone arch—Kolob Arch. Walking among the cliffs at Zion is the most amazing hike ever! The cliffs change color from cream to pink to red. It's like being in a fairytale landscape.

Write F if the sentence below is a fact. **Write O** if it is an opinion.

_____ **A.** The prettiest national park in the country is Zion National Park.

_____ **B.** The park has the world's largest stone arch.

_____ **C.** The cliffs change color from cream to pink to red.

_____ **D.** It's like being in a fairytale landscape.

© Pearson Education, Inc., 2

Home Activity Your child read a story with facts and opinions in it. Help your child write a paragraph with both facts and opinions—for example, a paragraph describing the child's favorite food or favorite place.

Comparative and Superlative Adjectives

Mark the letter of the adjective that best completes each sentence.

1. Summer is our _____ season.
   - ○ **A** warm
   - ○ **B** warmer
   - ○ **C** warmest

2. Ice can make the cracks in rocks _____.
   - ○ **A** big
   - ○ **B** bigger
   - ○ **C** biggest

3. It is _____ under the ground than above it.
   - ○ **A** dark
   - ○ **B** darker
   - ○ **C** darkest

4. The mountains are _____ than hills.
   - ○ **A** high
   - ○ **B** higher
   - ○ **C** highest

5. Sand has a _____ texture than clay.
   - ○ **A** rough
   - ○ **B** rougher
   - ○ **C** roughest

6. Clay particles are the _____ particles in soil.
   - ○ **A** small
   - ○ **B** smaller
   - ○ **C** smallest

© Pearson Education, Inc., 2

School + Home **Home Activity** Your child prepared for taking tests on adjectives that compare. Use words on this page that end in *-er* and *-est*. With your child, make up sentences about plants and animals.

Name _____

<u>su</u>/per   s<u>u</u>p/per   b<u>a</u>s/ket   p<u>a</u>/per

Pick a word from the box to match each clue.
Write the word on the line.

> cowboy   magnet   picnic   blanket   painting
> begin   tiger   oatmeal   boyhood   joyful

1. This is a wild animal.	2. Some people eat this for breakfast.	3. This is the same as happy.	4. A nail sticks to this.

5. This is when you eat outside in the park.	6. He rides a horse and herds cows.	7. This can keep you warm in bed.	8. This word is opposite of **end**.

Home Activity Your child used syllable patterns to write and identify words. Point to some two-syllable words in a favorite book. Help your child identify the first vowel sound, pronounce each syllable, and read the word. Have your child use each word in a sentence.

© Pearson Education, Inc., 2

Name _____

Pick a word from the box to complete each sentence. **Write** the word on the line.

> balance   canyons   coral   rattle
> slivers   sway   whisper

1. When school is out, my friend and I hike in the deep

   _____

   _____ near our home.

2. When hiking, we do not move if we hear the

   _____

   _____ of a snake.

3. We love to hear the wind _____ through the trees.

4. Yesterday we saw a baby bird try to _____ on
   a twig.

5. The bird was lucky that the tree did not _____ too
   much in the wind.

6. My friend had to pull some _____ of wood out of
   her socks.

7. Tomorrow, we will hike to a beach with pretty

   _____

   _____ in the water.

School + Home

Home Activity Your child used lesson vocabulary to complete sentences. Work with your child to use these words in his or her own story.

© Pearson Education, Inc., 2

Read the myth. **Follow** the directions.

A Native American Myth

In early times, Native Americans made up stories about things in nature. One story that the Lakota Indians told was about plants, grass, and trees. In the story, the plants and grass were happy during the sunny days of summer. But when the cold days of winter began, they felt sick. The Great Spirit, who takes care of all things in nature, saw that the plants and grass were dying. He decided to make the leaves fall from the trees and cover the grass and plants like a blanket. The Great Spirit felt sorry then for the trees who had to lose their leaves. To thank the trees, he turned their leaves into beautiful colors before they fell. Every fall after that, the trees glowed with bright red, orange, yellow, and gold leaves.

I. **Underline** the sentence that tells the big idea of the story.

The Great Spirit takes care of things in nature.

Why leaves change color and fall off trees in the fall.

2. **Write** the name of the main character in the story.

_____

_____

3. **Write** the correct word to finish the sentence.

The purpose of this myth is to explain something about

_____

_____ .

© Pearson Education, Inc., 2

Home Activity Your child read a myth and identified its theme. Reread the myth and discuss what similar events in nature a myth might explain.

Writing • Narrative Poem

Time to Move

We're moving away.
This is the date.
We're moving away,
And can't be late.

I try to feel happy,
But really I'm sad.
I try to feel happy,
Still I'm a little mad.

Today, I'm leaving my friends.
It's hard to say good-bye.
Today, I'm leaving my friends.
I hope I don't cry.

New things are good,
Like friends and school.
New things are good.
It'll be pretty cool!

Key Features of a Narrative Poem

• tells a story

• may have rhyming words

• can describe something or can express feelings

© Pearson Education, Inc., 2

Name _____

Syllable Patterns

Write a list word to complete each sentence.

1. I went _____ to the basement.

2. The _____ rode on the horse.

3. There was a _____ after the storm.

4. I ate _____ for breakfast.

5. We played _____ after school.

6. We drove on the _____ .

7. She lived on the _____ .

Spelling Words
downstairs
boyhood
football
oatmeal
cowboy
soybean
houseboat
roadway
railroad
outplay
rainbow
daydream

Write the compound word that is made from joining the two smaller words.

8. out + play _____

9. day + dream _____

10. rail + road _____

11. boy + hood _____

12. soy + bean _____

Home Activity Your child is learning how to spell compound words. Have your child circle the two smaller words that make up each compound word.

© Pearson Education, Inc., 2

Name _____

Read the sentence. **Circle** the correct meaning of the underlined word. **Write** your own sentence for the underlined word. Make sure you include words that will help others figure out the correct meaning of the word.

1. Be careful not to <u>slip</u> on the ice.

    a. to make a mistake   b. to slide and fall   c. small piece of paper

_____

- -

_____

2. Dean can ice <u>skate</u> across the pond.

    a. a fish   b. to glide   c. a shoe with a metal blade

_____

- -

_____

3. We like to skate by the <u>light</u> of the moon.

    a. to start burning   b. not heavy   c. glow

_____

- -

_____

4. If you move too quickly, you might <u>fall</u>.

    a. the season before winter   b. drop down   c. a wig

_____

- -

_____

© Pearson Education, Inc., 2

Home Activity Your child used context clues to figure out the correct meanings of words that have more than one meaning. Ask your child to explain how he or she chose the correct meaning of each underlined word.

Name _____

Adverbs That Tell When and Where

Adverbs tell more about a verb. Some adverbs show **when** or **where**.

> The moon shines **tonight**.
> **Tonight** tells when.
>
> The moon shines **outside**.
> **Outside** tells where.

Circle the adverb in each sentence that tells when or where.
Write the adverbs in the chart. **Say** a sentence with an adverb you wrote.

1. Luna hummed somewhere.

2. The stars twinkled everywhere.

3. The moon is shining now.

4. It will shine here.

5. The moon jumped first.

6. The stars jumped next.

Adverbs That Tell When	Adverbs That Tell Where

© Pearson Education, Inc., 2

School + Home **Home Activity** Your child learned about adverbs that tell when and where. With your child, add more words to the chart that tell when or where. Start with *tomorrow* and *inside*.

Name _____

Story Sequence

Title_____

Characters	Setting

Events

1. First

↓

2. Next

↓

3. Then

↓

4. Last

Home Activity Your child is learning to write stories, poems, brief reports, nonfiction paragraphs, letters, and other products this year. Ask what your child is writing this week

© Pearson Education, Inc., 2

Name _____

Look at the e-mail. **Write** the answer to each question.

⊠ ⊟ ⊕

| Write | Reply | Send | Forward | Delete | Address Book | Print | ▲ |

FROM: Tyler Becker
TO: Jim Alcott
SUBJECT: Moving

Hi Jim,
I have some good news and some bad news. The good news is that my dad got a new job! The bad news is that we're moving. I will miss you. I'll tell you the rest when I see you at school.

Your friend,
Tyler

▼

1. Who is Tyler Becker?

_____
- -

2. What is he writing about? How do you know?

_____
- -

3. Who is Jim Alcott? How do you know?

_____
- -

4. How is an e-mail different from a letter?

_____
- -

5. How could Jim find out where Tyler is moving?

_____
- -

School + Home **Home Activity** Your child learned how to use e-mail. Discuss ways you or your child could use e-mail. Write a pretend e-mail message together. Discuss the advantages and disadvantages of e-mail compared to regular postal mail.

© Pearson Education, Inc., 2

Name _____

Syllable Patterns

Read about the life of a cowboy. **Circle** three spelling mistakes. **Write** the words correctly. **Circle** the word that should be capitalized. **Write** that word correctly.

Spelling Words	
downstairs	boyhood
football	oatmeal
cowboy	soybean
houseboat	roadway
railroad	outplay
rainbow	daydream

> Once there were no roadways or raleroads. Cowboys ruled the plain. Cowboys looked after cattle. they ate simple meals like otmeal, beans, or rice. Sometimes I daidream about what it would be like to be a cowboy.

Frequently Misspelled Words

one

once

first

1. _____   2. _____

3. _____   4. _____

Circle the list word that is spelled correctly.

5. outplay   owtplay   6. futball   football

7. housebot   houseboat   8. rainbow   ranbow

9. soibean   soybean   10. rodeway   roadway

11. boyhood   boihood   12. cowboy   cowboi

© Pearson Education, Inc., 2

School + Home **Home Activity** Your child identified misspelled compound words. Take turns pointing to and spelling the list words.

Read the myth. **Follow** the directions.

Coyote and the Stars

Long, long ago, people made up stories, or myths to explain how some things came to be. The Hopi Indians told many myths. One was about Coyote and the stars. One night, Coyote stole a very heavy stone jar from the world's creator. The jar was so heavy he soon got tired of carrying it. He decided to leave the jar behind. He set the jar on the ground and began to walk away. However, Coyote was too curious. He went back to the jar and pulled on the top. The jar burst open. Shining pieces of fire flew out into the night sky. As they flew past Coyote, the pieces of fire burned the fur on his face. That's why Coyote's face is black and there are stars in the sky.

I. Write the name of the main character in the story.

_____

- -

_____

2. Underline the sentence that tells the big idea of the story.

The Hopi Indians told many myths.

Long ago, people made up stories to explain how some things came to be.

That's why Coyote's face is black and there are stars in the sky.

Home Activity Your child read a myth and identified its theme. Reread the myth and discuss what other things in nature a myth could explain.

© Pearson Education, Inc., 2

Name _____

Adverbs That Tell When and Where

Mark the letter of the word that is an adverb that tells when or where.

1. Today the sky became black.
   - ○ **A** Today
   - ○ **B** became
   - ○ **C** black

2. The stars looked here.
   - ○ **A** here
   - ○ **B** looked
   - ○ **C** stars

3. The stars looked there.
   - ○ **A** looked
   - ○ **B** stars
   - ○ **C** there

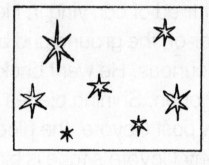

4. The stars whispered outside.
   - ○ **A** whispered
   - ○ **B** outside
   - ○ **C** stars

5. Then the world waited.
   - ○ **A** world
   - ○ **B** Then
   - ○ **C** waited

6. The moon's friends swam nearby.
   - ○ **A** friends
   - ○ **B** swam
   - ○ **C** nearby

Home Activity Your child prepared for taking tests on adverbs that tell when and where. Read a story together. Have your child look for the adverbs *then* and *now* and for the adverbs *here* and *there*.

336 **Conventions** Adverbs That Tell When and Where

© Pearson Education, Inc., 2

Name _____

moon   gl**ue**   fr**ui**t   scr**ew**

Circle the word that has the same vowel sound as **moon**.
Write the word on the line.

1. uncut   untrue   unplug

    _____

    - - - - - - - - - - - - - - - - - -

2. grew   grow   grain

    _____

    - - - - - - - - - - - - - - - - - -

3. stood   spoon   spun

    _____

    - - - - - - - - - - - - - - - - - -

4. just   joy   juice

    _____

    - - - - - - - - - - - - - - - - - -

Circle a word to finish each sentence. **Choose** a word that has the same vowel sound as **new**. **Write** the word on the line.

    _____

    - - - - - - - - - - - - - - - - - -

5. I _____ home from Roy's house on a plane.

    flow   fun   flew

    _____

    - - - - - - - - - - - - - - - - - -

6. I just unpacked my _____.

    sudden   suitcase   supper

    _____

    - - - - - - - - - - - - - - - - - -

7. I want to _____ the library book about a cow.

    renew   repeat   recess

School + Home

Home Activity Your child wrote words that have the same vowel sound spelled *oo* as in *moon*, *ue* as in *glue*, *ui* as in *fruit*, and *ew* as in *screw*. Help your child write sentences using these words: *blue, food, bruise, drew*.

Phonics Vowel Digraphs *oo, ue, ui, ew*   **337**

© Pearson Education, Inc., 2

Name _____

Pick a word from the box to complete each sentence. **Write** the word on the line.

> awaken volcano mountain cliffs
> suffer rainbow prize

1. This morning, Jim's mother will _____ him with good news.

2. Jim won a _____ for a picture he took.

3. The picture shows a colorful _____ in the sky.

4. A tall, snowy _____ is in the picture.

5. It was formed over time from hot mud and ashes that came _____ out of a _____.

6. Some high, rocky _____ show in the distance.

7. He had to _____ in his cold, wet clothes, but he thought the picture was worth it.

© Pearson Education, Inc., 2

Home Activity Your child used lesson vocabulary words to complete sentences. Name a word from the box. Have your child find the sentence that uses that word and read it aloud.

Name _____

Read the legend. **Follow** the directions.

A Flood Legend

Through the years, storytellers in South America have passed down a legend about a great flood. In the story, some people lived at the bottom of a mountain range. These people began doing evil things. The gods did not like the way these people behaved. Other people lived up high in the mountains. These people did not do evil things. They were shepherds who took care of llamas. One day, two brothers noticed their llamas were behaving in a strange way. They asked their llamas what was wrong. The llamas said the stars had warned them that a great flood would soon cover the earth. Quickly the brothers took their families and llamas into a cave. Then it rained for four months! The flood never reached the cave because the mountains grew taller. These people and animals were saved, but the flood had destroyed all the rest of life on earth.

1. **Underline** the sentence that tells the big idea of the story.

    It can rain for a very long time.

    Llamas are smart animals.

    Evil people will be punished.

2. What happened before the brothers talked to their llamas?

    _____

    _____

    _____

    _____

    _____

© Pearson Education, Inc., 2

School + Home **Home Activity** Your child read a legend and identified its theme and plot. Reread the story with your child. Ask your child to underline sentences that tell story events.

Name _____

Writing • Thank-You Note

March 7, 2011

Dear Uncle Roy,

Thank you for making my favorite soup for lunch yesterday. I knew you made the soup as soon as I walked into the kitchen. The air was filled with the wonderful smell of simmering vegetables. The carrots tasted so sweet, and the broth had a tangy flavor from the onions and spices.

You must have put a lot of time into preparing the lunch. First, you carefully chose fresh vegetables. Next, you cut the vegetables evenly into little chunks. Then, you cooked the soup slowly for hours. It was so delicious that we ate it much too quickly. You are a great cook!

Love,
Mike

© Pearson Education, Inc., 2

Key Features of a Thank-You Note

• a short message that thanks someone

• has a greeting and a closing, like a letter

Name _____

Vowel Digraphs *oo, ue, ew, ui*

Spelling Words					
too	new	fruit	blue	true	fool
suit	spoon	clue	juice	drew	flew

Write a list word that means the same as the underlined word.

1. May I play <u>also</u>?

      1. _____

2. He <u>painted</u> a picture.

      2. _____

3. Is it <u>correct</u> that we tied?

      3. _____

4. Let's start a <u>fresh</u> game.

      4. _____

Add a list word to each group.

5. milk, water, _____

6. red, yellow, _____

7. soup, bread, _____

8. dress, skirt, _____

9. fork, knife, _____

10. ran, swam, _____

11. trick, joke, _____

12. tip, hint, _____

Home Activity Your child spelled words with the vowel sound in *moon* spelled *oo, ue, ew,* and *ui.* Have your child point out these letter combinations in the list words.

© Pearson Education, Inc., 2

Name _____

Read the word at the beginning of each row.
Fill in the rest of the table.

Word	Prefix	Base Word	Meaning
1. reawaken			
2. disapprove			
3. rewrite			
4. unable			
5. disallow			
6. restart			
7. unlike			
8. distrust			
9. reapply			
10. unclear			

Home Activity Your child learned about words with prefixes. Have your child choose three words on this page starting with *re-*, *dis-*, and *un-*. Have him or her make up a sentence for each word.

© Pearson Education, Inc., 2

Name _____

Adverbs That Tell How

An **adverb** can tell more about a verb by telling how an action is done. **Adverbs** that tell how usually end in **-ly**.

> Jade moved **quickly**.
> **Quickly** tells how Jade moved.

Write the adverb from the box that completes each sentence.

> rapidly   brightly   loudly

1. The earth rumbled _____ .

2. The sun shone _____ .

3. Jade worked _____ .

Underline the adverb that tells how in each sentence.
Say a sentence with that adverb.

4. The hummingbird chirped quietly.

5. Jade slowly climbed the mountain.

6. The lava suddenly flowed.

© Pearson Education, Inc., 2

Home Activity Your child learned about adverbs that tell how. With your child, use the words in the box and the words that were underlined on this page. Make up sentences that tell how people do things.

Name _____

Web

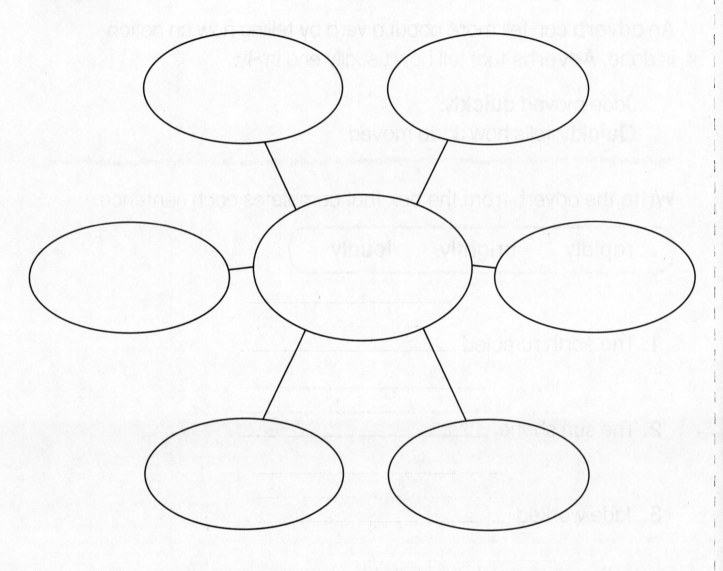

 Home Activity Your child is learning to write stories, poems, brief reports, nonfiction paragraphs, letters, and other products this year. Ask what your child is writing this week

344 Writing Plan

Name _____

Pick a word from the box to
answer each question.
Write the word on the line.

> almanac   computer   dictionary
> thermometer   wind sock

1. Where would you find Web sites about storms?

_____

_____

2. What source would you use to find the meaning of **temperature**?

_____

_____

3. What would you use to find the temperature in your classroom?

_____

_____

4. Where would you most likely find a collection of weather
   patterns over a period of time?

_____

_____

5. What would you look at to see which way the wind is blowing?

_____

_____

Home Activity Your child learned how to gather evidence from natural sources, sources usually found in
a classroom, and personal sources found at home. Together with your child, collect information about the
weather in your area for one week. If possible, use a computer, the newspaper, or a thermometer to record
the temperature as well as any interesting weather patterns that occur.

© Pearson Education, Inc., 2

Vowel Digraphs *oo, ue, ew, ui*

Read the invitation. **Circle** two spelling mistakes. **Circle** a word with a capitalization error. **Write** the words correctly.

Spelling Words	
too	suit
new	spoon
fruit	clue
blue	juice
true	drew
fool	flew

> Please come too the class picnic Saturday at 4:00 PM.
> The menu includes hot dogs, fruit salad, and jiuce.
> bring your own plate, fork, and spoon.

_____   _____   _____

1. _____   2. _____   3. _____

Frequently Misspelled Words
too   to
two

Fill in the circle next to the word that is spelled correctly. **Write** the word.

4. ○ clew   ○ clue   ○ clui   _____

5. ○ trew   ○ true   ○ tru   _____

6. ○ floo   ○ fue   ○ flew   _____

7. ○ fool   ○ ful   ○ fewl   _____

8. ○ bluw   ○ bloo   ○ blue   _____

9. ○ suit   ○ sute   ○ siut   _____

10. ○ drew   ○ dru   ○ drue   _____

School + Home **Home Activity** Your child has identified misspelled words with the vowel sound in *moon* spelled *oo, ue, ew,* and *ui*. Have your child identify and spell one or more words with each of these letter combinations.

© Pearson Education, Inc., 2

Name _____

Read the legend. **Follow** the directions.

A Mountain Legend

   In North Carolina, a legend has been passed down about a light that shines from a mountain at night. In this tale, a young woman lived on the mountain with her father. Every evening, her sweetheart, a nice young man, came to visit her there. To get to her home, he would have to walk on a forest path filled with snakes and dangerous animals. The young woman would light a torch and stand on her porch to welcome him. One night, the young man never showed up. The young woman was heartbroken. After that, every night at sunset, she would light a torch and wander the mountain looking for him. Even after her death, the light still shone on the mountain after dark.

1. Underline the sentence that tells the big idea of the legend.

   It's dangerous to walk in the woods at night.

   True love lasts forever.

   Never walk around with a torch on a mountain.

2. What does this legend explain?

   _____

   _____

Home Activity Your child read a legend and identified its theme and plot. Reread the story with your child. Then discuss any legends that you or your child may have known.

© Pearson Education, Inc., 2

Comprehension Plot and Theme   **347**

Adverbs That Tell How

Mark the letter of the sentence that has an adverb that tells how.

1. ○ **A** Loud thunder crashed.
   ○ **B** Thunder suddenly crashed.
   ○ **C** The thunder crashed.

2. ○ **A** I quickly covered my ears.
   ○ **B** I covered my ears.
   ○ **C** My ears were covered.

3. ○ **A** The wind howled.
   ○ **B** The wind blew.
   ○ **C** The wind raged fiercely.

4. ○ **A** People welcomed the rain.
   ○ **B** People happily welcomed the rain.
   ○ **C** People welcomed the heavy rain.

5. ○ **A** The storm ended.
   ○ **B** The storm slowly ended.
   ○ **C** The big storm ended.

6. ○ **A** I uncovered my ears.
   ○ **B** I uncovered my warm ears.
   ○ **C** I bravely uncovered my ears.

Home Activity Your child prepared for taking tests on adverbs that tell how. Take turns with your child making up sentences about family members using the words *neatly*, *sweetly*, *nicely*, and *gladly*.

© Pearson Education, Inc., 2

Name _____

Pick a word from the box to match each clue.
Write the word on the line.

> ankle   bubble   table   puzzle   title   turtle

1. blow a _____

_____

_____

2. knee, _____, foot

_____

_____

3. a piece of a _____

_____

_____

4. slow as a _____

_____

_____

5. sit at a _____

_____

_____

6. the _____ of the story

_____

_____

Read the story.

Dave and Ann went to the pond to see the ducks paddle. They rode blue bikes, and Ann's bike had purple handles. They steered their bikes around a puddle in the middle of the bike path. They rode well and did not tumble off their bikes. There were ripples and bubbles in the pond. A turtle swam in the middle of the pond. Ann and Dave sat down at a picnic table. They drank the bottles of milk Ann had in her backpack. Then it was time to ride home.

Home Activity Your child reviewed words that end in -*le* and have more than one syllable, such as *title*. Have your child write a story title and short story with words that end in *le*. Encourage your child to use as many words that end in *le* as possible. The story can be silly and fun.

© Pearson Education, Inc., 2

Name _____

Final Syllable *-le*

Spelling Words					
ankle	title	apple	cable	purple	able
bugle	bundle	bubble	giggle	sparkle	tickle

Read the clues. **Write** the list words in the puzzle.

Across

2. a small trumpet
3. the name of a book
5. body part above your foot
6. soap _____

Down

1. can do something
4. tingling or itching feeling

Write the words in the box in ABC order.

7. _____   8. _____

9. _____   10. _____

11. _____   12. _____

© Pearson Education, Inc., 2

| sparkle |
| cable |
| bundle |
| giggle |
| purple |
| apple |

Home Activity Your child has been learning to spell words that end with *-le*. Pick a list word. Have your child spell the word and use it in a sentence.

Name _____

Read the story. **Pick** a word from the box to complete each sentence. **Write** the word on the line.

> clearing   perfect   traveled   splashing
> pond   crashed   spilling

_____

Kim _____ to camp on a bus. The road wound

through the woods and stopped in a _____.

_____

The camp was near a _____ with ducks resting beside it. When Kim came close, the ducks jumped into the

_____

pond, _____ water on Kim. It was warm, and Kim poured a cold cup of water to drink. Just then, a deer

_____

_____ through the brush into the clearing. Kim

jumped, _____ her water on the grass. The deer

_____

came up close to Kim. What a _____ end to the day!

Home Activity Your child reviewed vocabulary learned earlier in this unit. Tell your child to pretend that he or she is at a camp. Have your child write a short description of what happened using as many of the vocabulary words as possible.

© Pearson Education, Inc., 2

Name _____

Read the fable. **Answer** the questions.

Greedy Groundhog

The forest animals were very quiet. All the animals were resting in the shade of an old barn. The summer sun was hot like a fire even though it was early in the morning. For a long time, there had been no rain. The soil was dried and cracked. Plants had died because they couldn't grow without water.

The animals that ate plants were very hungry. Those who nibbled on trees were hungry, too. They had eaten the last of the leaves, twigs, and bark.

Then one of the deer, Miss White Tail, stood up in her graceful way. "Wake up, my dear friends," she said. "We can't wait for the rain to come. We shall have to leave this place and look for food in another place."

"Good idea," Mr. Porcupine replied.

"My family is ready!" Mrs. Long Ears exclaimed.

All the animals agreed it was a good plan. So when all were gathered together, they hopped, bounced, and trotted after Miss White Tail. Soon they came to a magnificent garden! They couldn't believe their eyes. Big, bright vegetables and tall, green grass filled the garden. There were even trees in the garden with crisp leaves and bushes with juicy berries.

But the garden had a metal fence all around it. And sitting at the gate of the garden was a big, fat groundhog. "Go away!" he shouted. "I found the garden, and this is my food." He growled and scared the animals. They all ran away as fast as they could.

© Pearson Education, Inc., 2

Home Activity Your child used text to draw conclusions and make inferences about a fable. Read aloud a portion of a story your child has not read. Work with your child to draw conclusions and make inferences about a character or event. Pause often to ask *why, what,* and *how* questions.

Name _____

When the animals were safely away from the groundhog, Miss White Tail said, "Let's go back tomorrow. I have an idea."

Early the next morning, Miss White Tail went to the garden, carrying several large bags. "Run, Groundhog!" she yelled. "A fierce rainstorm is coming. I'm going to cover the animals with these bags to keep them from being soaked to death."

"Give me a bag!" the groundhog demanded.

"Well, OK," she said calmly. "If you really want one, let me help you put it on." Miss White Tail carefully put the bag over the groundhog. Then she quickly tied a rope around and around the groundhog's body so he couldn't move.

All the animals came running to help tie the groundhog to the fence. After that, Miss White Tail opened the garden gate, and all the hungry animals ate a delicious meal. **Moral: It is not right to be selfish.**

1. Why were the animals quiet?

2. Why do you think the animals decided not to wait for rain?

3. How was Miss White Tail able to get into the garden?

4. What words do you think describe Miss White Tail?

© Pearson Education, Inc., 2

Name _____

Adjectives and Our Senses

Find an adjective in each sentence that tells how something looks, sounds, tastes, feels, or smells. **Underline** the adjectives.

1. Frog liked the cool pond.

2. Frog made a big breakfast.

3. Frog took a short nap.

Choose the adjective in ( ) that makes sense in the sentence. **Write** the sentence.

4. Otters sat in the (warm, loud) pond.

_____

- -

_____

5. Frog saw (hot, tiny) bugs.

_____

- -

_____

6. Frog liked (red, nice) changes.

_____

- -

_____

© Pearson Education, Inc., 2

Name _____

Day 1 Unit 4 Week 1 — A Froggy Fable

Copy the words. Make sure you form your letters correctly.

he   he   he   he   he   he

heel   heel   heel   heel

Day 2 Unit 4 Week 2 — Life Cycle of a Pumpkin

Copy the words. Make sure you space the letters the same way.

hill   it   tell   the

hull   hut   till   let

Home Activity Your child practiced writing letters *l, h, k, t, i, u, e, j, p, a, d, c, n, m,* and *x.* Have your child practice writing the following words, focusing on letter formation and spacing: *pad, that, text, men, like, jam, come, cup.*

© Pearson Education, Inc., 2

Handwriting 355

Name _____

Day 3 Unit 4 Week 3   **Soil**

Copy the words. Make sure you form your letters correctly.

kite   pet   jet   put

_____
- -
_____

kit   help   jute   pile

_____
- -
_____

Day 4 Unit 4 Week 4   **The Night the Moon Fell**

Copy the phrases. Make sure you space your words correctly.

cute cat | tame pet

_____ | _____
- - - - - - - - - - - - - - - | - - - - - - - - - - - - - - -
_____ | _____

Day 5 Unit 4 Week 5   **The First Tortilla**

Copy the phrases. Make sure your letters are the same size.

pink jam | like to hike

_____ | _____
- - - - - - - - - - - - - - - | - - - - - - - - - - - - - - -
_____ | _____

© Pearson Education, Inc., 2

Name _____

Pick a word from the box to match each picture.
Write the word on the line.

> pudding   bush   herd   hood   hook   push   wood

1. _____

2. _____

3. _____

4. _____

5. _____

6. _____

Read the story.

Woody and Carla went to the brook. It was chilly, so they wore jackets with hoods. Woody had a booklet about what to look for in brooks. He had a hook to pull things out of the brook. Woody took a look under a bush. A turtle was hiding under it. It needed to be in the brook, so Carla gave it a little push with her foot. It scrambled away and into the brook. Then it was time for a snack. Carla was a good cook, and she had made some pudding and cookies. They were really good. Woody and Carla had a good time on the way home.

Home Activity Your child reviewed words that have the vowel sound in *book*, spelled *oo* and *u* as in *pull*. Say a word from the box on the page above. Ask your child to use the word in a sentence. Repeat the word and have your child write it. Continue the activity with other words from the box.

© Pearson Education, Inc., 2

Vowel Patterns *oo, u*

Spelling Words					
put	cook	stood	full	wood	July
shook	push	pull	brook	book	hood

Read the story. **Write** the missing list words.

I go to summer camp every year in **1.** _____ . This year, I will

learn how to use **2.** _____ to make a fire. A **3.** _____

flows near the camp. I will read a **4.** _____ and learn how to

5. _____ a fish. My backpack is **6.** _____ of things

I **7.** _____ in it.

Read the clues. **Write** the list words.

8. can be found on your jacket or on a car _____

9. can mean **shivered** _____

10. rhymes with **wood** but starts like **step** _____

11.–12. are opposites _____ _____

Home Activity Your child has been learning to spell words with the vowel sound in *book,* spelled *oo* and *u.* Write the words *look, took, cookie, put,* and *push.* Read them to your child. Have your child sort the words by spelling pattern.

© Pearson Education, Inc., 2

Name _____

Write a word from the box to finish each sentence.

> bumpy   fruit   harvest
> root   smooth   soil   vine

1. Apples and grapes are two kinds of _____.

2. Apples grow in trees, but grapes grow on a _____.

3. A banana peel feels _____.

4. An orange peel feels _____.

5. Farmers need good _____ for plants.

6. Farmers _____ fruits when they are ripe.

7. The part of the plant that grows under the ground is the _____.

Home Activity Your child reviewed vocabulary words learned this week. Have your child draw pictures of his or her favorite fruits and write sentences to describe them using words learned this week.

© Pearson Education, Inc., 2

Vocabulary 359

Name _____

Read the story. **Follow** the directions and **answer** the questions.

A Class Mural

My class was learning about cities. Our teacher, Mr. Mendez, asked if we thought we could make a mural to show what city life was like. We told him we could make a great mural. Mr. Mendez said we could hang the mural in the hall when it was finished. Our mural would let other children in the school see what a city looks like.

Mr. Mendez put us in groups and gave each group one part of the mural to work on. He had put up a long sheet of mural paper on one wall. We were to use pencils, crayons, drawing paper, scissors, and paste.

The class decided to show a city street. The first thing we did was make a plan for the mural. We made a list of things to include. Our city street would be a busy place with a lot of people and traffic. There would be cars, taxis, trucks, and buses on the street. There would be people walking on the sidewalk and going into different kinds of buildings.

Next, each group went to the mural paper and used pencils to draw the buildings along the street. My classmates and I drew many kinds of buildings. The buildings included tall office buildings, big stores, and small shops. We drew a bank, a movie theater, and a museum. Then we colored the buildings with crayons.

After that, we drew people on sheets of colored paper. Some of us drew adults, and others drew children. We drew tall people and

© Pearson Education, Inc., 2

 Home Activity Your child identified the sequence of events in a story. Ask your child to tell you about an art or science project he or she did in school. Encourage your child to use order words such as *first, next, then,* and *last* to show the sequence of events.

Name _____

short people. We drew people dressed for shopping and people dressed for work. I drew a worker who was fixing part of the sidewalk.

Finally, everyone cut out his or her drawings. And last of all, each group pasted people on the city street. Our mural was finished! We thought it was a great mural. Mr. Mendez said it was wonderful.

The next day, Mr. Mendez hung the mural in the hall by our classroom. Our friends in other classes stopped to look at it. They said it was awesome.

___

1. **Circle** the words in the story that give clues to the order in which things happened.

2. What happened after the class made a plan for the mural?

_____
- -
_____

3. What happened before the children drew people for the mural?

_____
- -
_____

4. What did the children do after they drew people for the mural?

_____
- -
_____

5. What happened after the mural was finished?

_____
- -
_____

© Pearson Education, Inc., 2

Name _____

Adjectives for Number, Size, and Shape

Write an adjective to complete each sentence. **Use** a word in ( ).

1. I planted _____ seeds. (oval, slowly)

2. _____ vines grew on the wall. (Who, Tall)

3. I counted _____ vines! (pulled, sixty)

Underline adjectives that describe the number, size, or shape of something. **Write** the adjectives in the chart.

4. I picked short pods.

5. I snapped open twenty pods.

6. I found round peas inside.

Describe Number	Describe Size	Describe Shape

© Pearson Education, Inc., 2

Name _____

Say the name of the picture. **Circle** the word that has the same vowel sound as the name of the picture.

1.		
top	toy	tower

2.		
soybean	sow	soap

3.		
goal	boil	allow

4.		
cloudy	royal	joggle

Read the story.

Cho went to visit Kengo Brown on his farm. The Browns had a lot of cows. Cho and Kengo walked around the cows to the soybean patch. The tractor was making a loud noise. The plants had flowers but no beans. Kengo put his finger in the ground to see if the soil was moist. It was dry. He pointed at the clouds and said, "If it rains, I will not need to sprinkle the soybeans." Now it was time to broil some beef on the outside grill. Kengo's dad was boiling beans inside. "Chow time!" said Kengo's mom. They sat down to eat.

© Pearson Education, Inc., 2

Home Activity Your child reviewed words that have the vowel sounds in *gown, house, joy,* and *soil*. Ask your child to draw pictures representing words with these sounds. Help your child write words to label each picture. Have your child use each word in a sentence.

Name _____

Diphthongs *ou, ow, oi, oy*

Spelling Words					
around	out	gown	sound	flower	howl
toy	noise	royal	moist	coil	cow

There are stars where the letters that make the vowel sounds should be. **Write** the list word with the correct letters.

1. ar ★ ★ nd _____

2. m ★ ★ st _____

3. r ★ ★ al _____

4. s ★ ★ nd _____

5. n ★ ★ se _____

Write the missing list words.

There once was a queen with a golden crown,
who dressed every day in a long blue ___(6)___.
One day she decided she wanted a ___(7)___,
so she planted a seed and waited an hour.
After that time she started to pout,
It had been 60 minutes and nothing came ___(8)___.
She stamped and cried and let out a ___(9)___.
"Where is my flower?" she asked with a scowl.
"Just wait!" said the king. "I'm sure it will come."
"It just needs some rain and perhaps some more sun."
Twenty days later a small sprout did ___(10)___
Up from out of the dark and rich soil.

6. _____

7. _____

8. _____

9. _____

10. _____

Home Activity Your child has been learning to spell words with the vowel sounds in *gown* and *toy*. Give clues about a list word. Ask your child to name and spell the word.

© Pearson Education, Inc., 2

Name _____

Pick a word from the box to match each clue.
Write the letters of the word in the puzzle.

> grains   materials   particles
> seep   substances   texture

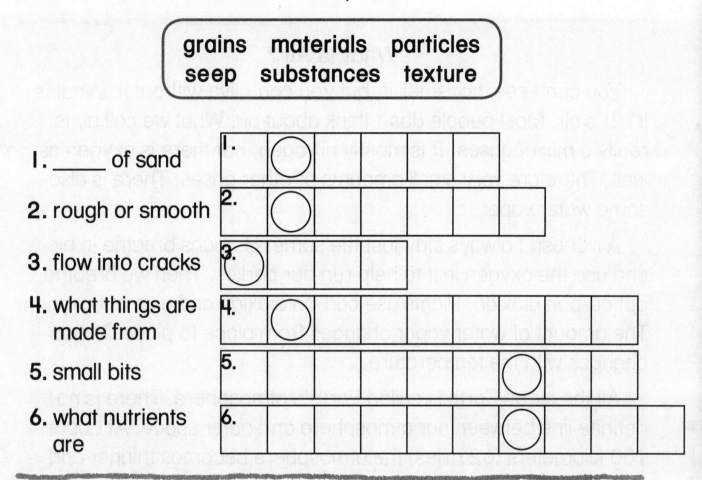

1. _____ of sand
2. rough or smooth
3. flow into cracks
4. what things are made from
5. small bits
6. what nutrients are

Put the circled letters in order to write a word.
HINT: The first letter is shown.

I _____

© Pearson Education, Inc., 2

Home Activity Your child reviewed vocabulary words learned this week. Choose library books about soil. Encourage your child to look for these vocabulary words when reading about soil.

Vocabulary 365

Name _____

Read the article.
Answer the questions.

What Is Air?

You can't see it or smell it, but you can't live without it. What is it? It's air. Most people don't think about air. What we call air is really a mix of gases. It is mostly nitrogen, but there is oxygen as well. There are very small amounts of other gases. There is also some water vapor.

Air doesn't always stay just the same. Humans breathe in air and use the oxygen in it to help run our bodies. Then we breathe out carbon dioxide. Plants use carbon dioxide and give out oxygen. The amount of water vapor changes from place to place. It also changes with the temperature.

All the air on Earth is called Earth's atmosphere. There is no definite line between our atmosphere and outer space. At about 100 kilometers (62 miles) the atmosphere becomes thinner and fades into space.

Although you can't see air itself, sometimes you can see substances that hang in the air. When the air looks like a white haze, we call it fog. Many people are afraid of fog. Fog is made up of tiny drops of water, and it can be hard to see through. Fog is like a cloud that is close to the ground.

© Pearson Education, Inc., 2

School + Home **Home Activity** Your child identified facts and opinions in an article. Have your child tell his or her opinion of this article.

Name _____

When the air looks like a brownish yellow haze, we call it smog. Smog is made up of tiny grains of dust and particles of liquid in the air. It can be caused by air pollution from cars, factories, forest fires, volcanoes, and so on. Then it almost feels as if the air has a texture. Smog can be dangerous to human health. How? People can die from breathing the kinds of material that hang in the air. Smog also damages the leaves of plants.

1. Look at the first paragraph. Write one fact about air.

_____
_____
_____
_____

2. Write one fact about fog.

_____
_____
_____
_____

3. Write one fact about smog.

_____
_____
_____
_____
_____

4. Underline one opinion stated in the article.

© Pearson Education, Inc., 2

Comparative and Superlative Adjectives

Underline the word in ( ) that completes each sentence.

1. The (larger, largest) particles in soil are minerals.

2. Sand feels (rougher, roughest) than clay.

3. Clay particles are the (smaller, smallest) of all particles in soil.

Add -er or **-est** to the word in ( ) to complete each sentence.
Write the word.

4. Water moves slowly through the _____ air
   spaces. (small)

5. A steep mountain is _____ than a hill.
   (high)

6. Clay feels _____ than sand. (smooth)

© Pearson Education, Inc., 2

Name _____

Pick a word from the box to match each picture.
Write the word on the line.

> boyhood   picnic   label   music
> tiger   insect   signal   oatmeal

1. _____

2. _____

3. _____

4. _____

5. _____

6. _____

7. _____

8. _____

Read the story.

   Music is Nancy's best subject. Lupe sits next to her in class. Nancy did Lupe a favor. She lent her a pencil and paper to write down the words to her solo. Lupe was in a contest and wanted to practice at home. Nancy slept over at her house to help her. In the morning they had donuts, cider, and bacon. Then they went to the school for the contest. Lupe won the contest with her solo.

School + Home **Home Activity** Your child used syllable patterns to write and identify words. Point to some two-syllable words in a favorite book. Help your child identify the first vowel sound, pronounce each syllable, and read the word. Have your child use each word in a sentence.

© Pearson Education, Inc., 2

Name _____

Syllable Patterns

Spelling Words
downstairs football cowboy houseboat railroad rainbow
boyhood oatmeal soybean roadway outplay daydream

Draw a line to connect two words that make a compound word.
Write the compound word.

1. day way   1. _____

2. out ball   2. _____

3. road bean   3. _____

4. soy dream   4. _____

5. foot stairs   5. _____

6. down bow   6. _____

7. rain play   7. _____

Divide the compound word into two shorter words.

8. oatmeal _____ + _____   9. cowboy _____ + _____

10. railroad _____ + _____   11. houseboat _____ + _____

School + Home **Home Activity** Your child has been learning to spell compound words. Together, look for compound words in a favorite book. Ask your child to say each compound word. Then ask him or her to name the two words that make up each compound word.

© Pearson Education, Inc., 2

370 Spelling

Name _____

Write a word from the box to complete each sentence.

> balance canyons coral rattle
> slivers sway whisper

1. After school, my friend and I looked at the pretty _____ in the tide pools.

2. We had to _____ to keep from scaring the birds away.

3. The sand had washed down from some deep _____.

4. We watched the sea plants _____ in the moving water.

5. I shook my can of nuts and heard them _____ inside.

6. The nuts were cut into small _____.

7. My friend showed me how to _____ the can of nuts on my head.

School + Home

Home Activity Your child reviewed vocabulary learned earlier in this unit. Take turns making up a riddle about a vocabulary word and guessing the word.

© Pearson Education, Inc., 2

Name _____

Read the text. **Follow** the directions and **answer** the questions.

The Monster in the Maze

An Ancient Greek Myth

There once was a king who was mean to the people he ruled. All the people in the kingdom were afraid of the king. And they were afraid of something else, too. The king had a terrible monster. The people thought they had to obey the king, or he would send the monster after them.

The monster was VERY SCARY! It had a huge head with horns like a bull and a strong body like a man's body. This creature was called a minotaur, and the king kept it trapped in the middle of a maze.

One day, a Greek hero named Theseus came to help the people of this kingdom. He declared he would go into the maze and fight the minotaur. The king's daughter, a kind young maiden, heard this news. She called Theseus to meet with her. When Theseus came, she gave him a ball of string.

"You will get lost in the maze," she said. "Take this ball of string and unwind it behind you. Then you can follow the string to find your way out."

Theseus thanked the king's daughter and accepted the ball of string. Then brave Theseus headed for the maze. He entered the maze, unafraid of what might happen. He was determined to set the people free from the mean king.

Inside the maze, Theseus walked up one path and down another. But no path led him to the minotaur. Each path he took

© Pearson Education, Inc., 2

School + Home **Home Activity** Your child identified the plot and theme--the big idea--of a story. Read a short fiction story with your child. Discuss the theme of the story and the events that happened.

Name _____

ended at a wall. Theseus twisted his way through the maze for a long time, unwinding the ball of string behind him as he went.

Suddenly, Theseus heard stomping and a tremendous roar. He had found his way to the middle of the maze. And now he was face-to-face with the frightening minotaur!

───────────────────────────────────

1. Underline the sentence that tells the big idea of the story.

A king can be mean to people.
A hero helps people in trouble.
Monsters are scary creatures.

2. How did the king make sure the people would obey him?

_____

- -

_____

3. What happened when Theseus went to see the king's daughter?

_____

- -

_____

- -

_____

4. Why did it take a long time for Theseus to find the minotaur?

_____

- -

_____

5. What do you think happened at the end of the story?

_____

- -

_____

© Pearson Education, Inc., 2

Name _____

Adverbs That Tell When and Where

Complete each sentence. **Write** an adverb in ( ) that tells when or where.

1. _____ I will look for the moon. (Closely, Tonight)

2. The moon shone _____ else. (everywhere, softly)

3. The stars will _____ twinkle. (forward, soon)

Circle adverbs that tell when or where.
Write the adverbs in the chart.

4. The moon fell yesterday.

5. It landed here in the sea.

6. Later, it got back in the sky.

Adverbs That Tell When	Adverbs That Tell Where

© Pearson Education, Inc., 2

Name _____

Say the word for each picture.
Write oo, ue, ew, or **ui** to finish each word.

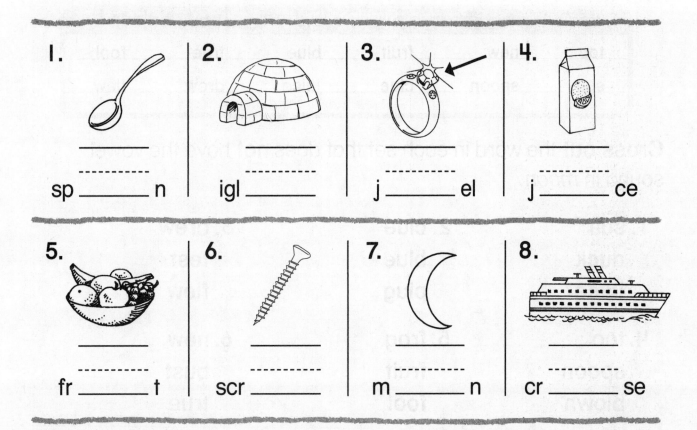

1. sp _____ n

2. igl _____

3. j _____ el

4. j _____ ce

5. fr _____ t

6. scr _____

7. m _____ n

8. cr _____ se

Read the story.

Sue got a new blue swimsuit. Trudy got a new swimsuit too. Trudy had a pool at her house. Sue went over to swim after school. The newspaper said it was a hot day, but that was untrue. It was quite cool. The jewel on the strap of Trudy's sandal came unglued. Her dad fixed it. After swimming, the girls drank fruit juice and ate oatmeal with a spoon. Then it was time for Sue to go home. Trudy asked her to visit again soon.

© Pearson Education, Inc., 2

Home Activity Your child reviewed words that have the same vowel sound as in *moon*, spelled *oo* as in *moon*, *ue* as in *glue*, *ui* as in *fruit*, and *ew* as in *screw*. Help your child write sentences using these words: *blue, food, bruise,* and *drew.*

Name _____

Vowel Digraphs *oo, ue, ew, ui*

Spelling Words					
too	new	fruit	blue	true	fool
suit	spoon	clue	juice	drew	flew

Cross out the word in each set that does **not** have the vowel sound in *moon*.

1. suit
   duck
   juice

2. clue
   blue
   plug

3. drew
   test
   flew

4. too
   spoon
   blown

5. frog
   fruit
   fool

6. new
   bust
   true

Write the missing letters to make a list word.

7. something you eat with   __ __ o __ o __

8. trick   __ o __ o __

9. a color   __ __ u __ e

10. also   __ o __ o

11. not old   __ e __ w

12. something to drink   __ u __ i __ __

Home Activity Your child has been learning to spell words with the vowel sound in *moon* spelled *oo, ue, ew,* and *ui*. Write or say more sets of three words like the words in items 1–6. Have your child identify the word that does not have the vowel sound in *moon*.

© Pearson Education, Inc., 2

Name _____

Pick a word from the box to answer each riddle.
Write the word on the line.

1. You get this when you win. _____

2. You do this before you
   get up in the morning. _____

3. This is very tall and
   may have snow on top. _____

4. This has many colors and
   you see it after it rains. _____

5. This blows hot gas and
   ashes out its top. _____

6. These are very high and
   you do not want to fall
   off of them. _____

7. You do this when you are
   hurt or unhappy. _____

awaken
volcano
mountain
cliffs
suffer
rainbow
prize

© Pearson Education, Inc., 2

School + Home **Home Activity** Your child reviewed vocabulary learned earlier in this unit. Encourage your child to use many of the vocabulary words in his or her own story.

Read the legend. **Follow** the directions and **answer** the questions.

A Tale of Tails

A Native American Legend

Opossum had always thought Raccoon had a very fine tail. Although she had a furry tail like Raccoon's tail, she admired the beautiful black rings around Raccoon's tail. Opossum wanted a tail just like it.

One night, when Opossum was searching for food, she spied Raccoon by a brook, having a meal of nuts, fruit, and plants. Although she was usually a shy animal, Opossum went right up to Raccoon.

"Hello, Raccoon," she said. "Nice night, isn't it?"

"Yes, it is," Raccoon replied. "I'm having good luck finding delicious things to eat."

Opossum went on to say, "I think you have a magnificent tail, Raccoon. How did you get such lovely black rings around it?"

Raccoon smiled and answered, "Well, I'd be happy to tell you, Opossum. I went looking for some long, narrow strips of bark. After I found ones that were just the right size, I wrapped them around my tail."

"Now I know!" Opossum exclaimed. "The bark left black marks in rings around your tail, didn't it?"

"You didn't let me finish," Raccoon said. "The next thing I did was make a fire. Then I stuck my tail right into that fire. Soon all the fur between the strips of bark burned and turned black. I peeled off the bark and the black fur had become black rings."

Home Activity Your child read a story and identified the plot and theme of the story. Read a short fiction story with your child. After reading, have your child tell you what happened at the beginning, in the middle, and at the end of the story.

© Pearson Education, Inc., 2

Name _____

"That's what I'll do, too." Opossum thought to herself.

Opossum thanked Raccoon for the information and scurried off to gather some long, narrow strips of bark. Opossum carried the bark home and then carefully wrapped the strips around her furry tail.

Opossum made a fire and then stuck her tail into the flames. But she had made the fire too hot! The fire burned every inch of fur off her tail! For days and days, she waited and waited and waited for the fur to grow back. The fur never grew back.

1. **Underline** the sentence that tells the theme of the story.

Why the opossum has a tail without fur.

Why the raccoon has a furry tail.

How fire can hurt animals.

2. **Write** the sentence from the story that gives a clue to the story's theme.

_____

_____

3. What does Opossum do at the beginning of the story?

_____

_____

4. What happens after Opossum and Raccoon talk to each other?

_____

_____

5. What event takes place at the end of the story?

_____

_____

© Pearson Education, Inc., 2

Adverbs That Tell How

Choose the adverb in ( ) that completes each sentence.
Write the sentence.

1. Rain pinged ____. (plainly, loudly)

   _____

   _____

2. Jade ____ ran inside. (gladly, sweetly)

   _____

   _____

3. She grumbled ____ about rain. (oddly, crossly)

   _____

   _____

Write the adverb from the box that completes each sentence.

   brightly   softly   suddenly

   _____

4. The gentle wind blew _____ .

5. Then, _____, the wind raged.

6. Lightning flashed _____ .

© Pearson Education, Inc., 2

Name _____

Details Web

Fill out this details web to help you organize your ideas.

© Pearson Education, Inc., 2

Name _____

Use Strong Adjectives

Look at the adjectives in dark type.
Which sentence in each pair has a stronger adjective?
Underline the sentence.

1. We looked at the **colorful** garden.

   We looked at the **pretty** garden.

2. She ate a **good** apple.

   She ate a **crisp** apple.

3. My grandmother made me a **nice** quilt.

   My grandmother made me a **blue and white** quilt.

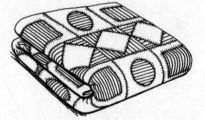

4. The thunder made a **booming** sound.

   The thunder made a **loud** sound.

5. The pumpkin pie smelled **good.**

   The pumpkin pie smelled **spicy.**

© Pearson Education, Inc., 2

Name _____

Deleting Words, Phrases, or Sentences

When you revise, delete words, phrases, and sentences that are not needed or do not tell about your topic.

Follow the directions.

1. Read the sentence. Draw a line through the words that are not needed.
   Seeds were planted in the school's very own real garden.

2. Read the sentence. Draw a line through a phrase that is not about the topic.
   The seeds needed bright sunlight, warm soil, fresh bread, and water.

3. Read the sentence. Draw a line through the words that make the sentence too wordy.
   The seeds sprouted, and the little plants began to grow and grow.

4. Read the sentences. Draw a line through the sentence that does not belong.
   Soon tiny green leaves appeared. They grew bigger. Trees have leaves.

5. Read the sentences. Draw a line through the sentence that is too wordy.
   The garden was finally complete when many beautiful white flowers began to bloom all over the plants.
   Finally, beautiful white flowers bloomed.

© Pearson Education, Inc., 2

Name _____

Editing 3

Proofreading Marks	
Delete (Take out)	੭
Add	^
Spelling	⬭
Uppercase letter	≡
Lowercase letter	/

This is part of a description. **Edit** the paragraph. **Look** for errors in grammar, punctuation, capitalization, and spelling. **Use** proofreading marks to show the corrections.

Spring begins dering the last chills of Winter. At first the trees are

still bair and the air is still cool. But soon the sun shine more warmly

and rain showers made the grass turn green. The trees start to

burst out in buds colorful tulips and daffodil shoot out of the dirt

toward the sun. Birds sung happy songs of spring and hurry to bild

their nests. Wait! Did you here that sound. It was the crack of a

baseball bat. Now you know spring is hear.

Now you'll edit the draft of your description as your teacher directs you. Next you'll use your draft to make a final copy of your description. Finally, you'll publish your work and share it with others.

© Pearson Education, Inc., 2

Name _____

teach + er = teach**er**   child + ish = child**ish**   sail + or = sail**or**

Add -er, **-or**, or **-ish** to each word to make a word from the box.
Write the new word on the line.

> actor   foolish   selfish   helper   singer   visitor

visit
_____

1. _____

sing
_____

3. _____

self
_____

5. _____

fool
_____

2. _____

act
_____

4. _____

help
_____

6. _____

---

slow + ly = slow**ly**   cheer + ful = cheer**ful**

Add -ly or **-ful** to each word to make a new word.
Write the new word on the line.

Add -ly

week
_____

7. _____

quick
_____

9. _____

Add -ful

joy
_____

8. _____

hope
_____

10. _____

© Pearson Education, Inc., 2

School + Home **Home Activity** Your child wrote words with the suffixes *-ly*, *-ful*, *-er*, *-ish*, and *-or*. Help your child write sentences, using the words from this page. Ask your child to read each sentence and circle the *-ly*, *-ful*, *-er*, *-ish*, or *-or* suffix in each lesson word.

Name _____

Pick a word from the box to finish the sentence.
Write the word on the line.

> building burning masks
> quickly roar station tightly

1. A call comes to the fire _____ .

2. A _____ is on fire!

3. The firefighters move _____ .

4. They grab their boots and _____ .

5. The truck races to the _____ home.

6. You can hear the siren _____ .

7. They hold on _____ to the hoses.

School + Home **Home Activity** Your child used lesson vocabulary words to complete sentences. Ask your child to use the vocabulary words to make up sentences about the jobs that firefighters do. Work together to write the sentences, and encourage your child to illustrate them.

© Pearson Education, Inc., 2

Name _____

Read the story. **Write** the answer to each question.

House Rabbits

House rabbits are the best pets. Rabbits are good pets for someone who lives in an apartment building because they are quiet. They have fur on the bottom of their feet, so neighbors won't hear them hopping around. Rabbits are clean animals. Just like cats, rabbits keep their fur clean by grooming. Their long ears are beautiful. A rabbit looks very cute when it pulls down an ear and licks it. Like all pets, rabbits require special care, but they are worth it.

1. What does this story try to make you believe?

_____

_____

2. What fact tells you that rabbits are quiet animals?

_____

_____

_____

3. The writer says that rabbits have beautiful ears. Is this a fact or an opinion? How do you know?

_____

_____

_____

_____

© Pearson Education, Inc., 2

Home Activity Your child read a persuasive piece of writing and answered questions about it. Have your child write a few sentences about the kind of animal he or she feels is the best pet. The sentences should give facts about why the animal is a good pet.

Name _____

Writing • Narrative Nonfiction

A Bus Ride with Mr. Dee

Mr. Dee is our bus driver. Beep! Beep! Beep! Better move fast! Mr. Dee is waiting, and he can't wait long. He has a schedule to keep.

Mr. Dee says hello and whistles as he drives. He follows the route and picks up all my friends. We're just minutes away from school when we hear a siren blaring and see flashing lights. There is a car stopped sideways in the middle of the road. No one is hurt, but traffic is stopped.

Mr. Dee thinks fast and makes a quick turn. He gets us to school safely and on time.

Key Features of Narrative Nonfiction

• It tells a story about real people or events.

• It usually tells about events in the order they happened.

© Pearson Education, Inc., 2

Name _____

Suffixes *-ly, -ful, -er, -or*

Spelling Words					
cheerful	visitor	slowly	weekly	teacher	helper
hardly	graceful	yearly	quickly	fighter	sailor

Write a list word that means the same as each phrase.

someone who teaches

1. _____

every 365 days

2. _____

someone who helps

3. _____

someone who fights

4. _____

someone who sails

5. _____

full of happiness

6. _____

Write list words that mean the same as the underlined words.

7. We meet <u>every seven days</u>.

_____

8. We have a <u>guest</u>.

_____

9. The turtle moves <u>with little speed</u>.

_____

10. I <u>barely</u> had time to finish.

_____

11. She walks <u>rapidly</u>.

_____

12. The dancer is <u>not awkward</u>.

_____

Home Activity Your child spelled words with the suffixes *-ly, -ful, -er,* and *-or*. Point to a word. Ask your child to identify the suffix and spell the word.

© Pearson Education, Inc., 2

Name _____

Read the sentence and the question.
Fill in the blank to correctly answer the question.

---

1. Sentence: The fire engine moved quickly down the street.

   Question: How did the fire engine move?

   Answer: It moved in a _____ way.

2. Sentence: The firefighters went carefully into the building.

   Question: How did the firefighters go into the building?

   Answer: They went in a _____ way.

3. Sentence: People watched closely as they put out the fire.

   Question: How did the people watch?

   Answer: They watched in a _____ way.

4. Sentence: Everyone happily left when the fire was out.

   Question: How did everyone leave?

   Answer: They left in a _____ way.

School + Home

Home Activity Your child read and identified words with the suffix *-ly*. Have your child circle the word in each sentence with the suffix *-ly* and then define the word.

390 **Vocabulary**

© Pearson Education, Inc., 2

Name _____

Pronouns

A **pronoun** is a word that takes the place of a noun or nouns. The words **he, she, it, we, you,** and **they** are pronouns.

> **Carlos** is a vet. **He** helps animals.
> **He** takes the place of the noun **Carlos.**

> **Keesha** and **Paul** are zookeepers. **They** also help animals.
> **They** takes the place of the nouns **Keesha** and **Paul.**

Write the pronoun that can take the place of the underlined word or words. **Use he, she, it, we,** or **they.**

1. <u>Len Smith</u> has a sick dog.   _____

2. <u>Len and I</u> will take the pet to the vet.   _____

3. <u>People</u> are waiting for the doctor.   _____

4. <u>Gina Jones</u> helps the vet.   _____

5. "Put the dog on <u>the table</u>," said Gina.   _____

6. <u>Carlos Lopez</u> helped the dog.   _____

Say sentences using the pronouns you wrote.

© Pearson Education, Inc., 2

School + Home **Home Activity** Your child learned about pronouns. Together look for names of story characters in books. Ask your child to replace each name with the pronoun *he, she, it, we,* or *they.*

Name _____

Story Chart

Title _____

```
┌─────────────────────────────────────────┐
│  Community Worker                         │
│                                           │
│                                           │
│                                           │
└─────────────────────────────────────────┘

┌─────────────────────────────────────────┐
│  Beginning                                │
│                                           │
│                                           │
│                                           │
│                                           │
└─────────────────────────────────────────┘
                    ↓
┌─────────────────────────────────────────┐
│  Middle                                   │
│                                           │
│                                           │
│                                           │
│                                           │
└─────────────────────────────────────────┘
                    ↓
┌─────────────────────────────────────────┐
│  End of Story                             │
│                                           │
│                                           │
│                                           │
│                                           │
└─────────────────────────────────────────┘
```

© Pearson Education, Inc., 2

School + Home **Home Activity** Your child is learning to write stories, poems, brief reports, nonfiction paragraphs, letters, and other products this year. Ask what your child is writing this week

Name _____

You will be presenting a dramatization answering the Question of the Week, *Why should we be responsible for doing a good job?* Use the following steps to help you plan your dramatization.

Step 1 What did you learn that interests you most about why we should be responsible for doing a good job? Write the information you would most like to share with the class. Create a group with 3–4 other students who would like to share the same information.

I want the class to know _____.

Step 2- As a group, create a situation to show what you think is most interesting about why we should be responsible for doing a good job. Where does the situation take place? What people, or characters, are involved? What is the problem? What do the characters do?

The setting is _____.

The characters are _____.

The problem is _____.

The characters' actions are _____.

Step 3 Choose a character. Think about what he or she might say in the situation your group created.

My character is _____.

My character says, "_____."

Step 4 Present the situation to the class.

Home Activity Your child learned how to create a dramatization based on research results. Together find and read a newspaper, magazine, or Internet article. Plan and present a dramatization of the events in the article.

© Pearson Education, Inc., 2

Name _____

Suffixes *-ly, -ful, -er, -or*

Spelling Words					
cheerful	visitor	slowly	weekly	teacher	helper
hardly	graceful	yearly	quickly	fighter	sailor

Read about Tracy's job. **Circle** three spelling mistakes. **Write** the words correctly. Then write the last sentence using correct grammar.

Frequently Misspelled Words
beautiful
through

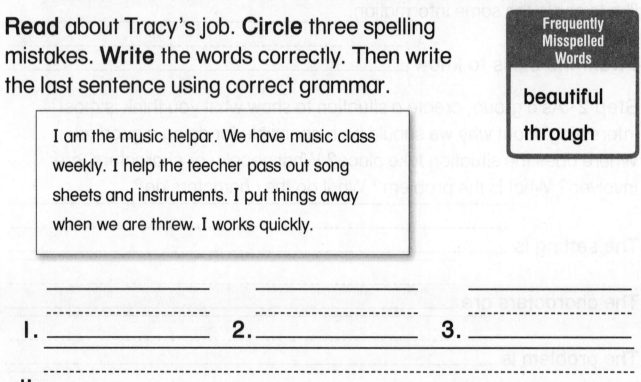

I am the music helpar. We have music class weekly. I help the teecher pass out song sheets and instruments. I put things away when we are threw. I works quickly.

1. _____ 2. _____ 3. _____

4. _____

Circle the word that is spelled correctly.

5. I can get ready _____. quickly quickle

6. Who was your _____? visiter visitor

7. The _____ cleaned the deck. sailor sailer

8. It _____ ever snows there. hardly hardlie

9. We saw a _____ plane. fightor fighter

10. This is a _____ room. cheerfull cheerful

© Pearson Education, Inc., 2

Home Activity Ask your child to name the three words they find the most difficult. Have your child divide each word and spell the base word and the suffix separately.

Name _____

Read the story. **Follow** the directions.

Camel Safari

Jaisalmer, India is a magical place. Jaisalmer is an old city in the Thar Desert. It has many beautiful houses, called havelis, made of sandstone. Many years ago, I went on a camel safari near Jaisalmer. We rode camels into the desert. During the day the sun was hot, but when we camped at night it was cold. We cooked dinner over a campfire. We slept wrapped in blankets under the stars. Riding a camel wasn't very comfortable, but the desert was amazing. It was best in the late afternoon. Then the setting sun turned the sky pink and the sand gold. Anyone who went on a camel safari there would agree that it was unforgettable!

1. What are two facts from the story?

_____
- -
_____
_____
- -
_____

2. What are two opinions from the story?

_____
- -
_____
_____
- -
_____

© Pearson Education, Inc., 2

Home Activity Your child read a memoir and identified some facts and opinions in it. Have your child write his or her own paragraph about an unforgettable experience. Help them include some facts and some opinions.

Comprehension Fact and Opinion   **395**

Name _____

Pronouns

Mark the letter of the pronoun that can take the place of the underlined word or words.

1. What do <u>Carla and Denny</u> want to be?
    - ○ **A** he
    - ○ **B** she
    - ○ **C** they

2. <u>Carla</u> wants to be a teacher.
    - ○ **A** He
    - ○ **B** She
    - ○ **C** You

3. <u>Denny</u> wants to be a pilot.
    - ○ **A** He
    - ○ **B** She
    - ○ **C** We

4. <u>The job</u> would be fun and exciting.
    - ○ **A** You
    - ○ **B** It
    - ○ **C** They

5. <u>Juan and I</u> want to write books.
    - ○ **A** You
    - ○ **B** She
    - ○ **C** We

6. <u>Paul, Beth, and Ryan</u> are not sure.
    - ○ **A** They
    - ○ **B** You
    - ○ **C** He

Say a sentence with a pronoun.

Home Activity Your child prepared for taking tests on pronouns. Ask your child to write sentences about one or more people and then to replace their names with the pronouns *he, she, it, we, you,* or *they.*

© Pearson Education, Inc., 2

Name _____

un + happy = <u>un</u>happy over + time = <u>over</u>time re + paint = <u>re</u>paint

pre + game = <u>pre</u>game   dis + appear = <u>dis</u>appear

> disagree disloyal overripe overweight prepay
> preteen replay reread unsafe unlocked

Write words with **un-, re-, pre-, over-,** or **dis-** to match each clue.
Use the words in the box if you need help.

1. play again

2. not agree

3. opposite of thin

4. pay in advance

5. not locked

6. not loyal

7. not yet a teen

8. too ripe

9. not safe

10. read again

© Pearson Education, Inc., 2

Home Activity Your child wrote words with the prefixes *un-, re-, pre-, over-,* and *dis-*. With your child, look for words like these in ads and signs. Help your child pronounce the words and figure out what they mean. Encourage your child to use the meaning of the prefix to help define the word.

Name _____

Pick a word from the box to finish each sentence.
Write the word on the line.

> complain   P.M.   mumbles
> signature   shrugs   annoy

1. Jay sees a girl drop an empty chip bag on the sidewalk. "People

   _____

   -

   who litter really _____ me," says Jay.

   _____

   -

2. Jay stops the girl to _____ to her.

   _____

   -

3. She _____ that she could not find a

   trash can.

   _____

   -

4. She then _____ her shoulders and

   walks away.

5. Jay writes a letter to the city council to ask for more trash cans.

   _____

   -

   He puts his _____ at the bottom of

   the letter.

6. He drops the letter in the mailbox in time for the

   _____

   -

   3 _____ mail pickup.

© Pearson Education, Inc., 2

School + Home   **Home Activity** Work together with your child to write a story using the vocabulary words in this list. Ask your child the meaning of the words before you start working on the story.

398 Vocabulary

Name _____

Read the story. **Write** the answer to each question.

Camping in the Rain

   Last week, my family and I went on a camping trip. Although we arrived at the campground in the afternoon, the sky was getting dark. We thought it was going to rain very soon. So we decided to set up our tent right away. It was hard to do. The tent cover kept flapping because a strong wind was blowing. But we got it set up and crawled inside just before big raindrops started to fall. I was glad to be out of the rain, but I was shivering. I was cold because I had left my jacket in the car. Mom told me to get into my sleeping bag. Then I was very warm and cozy.

1. Where do the story characters go that people could go to in real life?

_____

- -

_____

2. What causes the tent cover to flap open?

- -

_____

3. Why is one character cold?

_____

- -

_____

Home Activity Your child read a story that is realistic fiction. Reread the story together. Then encourage your child to identify other cause and effect relationships in the story.

© Pearson Education, Inc., 2

Writing • Realistic Story

A Green Thumb

Genay has a green thumb. She really likes to grow things. She is good at it, but she lives in a building that does not have a garden.

"Come with me," Mom said one morning. "I have a surprise for you."

Mom led Genay to Riveredge Park. First, they went down a set of stairs. Then they entered a space with a sign that read "Riveredge Community Garden." In one corner, Genay saw her neighbor Mr. Diaz planting seeds. Mom pointed to another corner.

"This is our spot," Mom said. "Let's make it beautiful."

Genay smiled as she began pulling out weeds.

Key Features of a Realistic Story

· The characters and the setting seem real.

· The characters do things that could really happen.

· The story tells events one after another.

© Pearson Education, Inc., 2

Name _____

Prefixes *un-*, *re-*, *pre-*, *dis-*

Write the list word.

Spelling Words	
unsafe	rewind
preheat	unpack
rerun	unplug
disappear	regroup
unlock	preschool
discolor	disagree

not safe

1. _____

wind again

2. _____

opposite of **pack**

3. _____

group in a new way

4. _____

Read the sentence. Make a list word by adding a prefix to the underlined word.

5. Did you <u>plug</u> the lamp?

6. I <u>agree</u> with that idea.

7. Let's <u>run</u> those home movies.

8. Eddie started <u>school</u> this year.

9. Be sure to <u>lock</u> the door.

10. My cat seems to <u>appear</u> at night.

11. Did the washer <u>color</u> the shirt?

12. Did you <u>heat</u> the oven?

Home Activity Your child spelled words with the prefixes *un-*, *re-*, *pre-*, and *dis-*. Have your child explain how the new word changes the meaning of the sentences in Exercises 5 to 12 above.

© Pearson Education, Inc., 2

Name _____

Look at the dictionary page.
Write the meaning for each underlined word.

---

bowl [bōl] *n.* a round container, *v.* to roll a ball

burn [birn] *n.* an injury caused by heat; anger; *v.* to be on fire

pack [pak] *n.* a crowd, a bundle; *v.* to fill a container with things

pin [pin] *n.* a thin metal stick, a badge, *v.* to attach something, to stop someone from moving

plan [plan] *n.* a layout or outline; *v.* to arrange, to make a drawing

shop [shop] *n.* a store; *v.* to visit a store, to try to see something.

---

1. Which <u>shop</u> do you like to go to best?

_____

_____

2. We will <u>plan</u> our vacation for next month.

_____

_____

3. My friends and I <u>bowl</u> every Saturday.

_____

_____

© Pearson Education, Inc., 2

School + Home **Home Activity** Your child learned to use a dictionary. Look at a dictionary together. Choose a word and discuss its meaning. Then have your child use the word in a sentence.

Singular and Plural Pronouns

He, she, and **it** are pronouns that name only one.
We and **they** are pronouns that name more than one.

Carl likes to play. **He** goes to the park.

He is a pronoun that names one person—Carl.

Carl and Dale are friends. **They** will go to the park.

They is a pronoun that names more than one—Carl and Dale.

Circle the pronouns that name only one. **Underline** the pronouns that name more than one. **Write** the pronouns in the chart.

Carl and Dale were unhappy. They wanted to play at the park, but it was closed. The park closed before sundown. "We should try to have the park stay open later," Dale said. He learned about petitions on the Internet. Carl and Dale started a petition. They asked neighbors to sign it. The city council read the petition and passed a new rule. Now the park stays open later.

Pronouns That Name Only One	Pronouns That Name More than One

© Pearson Education, Inc., 2

School + Home **Home Activity** Your child learned about pronouns for one and more than one. Ask your child to read aloud the story on this page. Have him or her continue the story by telling what happened next. Remind your child to use *he, she, it, we,* and *they.*

Name _____

Story Chart

Title _____

Topic

Beginning

↓

Middle

↓

End of Story

© Pearson Education, Inc., 2

Home Activity Your child is learning to write stories, poems, brief reports, nonfiction paragraphs, letters, and other products this year. Ask what your child is writing this week.

Name _____

You will be presenting a dramatization answering the Question of the Week, *How can we be responsible community members?* Use the following steps to help you plan your dramatization.

Step 1- What did you learn that interests you most about being a responsible community member? Write the information you would most like to share with the class. Create a group with 3–4 other students who would like to share the same information. _____

I want the class to know _____.

Step 2- As a group, create a situation to show what you think is most interesting about being a responsible community member. Where does the situation take place? What people, or characters, are involved? What is the problem? What do the characters do? _____

The setting is _____.

The characters are _____.

The problem is _____.

The characters' actions are _____.

Step 3- Choose a character. Think about what he or she might say in the situation your group created. _____

My character is _____.

My character says, " _____ "

Step 4- Present the situation to the class.

Home Activity Your child learned how to dramatize information. Have your child ask friends and relatives what kinds of things they recycle. Keep a tally of how many people respond. Help your child make a bar graph to show the results. Then have your child dramatize the results.

© Pearson Education, Inc., 2

Name _____

Prefixes *un-, re-, pre-, dis-*

Read Denny's note. **Circle** three spelling mistakes. **Write** the words correctly.
Write the word that needs a capital letter.

> Hey, I found out where your dogs go when they disapear. I saw them when I was riding my bike. they were playing with the boys at the preskool. I sed I'd find out, and I did!
>
> Denny

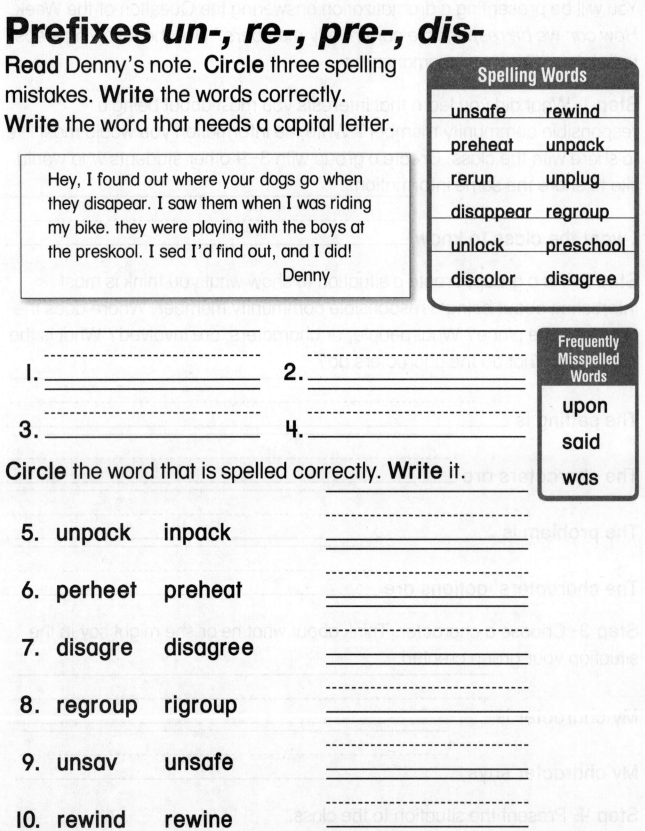

Spelling Words

unsafe	rewind
preheat	unpack
rerun	unplug
disappear	regroup
unlock	preschool
discolor	disagree

1. _____

2. _____

3. _____

4. _____

Frequently Misspelled Words

upon

said

was

Circle the word that is spelled correctly. **Write** it.

5. unpack   inpack   _____

6. perheet   preheat   _____

7. disagre   disagree   _____

8. regroup   rigroup   _____

9. unsav   unsafe   _____

10. rewind   rewine   _____

Home Activity Your child identified misspelled words with the prefixes *un-, re-, pre-,* and *dis-*. Pronounce a list word. Ask your child to identify the prefix and spell the word.

© Pearson Education, Inc., 2

Name _____

Read the story. **Follow** the directions.

The Statue Contest

Mona and her brother Anil were always fighting. One day, they got into an argument in the car. "You're putting your feet on my side," Mona said.

"No I'm not," said Anil. He stuck his tongue out at her.

Mona was mad. "Mom, Anil stuck his tongue out at me!" she cried.

Mom didn't look back. She was driving. "Why don't you have a statue contest?" she suggested. "The first person to move or talk loses."

Mona didn't like to lose. Neither did Anil. They were still and quiet the rest of the ride home.

"It's a tie!" Mom declared as she pulled into the driveway.

Fill in the blanks. _____

1. The characters in this story are _____,
_____ _____
_____, and _____.

2. Where does the story take place?

_____
_____

3. Why is Mona upset in the beginning?

_____
_____

School + Home

Home Activity Your child read a story that is realistic fiction. Reread the story together. Discuss the causes and effects of the events in the story.

© Pearson Education, Inc., 2

Name _____

Singular and Plural Pronouns

Mark the letter of the pronoun that can take the place of the underlined word or words.

1. <u>Dale</u> always looks on the bright side.
   - ○ **A** He
   - ○ **B** They
   - ○ **C** We

2. <u>Mother</u> was the first person to sign the paper.
   - ○ **A** They
   - ○ **B** We
   - ○ **C** She

3. After learning about petitions, <u>Dale and I</u> wrote one.
   - ○ **A** he
   - ○ **B** we
   - ○ **C** she

4. The sign said <u>the park</u> closed at 5 P.M.
   - ○ **A** it
   - ○ **B** they
   - ○ **C** we

5. <u>Those people</u> would not sign the petition.
   - ○ **A** It
   - ○ **B** She
   - ○ **C** They

6. <u>The petition</u> had 108 names for the meeting.
   - ○ **A** We
   - ○ **B** It
   - ○ **C** They

Say a sentence with a pronoun.

Home Activity Your child prepared for taking tests on pronouns for one and more than one. Ask your child to make up sentences about what family members like to do. Then change the names to the pronouns *he, she, we,* or *they.*

408 **Conventions** Singular and Plural Pronouns

© Pearson Education, Inc., 2

Name _____

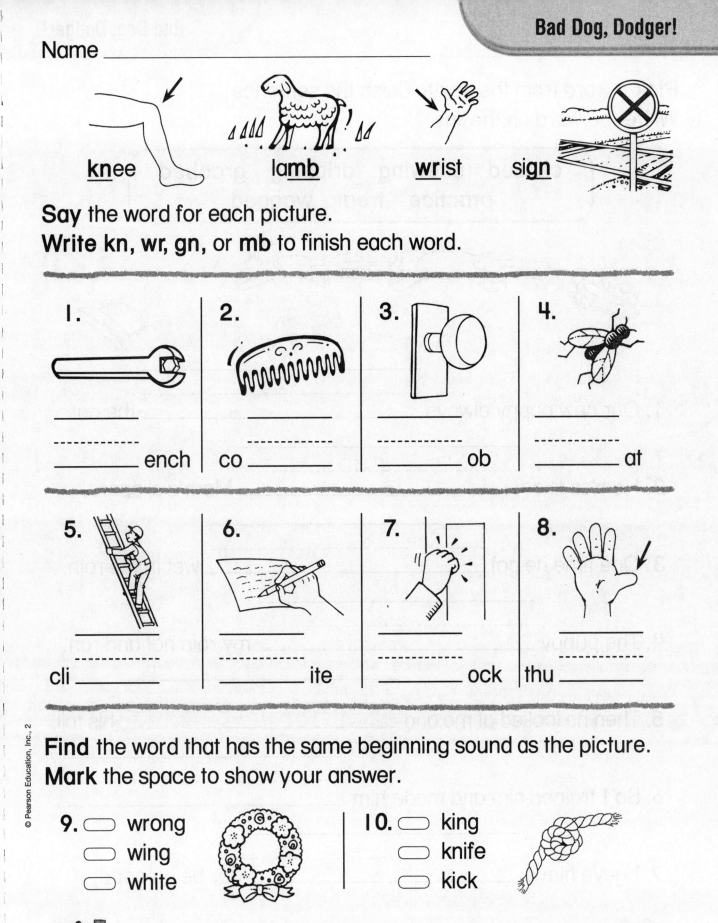

knee   lamb   wrist   sign

Say the word for each picture.
Write kn, wr, gn, or **mb** to finish each word.

1. _____ ench

2. co _____

3. _____ ob

4. _____ at

5. cli _____

6. _____ ite

7. _____ ock

8. thu _____

Find the word that has the same beginning sound as the picture.
Mark the space to show your answer.

9. ◯ wrong
   ◯ wing
   ◯ white

10. ◯ king
    ◯ knife
    ◯ kick

© Pearson Education, Inc., 2

School + Home **Home Activity** Your child completed words where two letters together stand for only one sound, as in *knee, wrist, sign,* and *lamb*. Work with your child to write sentences using the *kn, wr, gn,* and *mb* words on this page. Have your child read and illustrate each sentence.

Name _____

Pick a word from the box to finish the sentence.
Write the word on the line.

> chased   chewing   dripping   grabbed
> practice   treat   wagged

_____

1. Our new puppy always _____ the cat.

2. He also likes _____ Mom's slippers.

3. One time he got _____ wet in the rain.

4. The puppy _____ my rain hat and ran.

5. Then he looked at me and _____ his tail.

6. So I trained him and made him _____ .

7. I gave him a _____ for being good.

© Pearson Education, Inc., 2

School + Home **Home Activity** Your child used lesson vocabulary to complete sentences. Work with your child to use these vocabulary words in a poem or song about a playful puppy and to perform it for other family members or friends.

Name _____

Read the story.
Follow the directions.

Bill had a new puppy. Carmen was going to see it. Then her mom got sick and Carmen had to take care of her little brother. Carmen knew she needed to help out. She asked Bill to bring the puppy to her house. Carmen's mom took a nap. Everybody else had fun in the yard.

1. **Underline** the sentence that tells about Carmen's problem.

2. **Draw two lines** under the sentence that tells what Carmen did about her problem.

3. **Circle** the sentence below that tells how Bill helped Carmen.
   Bill got a new puppy.
   Bill asked Carmen to come to his house.
   Bill took the puppy to Carmen's house.

4. **Circle** the sentence below that tells the big idea of this story.
   Sometimes people get sick.
   Everyone likes puppies.
   Family members help each other.

5. **Circle** the parts of the story that helped you tell the big idea.

© Pearson Education, Inc., 2

Home Activity Your child identified the problem, solution, and big idea in a story. Work with your child to come up with an idea you both think is important, such as: *It's important to try.* Help your child write about something that has happened in his or her life that conveys that idea.

Writing • Journal Entry

 Monday, May 14

Mom forgot to set the alarm this morning. The whole family would have overslept, but Pepper came to the rescue! Pepper doesn't need a clock to know that it's time to get up. There she was at 6:30 A.M. patting my face with her paw. Once she saw that I was awake, she stretched, jumped off the bed, and meowed at me. Time for breakfast! I jumped out of bed to feed Pepper and to wake the rest of the family. It's a good thing that Pepper has me trained!

Key Features of a Journal Entry

• It tells about a personal event or idea.

• It tells what the writer thinks or feels.

• It may include the date.

© Pearson Education, Inc., 2

Name _____

Consonant Patterns *kn, wr, gn, mb*

Write list words to name the pictures.

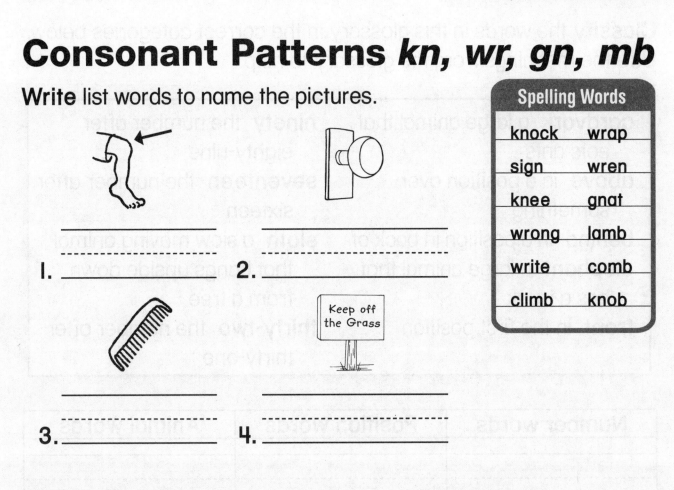

Spelling Words	
knock	wrap
sign	wren
knee	gnat
wrong	lamb
write	comb
climb	knob

1. _____

2. _____

3. _____

4. _____

Write the list word that means almost the same as each word or phrase.

5. tap _____

6. young sheep _____

7. print _____

8. little fly _____

9. incorrect _____

10. go up _____

11. small bird _____

12. cover with paper _____

Home Activity Your child spelled words with *kn, wr, gn,* and *mb*. Have your child point out examples of these letter combinations.

© Pearson Education, Inc., 2

Name _____

Classify the words in this glossary in the correct categories below.
Use the meanings from the glossary to help.

---

aardvark a large animal that eats ants

above in a position over something

behind in a position in back of

elephant a large animal that has a trunk

front in the first position

ninety the number after eighty-nine

seventeen the number after sixteen

sloth a slow moving animal that hangs upside down from a tree

thirty-two the number after thirty-one

Number words	Position words	Animal words

© Pearson Education, Inc., 2

Home Activity Your child learned to use a glossary to help classify words. Have your child add one more word to each category on the page. Ask your child what a glossary contains and why it might be helpful.

Using *I* and *Me*

The pronouns **I** and **me** take the place of your name. Use **I** in the subject of a sentence. Use **me** after an action verb. Always write **I** with a capital letter.

> **I** have a great dog. The dog follows **me**.

When you talk about yourself and another person, name yourself last. The pronouns **I** and **me** take the place of your name.

> My friends and **I** play after school.
> They see the dog and **me** do tricks.

Write *I* or *me* to complete each sentence.

_____

1. _____ have a smart dog.

2. Smarty and _____ play catch.

3. Smarty brings _____ the ball.

4. Then Smarty gives _____ his paw.

5. Smarty and _____ shake hands.

Home Activity Your child learned about using *I* and *me*. Take turns telling about animals you have seen do tricks. Use *I* and *me* as you tell your stories.

© Pearson Education, Inc., 2

Name _____

Story Chart

Title _____

Topic

Beginning

⬇

Middle

1.

2.

3.

⬇

End of Story

Home Activity Your child is learning to write stories, poems, brief reports, nonfiction paragraphs, letters, and other products this year. Ask what your child is writing this week.

© Pearson Education, Inc., 2

Name _____

Today, you reviewed the concept web that explored the Question of the Week, *How can we be responsible animal owners?* Use the following steps to help you add your interests to the list that the class started and create questions that you have about being a responsible animal owner.

Step 1- Ask yourself the following questions:

• What experiences have I had with animals? How did I act responsibly toward them?

• What stories have I read or movies have I seen about animals? How did the characters, or people in the stories, act responsibly toward them?

Step 2- Discuss these questions and your answers with a partner. What new ideas does your partner's responses lead to?

Step 3- Write down your new ideas and interests about the class topic.

_____   _____

- - - - - - - - - - - - - - - - - -   - - - - - - - - - - - - - - - - - -

_____   _____

- - - - - - - - - - - - - - - - - -   - - - - - - - - - - - - - - - - - -

Step 4- What do you want to know about being a responsible animal owner? Write four questions you have about being a responsible animal owner.

_____   _____

- - - - - - - - - - - - - - - - - -   - - - - - - - - - - - - - - - - - -

_____   _____

- - - - - - - - - - - - - - - - - -   - - - - - - - - - - - - - - - - - -

© Pearson Education, Inc., 2

School + Home **Home Activity** Your child learned how to generate a list of interests and create questions about topics that interest them. Discuss your experiences with animals and have your child add new ideas and questions to the lists.

Name _____

Consonant Patterns *kn, wr, gn, mb*

Read Jessie's report. **Circle** three spelling mistakes. **Write** the words correctly. **Cross out** the wrong verb in the second sentence. **Write** the correct verb.

Spelling Words	
knock	wrap
sign	wren
knee	gnat
wrong	lamb
write	comb
climb	knob

> I saw some people clim up a rock wall.
> One person done something rong. He hurt
> his knee. I woud like to try rock climbing.

Frequently Misspelled Words
Christmas
knew
would
what

1. _____

2. _____

3. _____

4. _____

Fill in the circle next to the word that is spelled correctly.

5. ○ knok   ○ knock   ○ nock   ○ knoke

6. ○ wrin   ○ ren   ○ wren   ○ rwen

7. ○ sign   ○ sine   ○ signe   ○ sien

8. ○ com   ○ komb   ○ kome   ○ comb

9. ○ lam   ○ lamm   ○ lamb   ○ labm

10. ○ writ   ○ write   ○ rite   ○ wriet

Home Activity Your child identified misspelled words with *kn, wr, gn,* and *mb*. Pronounce a list word. Ask your child to spell the word and name the "silent letter." (*k, w, g,* or *b*)

© Pearson Education, Inc., 2

Name _____

Read the story. **Follow** the directions.

Maria had a new puppy named Sunny. Sunny chewed Maria's doll. He ate her homework. Maria worked with Sunny. Sunny got better, but he still got into things. Then Maria trained herself. She picked up her toys and papers. Now Sunny no longer eats Maria's things.

1. **Circle** the sentence below that tells the big idea of this story.

   Puppies like to chew things.

   People and puppies may both need training.

   Puppies are a lot of work.

2. **Underline three sentences** in the story that show how Maria finally got the puppy to stop eating her things.

Write 1, 2, or **3** on the lines to show the right order.

_____

_____ **3.** Sunny chewed Maria's doll.

_____ **4.** Maria had a new puppy named Sunny.

_____ **5.** Now Sunny no longer eats Maria's things.

Write a sentence that tells something that happened in the middle of the story.

_____

6. _____

Home Activity Your child identified the big idea of a story and put story events in correct order. Read a story aloud to your child. Have your child tell what happened in the *beginning, middle,* and *end* of the story. Ask your child what he or she learned from the story.

Name _____

Using *I* and *Me*

Mark the letter of the word or words that complete the sentence.

1. ____ have a fish named Goldie.
   - ○ **A** I
   - ○ **B** Me
   - ○ **C** Mom and me

2. Goldie and ____ watch each other.
   - ○ **A** me
   - ○ **B** I
   - ○ **C** Mom and me

3. One day Goldie surprised ____ .
   - ○ **A** I
   - ○ **B** me
   - ○ **C** Mom and I

4. ____ saw her leap out of her bowl.
   - ○ **A** Me and Mom
   - ○ **B** Me
   - ○ **C** I

5. ____ put Goldie back in the bowl.
   - ○ **A** Mom and me
   - ○ **B** Mom and I

6. Goldie scared ____ .
   - ○ **A** me
   - ○ **B** I
   - ○ **C** I and Mom

School + Home

Home Activity Your child prepared for taking tests on using *I* and *me*. Ask your child to read the sentences on this page and to say the word or words that belong in the blank as he or she reads.

© Pearson Education, Inc., 2

Name _____

phone   cough   clock   ring

| backpack elephant laughter trophy |
| ticket hanger graph photo dolphin |

Pick a word from the box to match each clue.
Write the word on the line.

1. _____

2. _____

3. _____

4. _____

5. _____

6. _____

Pick a word from the box above to finish each sentence about the picture. **Write** the word on the line.

7. Roy wears a _____ .

8. Sue is taking a _____ of Roy.

Home Activity Your child wrote words with the consonant sound /ng/ spelled *ng* as in *ring*, /k/ spelled *ck* as in *clock*, /f/ spelled *ph* as in *phone*, and *gh* as in *cough*. Help your child look in a favorite book for words with these sounds. Write the words on a sheet of paper. Then read the list with your child.

© Pearson Education, Inc., 2

Phonics Consonant Patterns *ph, gh, ck, ng*   **421**

Name _____

Pick a word from the box to finish the sentence.
Write the word on the line.

adventure	climbed	clubhouse	exploring
greatest	truest	wondered	

1. Today we met at our _____ .

2. Only our _____ friends came.

3. We _____ what to do.

4. Then Max had the _____ plan.

5. We would go on an _____ !

6. We had fun _____ .

7. We _____ into bed and fell asleep.

© Pearson Education, Inc., 2

School + Home **Home Activity** Your child used lesson vocabulary words to complete sentences. Ask your child to describe an adventure he or she would like to take and write an adventure story together. Try to use as many of the vocabulary words as possible.

Name _____

Read the story. **Write** the answer to each question.

Where's Shadow?

One morning, Ricky went to Lenny's house. They were going to play the game checkers, but Lenny didn't feel like playing. His cat, Shadow, was missing. When Ricky heard this news, he almost started to cry. He told Lenny they should make "Lost Cat" signs and put them in places around the neighborhood. The boys found sheets of paper and crayons. Together they made several signs. Ricky wrote the words, and Lenny drew a picture of Shadow on each sign. After they put up the signs, Ricky stayed at his friend's house for a little while. While he was there, a woman called. She had found a black cat in her yard, and the name Shadow was on his tag!

I. What is the setting of the story?

_____

- -

_____

2. How did Ricky feel when he heard Shadow was missing?

_____

- -

_____

3. Why did Ricky stay at Lenny's house and make signs?

_____

- -

_____

- -

_____

Home Activity Your child described a character and setting of a story. Help your child write a short story about a kind person he or she knows. Have your child describe what the person did that was kind. Make sure your child tells the setting of the story.

© Pearson Education, Inc., 2

Name _____

Writing • Animal Fantasy

 Eating Out

Shimmy and Caleb are bears. They live in Big Berry National Park. One spring day, Shimmy said to Caleb, "Berries are boring. Let's eat out."

The two friends took a bus into the city. There they went into the most expensive restaurant. The waiter handed them a menu.

"Where are the acorns?" Shimmy asked.

"There's no honey," Caleb complained.

"Let's go home," Shimmy said.

The two friends took a bus back to the park. There they dined on berries topped with acorns and honey.

Key Features of an Animal Fantasy

• The characters are make-believe animals.

• The characters do things that real animals cannot do.

© Pearson Education, Inc., 2

Consonant Patterns *ph, gh, ck, ng*

Write a list word to answer the riddles.

Spelling Words
phone
enough
backtrack
laugh
ticket
duckling
graph
tough
photo
rough
cough
clang

What rhymes with **bone** and starts with **ph?**

1. _____

What rhymes with **rang** and starts with **cl?**

2. _____

What rhymes with **staph** and starts with **gr?**

3. _____

What rhymes with **stuff** and starts with **r?**

4. _____

Write the list word that best fits each sentence.

5. I have had _____ to eat.

6. I bought a _____ to ride the train.

7. The joke made me _____ .

8. I have a fever and a _____ .

9. John took a _____ of all of us together.

10. We make charts and _____ in math.

© Pearson Education, Inc., 2

School + Home

Home Activity Your child is learning words with the consonant patterns *ph*, *gh*, *ck*, and *ng*. Take turns with your child pointing to and spelling the word list.

Name _____

Choose a word from Column A and a word from Column B to make a compound word for each meaning below.
Write the compound word next to the meaning.

COLUMN A	COLUMN B
home	work
table	cloth
school	yard
tree	top
bird	house
snow	ball

1. a yard that belongs to a school _____

2. work that you do at home _____

3. a cloth that you put over a table _____

4. the top part of a tree _____

5. a house where a bird lives _____

6. a ball made of snow _____

Home Activity Your child learned about compound words. Have your child make compound words with the following small words and tell what each new word means: *plane, week, day, air, end.*

426 **Vocabulary**

© Pearson Education, Inc., 2

Different Kinds of Pronouns

The pronouns **I, he, she, we,** and **they** are used as subjects of sentences. The pronouns **me, him, her, us,** and **them** are used after action verbs. The pronouns **you** and **it** can be used anywhere in a sentence.

Morris has cheese. **He** shares **it.**
The pronoun **he** is the subject of the sentence.
The pronoun **it** is used after the action verb *shares.*

Morris met Doris. Morris showed **her** the cheese.
The pronoun **her** is used after the action verb *showed.*

___

Underline the pronoun in ( ) that can take the place of the underlined word or words.

1. "Where did you get cheese?" <u>Doris</u> asked. (she, they)

2. "I bought <u>the cheese</u>," Morris said. (them, it)

3. Morris also gave <u>Horace and Boris</u> cheese. (her, them)

4. <u>Horace, Boris, and Doris</u> thanked Morris. (They, Us)

5. "<u>My friends</u> are welcome," said Morris. (He, You)

© Pearson Education, Inc., 2

Home Activity Your child learned about different kinds of pronouns. Ask your child to make up new sentences using the pronouns he or she wrote on this page.

Name _____

Story Chart

Title _____

Characters

Beginning

↓

Middle
I.
2.
3.

↓

End of Story

Home Activity Your child is learning to write stories, poems, brief reports, nonfiction paragraphs, letters, and other products this year. Ask what your child is writing this week.

© Pearson Education, Inc., 2

Name ______________________________

Today, you will decide which sources of information might be relevant to answer your questions about the Question of the Week, *How can we be responsible friends and neighbors?* Use the following steps to help you choose a relevant source to answer your questions.

Step 1- Make sure it is clear what you want to learn about your topic. Write some of your inquiry questions below.

Step 2- Review the many sources of information that you have learned about this year. Write down four sources.

Step 3- Circle the sources that you think will help you answer your inquiry questions. Find these sources and use them to answer your inquiry questions.

Step 4- Are you able to find answers to all of your inquiry questions? If not, work with a partner to think about other sources you might use. Or, think about how a source might be more focused to answer your questions. For example, if you chose a web page, is the subject of the web page focused on friends and neighbors?

© Pearson Education, Inc., 2

School + Home **Home Activity** Your child learned to decide what sources of information might be relevant to answer his or her inquiry questions. Visit a Media Center or Library and discuss the various information sources that are available. Discuss with your child why some sources might be better than others.

Name _____

Consonant Patterns *ph, gh, ck, ng*

Read the poem. **Circle** three spelling mistakes.
Write the words correctly. Find a line with a
missing end mark. Add the end mark.

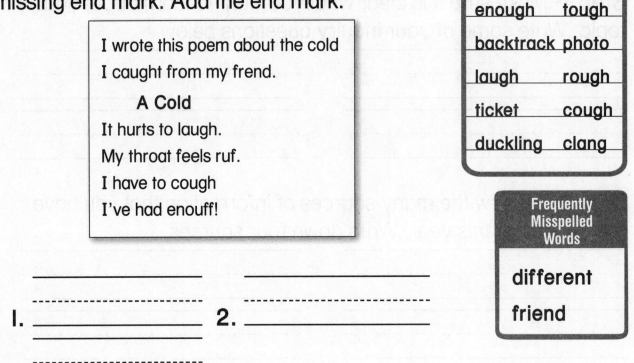

I wrote this poem about the cold
I caught from my frend.

A Cold
It hurts to laugh.
My throat feels ruf.
I have to cough
I've had enouff!

Spelling Words

phone	graph
enough	tough
backtrack	photo
laugh	rough
ticket	cough
duckling	clang

Frequently Misspelled Words

different

friend

_____ _____

1. _____ 2. _____

3. _____

Circle the word that is spelled correctly.

4. The _____ is ringing.	fone	phone
5. The _____ quacks loudly.	dukling	duckling
6. The pots made a _____.	claing	clang
7. I took a good _____.	photo	foto
8. The _____ showed the data.	graph	graff
9. We had to _____.	baktrak	backtrack
10. I have a _____ for the movie.	ticket	tiket

Home Activity Your child is learning words with the consonant patterns *ph, gh, ck,* and *ng*. Ask your child to find examples of these letter combinations in a book.

© Pearson Education, Inc., 2

Name _____

Read the story. **Follow** the directions.

Field Trip

Sara was excited. Her class was going on a field trip to the museum. She couldn't wait to see all the paintings. She wanted to be a painter too.

Ms. Jabs, their teacher, had them each pick a partner. Sarah picked Ines. Ines was the quiet, new girl. Sara hoped they could be friends.

The two girls sat next to each other on the way to the museum. When they got inside, they looked around the big entrance hall. "Wow, look at how high that ceiling is," Sarah said.

"Yes," said Ines, "and look at that painting. It's so tall. How do you think the artist painted the top?"

Ms. Jabs overheard Ines. "The artist stood on a ladder to paint that," she said.

"Cool!" Sara cried. "I want to stand on a ladder and paint someday."

Ines looked at Sara and smiled. "Me too," she said softly.

I. Why is Sara excited?

_____

- -

_____

2. Which word below best describes Ines?

_____

- - - - - - - - - - - - - - -

shy   mean   _____

School + Home **Home Activity** Your child described the characters and setting of a story. Help your child write a very short story. Make sure your child includes details about the characters and setting.

Name _____

Different Kinds of Pronouns

Mark the letter of the pronoun that can be used in place of the underlined word or words.

1. <u>Ana</u> started a craft club.
   - ○ **A** She
   - ○ **B** Her
   - ○ **C** We

2. Erin and Maria joined <u>the club</u>.
   - ○ **A** they
   - ○ **B** you
   - ○ **C** it

3. Maria wanted <u>Kevin</u> in the club.
   - ○ **A** them
   - ○ **B** him
   - ○ **C** he

4. <u>Kevin</u> liked crafts.
   - ○ **A** She
   - ○ **B** Him
   - ○ **C** He

5. "Kevin can teach <u>Ana, Erin, and me</u> paper folding," said Maria.
   - ○ **A** us
   - ○ **B** we
   - ○ **C** they

6. Kevin joined <u>Ana, Erin, and Maria</u>.
   - ○ **A** we
   - ○ **B** them
   - ○ **C** they

Say a sentence with a pronoun.

Home Activity Your child prepared for taking tests on different kinds of pronouns. Ask your child to choose three pronouns from this page and to use them in sentences that tell about things that are fun to make or do.

© Pearson Education, Inc., 2

Name _____

saw   **au**to   c**augh**t   ch**al**k

Write a word from the box to match each picture.

| daughter   draw   fall   naughty   raw   sauce   thaw   walk |

1. _____

2. _____

3. _____

4. _____

Write a word from the box that is the opposite of each word below.

freeze

rise

5. _____

6. _____

good

cooked

7. _____

8. _____

Mark the space for the word that has the vowel sound in **saw**.

9. ◯ fault
   ◯ find
   ◯ few

10. ◯ tray
    ◯ took
    ◯ taught

© Pearson Education, Inc., 2

School + Home **Home Activity** Your child wrote words with the vowel sound in *fall*, spelled *aw* as in *saw*, *au* as in *auto*, *augh* as in *caught*, and *al* as in *chalk*. Hold a spelling bee with your child. Say a word. Have your child repeat the word and then spell it aloud or write it.

Phonics Vowel Patterns *aw, au, augh, al*   **433**

Name _____

Pick a word from the box to finish the sentence.
Write the word on the line.

> afternoon   blame   idea   important
> signmaker   townspeople

1. An _____
   visitor was coming to town.

2. All the _____ met together.

3. They came up with an _____ .

4. They told the _____ what to write.

5. That _____ he held up his sign.

6. No one could _____ him for it.

Home Activity Your child used lesson vocabulary to complete sentences. Ask your child to read each sentence to you. Challenge him or her to explain the meaning of the vocabulary words and use each word in a new sentence.

© Pearson Education, Inc., 2

Name _____

Read the story.
Follow the directions.

Annie was going to wear a costume in a parade. She would look like a bunch of grapes. Annie's mom wrapped a strong brown ribbon around Annie's shirt. Next she attached eight purple balloons to the ribbon. These were the grapes. Soon Annie and her mom were off to the parade. When Annie got out of the car, one of the balloons popped! Then on her way to the float, a little dog jumped up and bit two balloons. Two more pops! After that, a boy bumped into Annie. Three pops! Finally Annie climbed onto the float and sat down. Pop! Pop! That was the last of the balloons. All that was left of Annie's costume was the brown ribbon. "You have a new costume," her mom laughed. "Now you're a grape vine!" Annie laughed too. Sometimes laughing is the best thing to do when things go wrong.

I. Circle the answer below that tells what the story is about.

Annie's costume   a parade's float   purple balloons

2. Write a sentence from the story that tells the main idea.

_____

- -

_____

_____

- -

_____

© Pearson Education, Inc., 2

Home Activity Your child identified the main idea of a story. Tell your child a story about something funny that once happened to you. Ask your child to tell you the main idea of your story. Together, brainstorm a good title.

Comprehension Main Idea   **435**

Name _____

Writing • Humorous Story

 An Amazing Morning

Writing Prompt: Write a humorous story about a character who has a good imagination.

Roberto got up late. He missed the bus and had to walk to school in the pouring rain.

What a walk! It was raining cats and dogs! Roberto just missed stepping on a poodle. A chihuahua nearly landed on top of his head! He saw his neighbor wrestling with an enormous tabby cat that was clinging to her umbrella.

When Roberto got to school, he had to wring out his jacket. His teacher, Miss Pierce, asked, "Roberto, why are you so late and how ever did you get so wet?"

Roberto grinned. "You'll never guess what happened on the way to school this morning," he said.

 Home Activity Your child is learning to write in response to a test prompt. Ask your child to tell you why this is a good example of a humorous story.

© Pearson Education, Inc., 2

Name _____

Vowel Patterns *aw, au, augh, al*

Spelling Words					
talk	because	August	caught	draw	walk
chalk	auto	taught	thaw	fault	launch

Read the word. **Write** a related list word.

1. blackboard: _____

2. mouth: _____

3. teach: _____

4. road: _____

5. month: _____

6. artist: _____

7. path: _____

8. warm: _____

Write the missing list words.

9. Let's _____ the boat!

10. It was his _____ that we missed the bus.

11. I am happy _____ I won the game.

12. She _____ three fish.

Home Activity Your child wrote words with the vowel patterns *aw, au, augh,* and *al*. Ask your child how all the list words are the same. (All have the vowel sound found in *fall;* all have an *a* in combination with other letters.)

© Pearson Education, Inc., 2

Name _____

Read the sentence. **Write** the correct word in the blank.
Write the meaning of the word you chose on the line below.

_____
- -

1. After losing the game the fans felt _____ .

   a. cheerful   b. cheerless

_____
- -
_____

_____
- -

2. Jim did not know how to swim. He was _____ in the water.

   a. helpful   b. helpless

_____
- -
_____

3. The painting has red, blue, yellow, and green.

   _____
   -
   It is so _____ .

   a. colorful   b. colorless

_____
- -
_____

Home Activity Your child learned about words with suffixes. Have your child choose four words he or she did not use for their answers and make up a sentence for each word. Then have him or her tell what the words they chose mean.

438 **Vocabulary**

© Pearson Education, Inc., 2

Contractions

A **contraction** is a short way to put two words together.
An **apostrophe** (') takes the place of one or more letters.
Contractions can be formed by putting together a pronoun and
another word, such as *will, are,* or *is.*

   I will get some flowers. **I'll** get some flowers.

Many contractions are formed with verbs and the word *not.*
   Otto **did not** read the sign. Otto **didn't** read the sign.

Replace the underlined words with a contraction from the box.

> He'll   he's   aren't   shouldn't   I'm

1. "Signs <u>are not</u> important," Otto said. _____

2. Otto said, "<u>I am</u> going to pick flowers." _____

3. People said he <u>should not</u> pick them. _____

4. Now <u>he is</u> just looking at the flowers. _____

© Pearson Education, Inc., 2

Home Activity Your child learned about contractions. Say sentences using the signtractions on this page and ask your child to identify the contraction and the two words that make up the contraction.

Name _____

Scoring Rubric: Humorous Fiction

	4	3	2	1
Focus/Ideas	The story ideas, characters, or events are very funny.	The story ideas, characters, or events are funny.	The story ideas, characters, or events are somewhat funny.	The story ideas, characters, and events are not funny.
Organization	The story has a strong beginning, middle, and end.	The story has a good beginning, middle, and end.	Some of the story events are out of order.	The events are not in any order.
Voice	The writing is strong, lively, and individual.	The writing is lively with some individuality.	The writing tries to show some personality.	The writing shows no sense of the writer.
Word Choice	The writer used vivid, descriptive words.	The writer used some descriptive words.	The writer used few descriptive words.	The writer's words are dull.
Sentences	Most sentences are different in length and begin differently.	Many sentences are different in length and begin differently.	Some sentences are different in length and begin differently.	Few sentences are different in length or begin differently.
Conventions	All contractions and quotations have correct punctuation.	Most contractions and quotations have correct punctuation.	Some contractions and quotations have correct punctuation.	Few contractions and quotations have correct punctuation.

© Pearson Education, Inc., 2

Home Activity Your child is learning to write a humorous story. Ask your child to describe the kind of astory he or she is writing. Your child's writing will be evaluated based on this four-point scoring rubric.

Name _____

Today, you will review your topic to check that you have found the answers to your original research topic. Use the following steps to help you review your topic and revise it if necessary.

Step 1- Make sure it is clear what you originally set out to learn about your topic. Write your research topic below.

I want to know _____.

Step 2- Review the list of questions you created about this topic and the answers from your research. Ask yourself the following questions:

• Do I have many unanswered questions?

• Did I learn something surprising that affects what I originally wanted to know?

• Based on what I learned, do I have new questions?

Step 3- Did you answer *yes* to any of the questions in Step 2? If so, you might want to consider revising your topic.

Step 4- Use your new questions and the surprising information you learned to revise your topic. You might need to just change a few words or you might need to rewrite the entire topic. Write your new topic and go back to Step 2. Can you answer *no* to all of the questions?

My new topic is _____.

Home Activity Your child learned how to revise a topic if needed. Discuss why it is important to revise a topic as a result of new information.

© Pearson Education, Inc., 2

Name _____

Vowel Patterns *aw, au, augh, al*

Read the letter. **Circle** three spelling mistakes and a word that needs a capital letter. **Write** the words correctly.

Spelling Words

talk	chalk
because	auto
August	taught
caught	thaw
draw	fault
walk	launch

August 5

Dear aunt Helen,
    Thank you for the big box of chauk. I used it to drawer pictures all over the walk. Everyone thot they were beautiful!
                                    Love,
                                    Janie

Frequently Misspelled Words

thought

caught

1. _____   2. _____

3. _____   4. _____

Circle the misspelled list word. **Write** each word correctly.

5. The ice will thau.   _____

6. Who talt you how to swim?   _____

7. I left becus I felt sick.   _____

8. He runs an aughto repair shop.   _____

© Pearson Education, Inc., 2

School + Home   **Home Activity** Your child identified misspelled words with the vowel patterns *aw*, *au*, *augh*, and *al*. Give clues about a spelling word. Ask your child to guess and spell it.

Name _____

Read the story. **Follow** the directions.

One day, Lucas was late for lunch at school. He ran into the cafeteria and right into Jerry. Jerry was the biggest, meanest boy in Lucas's class. Crash! Lucas's lunchbox fell to the ground. His lunch spilled everywhere. Jerry's did the same.

"Watch where you're going!" Jerry said.

"Sorry," Lucas mumbled. He quickly picked up his lunch. Then he went to sit at a table with his friends

"Wow, you ran into Jerry!" his best friend Chad said.

"Yeah," Lucas frowned absently. He was eating the broccoli from his lunch.

"What's the matter?" Chad asked.

Lucas smiled. "I think some of the peanut butter from Jerry's sandwich got on my broccoli. But you know what? It tastes really good!"

Chad laughed. "Something good comes out of everything!" he said.

1. Pick the best title for the story. **Circle** your answer below.

The Bully   Something Good   Run, Run, Run!

2. Write the sentence from the story that tells the main idea.

_____

- -

_____

- -

_____

_____

© Pearson Education, Inc., 2

School + Home **Home Activity** Your child identified the main idea of a story. Tell your child a story about something funny that once happened to you. Ask your child to tell you the main idea of your story. Together, brainstorm a good title.

Contractions

Mark the letter of the contraction that means the same as the underlined words.

1. <u>I am</u> a good helper to my dad.
   - ○ A I'm
   - ○ B I'll
   - ○ C It'll

2. <u>He will</u> ask me for tools.
   - ○ A He's
   - ○ B He'd
   - ○ C He'll

3. <u>They are</u> in a toolbox.
   - ○ A They'd
   - ○ B They're
   - ○ C They'll

4. I <u>could not</u> find a tool.
   - ○ A can'tv
   - ○ B couldn't
   - ○ C wouldn't

5. Dad said, "<u>It is</u> next to the hammer."
   - ○ A It'll
   - ○ B I'll
   - ○ C It's

6. "<u>I have</u> got it," I shouted.
   - ○ A I've
   - ○ B I'm
   - ○ C I'll

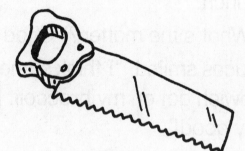

Home Activity Your child prepared for taking tests on contractions. Ask your child to use the contractions *I've* and *I'm* in sentences that tell how he or she helps you.

© Pearson Education, Inc., 2

Name _____

Write a suffix from the box to finish each word. You will need to use each suffix more than one time.

> **ly   er   ful   or   ish**

1. week _____   _____   2. child _____   _____

3. hope _____   _____   4. teach _____   _____

5. act _____   _____   6. self _____   _____

7. complete _____   _____   8. care _____   _____

9. sing _____   _____   10. invent _____   _____

Read the story.

Rex is a friendly puppy, but he is a handful of work. Rex's owner loves this little pup. When Rex wakes up, he quickly runs to his food dish. Rex starts barking loudly. Rex's owner swiftly jumps out of bed. She knows her cheerful puppy really wants food. She rapidly fills his colorful food dish. Rex is joyful with all the food, and he soon finishes it. Sometimes Rex feels sluggish, but his owner is always helpful. That is because Rex's owner is a doctor.

Home Activity Your child wrote words that end with the suffixes -ly, -ful, -er, -or, and -ish and read a story. Have your child write a sentence or short story using these words: *sculptor, graceful, foolish, gardener, suddenly.*

© Pearson Education, Inc., 2

Name _____

Suffixes *-ly, -ful, -er, -or*

Spelling Words					
cheerful	visitor	slowly	weekly	teacher	helper
hardly	graceful	yearly	quickly	fighter	sailor

Draw a line to match the base word to the suffix. **Write** the list word.

1. cheer   -or

2. week   -er

3. sail   -ly

4. fight   -ful

Add a suffix to the underlined word so the sentence makes sense.

5. The <u>visit</u> knocked on our door.

6. I thought the dancer was <u>grace</u>.

7. I will be a <u>help</u> for the school carnival.

8. John could <u>hard</u> wait for his birthday.

9. Who will be our new <u>teach</u>?

10. The rabbit moved very <u>quick</u>.

11. The snail moved very <u>slow</u>.

12. We take our <u>year</u> trip in June.

1. _____

2. _____

3. _____

4. _____

5. _____

6. _____

7. _____

8. _____

9. _____

10. _____

11. _____

12. _____

Home Activity Your child has been learning to spell words with the suffixes *-ly*, *-ful*, *-er*, and *-or*. Make a list of base words and a list of these suffixes. Say a base word and a suffix, and have your child point to each one. Say them together as a whole word.

© Pearson Education, Inc., 2

Name _____

Pick a word from the box to finish each sentence.
Write the word on the line.

> building   burning   masks   quickly
> roar   station   tightly

1. A fire started in a large factory _____.

2. Part of the roof was _____.

3. Firefighters heard the alarm and left the fire _____ _____.

4. The fire truck rushed _____ to the area.

5. The firefighters wore _____ on their faces.

6. They held the water hoses _____ with their hands.

7. They put out the fire fast. You could hear the people cheer and _____.

© Pearson Education, Inc., 2

School + Home **Home Activity** Your child reviewed vocabulary words learned earlier in this unit. Ask your child to write sentences about an event using these vocabulary words. Your child can illustrate his or her sentences.

Name _____

Read the story. Then **follow** the directions.

Palmer's Permanent Bridge

At one time many bridges were built of wood. In 1800 the city of Philadelphia, Pennsylvania, asked Timothy Palmer to build a bridge. The bridge was to cross the Schuylkill (SKOOL kil) River. It was to be 550 feet long.

Palmer was a skillful woodworker from Massachusetts. He had built many bridges before. Bridges are very important structures. He had even invented a way to brace bridges, or make them stronger. So he knew what he was doing. In about five years he had finished the bridge. Many people thought it was a beautiful bridge.

It was called the "Permanent Bridge." *Permanent* means "lasting a long time." Wooden bridges were not permanent. Rain and snow are harmful to wood. They cause it to rot, or break down. Then a bridge needs repair.

One day Palmer had a visitor. Judge Richard Peters lived near the bridge. He was president of the bridge company. "Mr. Palmer," he asked, "how long does a bridge like this usually last?"

"Oh, about ten or fifteen years," answered Palmer.

"What if you built walls?" the judge suggested. "That way, the wood would be protected from the weather."

© Pearson Education, Inc., 2

Home Activity Your child identified facts and opinions in a nonfiction story. Have your child tell other facts he/she learned about Timothy Palmer.

Name _____

Palmer quickly added walls to his bridge. Not only that, he built a roof. It looked like a building with open ends. Then he painted the whole thing. That sealed the wood tightly. He was the creator of the world's first covered bridge. The idea was successful. Hundreds of covered bridges were built after that.

The Permanent Bridge did not last forever. It did last for a long time, though—almost 70 years. It was finally destroyed in 1875. It wasn't weather that destroyed the bridge. It burned in a fire.

Write at least two facts and two opinions you find in this story.

Fact:	Opinion:

© Pearson Education, Inc., 2

Name _____

Pronouns

Write the pronoun that can take the place of the underlined word or words. **Use** *he, she, it, we,* or *they.*

1. <u>Our family</u> talked about a fire drill.   _____

2. <u>Mom</u> showed us where we should get out.   _____

3. <u>Dad</u> said, "Never open a hot door."   _____

Change the underlined word or words to a pronoun. **Write** the sentence. **Use** the pronoun *he, she, it, we,* or *they.*

4. <u>The Jackson family</u> practiced a fire drill.

_____

_____

5. <u>Leroy</u> ran to the meeting place.

_____

_____

6. <u>The fire drill</u> was a success.

_____

_____

© Pearson Education, Inc., 2

Name _____

Day 1 Unit 5 Week 1   **Fire Fighter!**

Copy the phrases. Make sure you form your letters smoothly.

mainly my quilt

_____
- -
_____

quietly getting my quill

_____
- -
_____

Day 2 Unit 5 Week 2   **Carl the Complainer**

Copy the words. Make sure your letters are spaced correctly.

an unhappy big owl

_____
- -
_____

the untied velvet bow

_____
- -
_____

© Pearson Education, Inc., 2

Home Activity Your child practiced writing all of the letters in the alphabet in lowercase and uppercase letters *A C E O H K M N*. Have your child copy and complete the following sentence about a story he or she read in school: *Carl the Complainer was about_____.*

Name _____

Day 3 Unit 5 Week 3   Bad Dog, Dodger!

Copy the phrases. Make sure you form your letters smoothly.

first lamb to zip by

_____
- -
_____

sign for the zoo

_____
- -
_____

Day 4 Unit 5 Week 4   Horace and Morris

Copy the sentences. Make sure your letters are the same size.

Chang and Al laugh.

_____
- -
_____

Every photo is of Oscar.

_____
- -
_____

Day 5 Unit 5 Week 5   The Signmaker's Assistant

Copy the sentences. Make sure your letters are straight.

How did Kate fall?

_____
- -
_____

My daughter is Nan.

_____
- -
_____

© Pearson Education, Inc., 2

Name _____

Pick two prefixes from the box to add to each base word.
Write the prefix on the line.

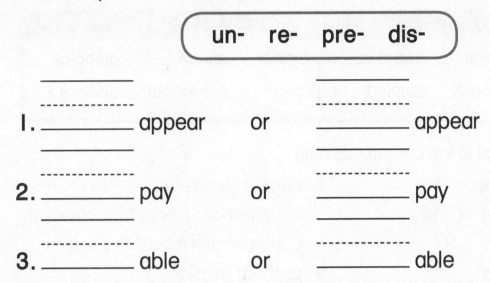

un-   re-   pre-   dis-

1. _____ appear   or   _____ appear

2. _____ pay   or   _____ pay

3. _____ able   or   _____ able

Write a word with one of the prefixes from the box above to match each meaning.

4. to not trust   _____

5. to heat before   _____

Read the story.

    Jan and Dan are unlike most twins. They disagree on many things. Jan thinks you should always prepay your bills. Dan disagrees. He prepaid a bill once. The check got lost. He had to rewrite the check. Then he had to resend it in the mail. Jan likes to reread a good book many times. She also likes to replay movies she has seen. Again, Dan is unlike Jan. He thinks it is uninteresting to reread the same book or replay the same movie.

School + Home   **Home Activity** Your child wrote words that had the prefixes *re-*, *un-*, *dis-*, and *-pre* and read a story. Write the following words and have your child tell you the prefix and what the word means: *unsafe, disloyal, preteen, restart.*

© Pearson Education, Inc., 2

Name _____

Prefixes *un-, re-, pre-, dis-*

Spelling Words

unsafe	preheat	rerun	disappear	unlock	discolor
rewind	unpack	unplug	regroup	preschool	disagree

Fill in the circle next to the correct meaning.

1. **disappear** means
   ○ to vanish completely
   ○ to arrive

2. **unplug** means
   ○ to remove a cord from a socket
   ○ to connect a cord to a socket

3. **rewind** means
   ○ to wind a tape back to the start
   ○ to run another race

4. **preheat** means
   ○ before the sun rises
   ○ to warm an oven before baking

5. **discolor** means
   ○ to change the color
   ○ to color outside the lines

6. **unpack** means
   ○ an old backpack
   ○ to remove clothes from a suitcase

Circle the hidden list words. Look across, down, and diagonally.

```
p  w  r  e  g  r  o  u  p
a  r  r  w  b  s  i  o  l
u  d  e  e  r  d  k  r  q
n  p  r  s  c  h  v  e  c
s  m  u  z  c  n  l  e  c
a  w  n  x  w  h  r  a  d
f  s  t  u  n  l  o  c  k
e  d  r  l  o  k  i  o  u
k  f  y  h  i  v  r  m  l
d  i  s  a  g  r  e  e  q
```

regroup
preschool
rerun
unlock
disagree
unsafe

© Pearson Education, Inc., 2

Home Activity Your child has been learning to spell words with the prefixes *un-, re-, pre-,* and *dis-*. Make a list of base words and a list of these prefixes. Say a base word and a prefix, and have your child point to each one. Say them together as a whole word.

Name _____

Pick a word from the box to match each of the scrambled words in the puzzle. **Write** the letters of the word in each row.

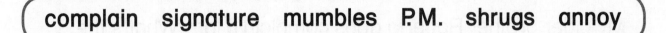

complain signature mumbles P.M. shrugs annoy

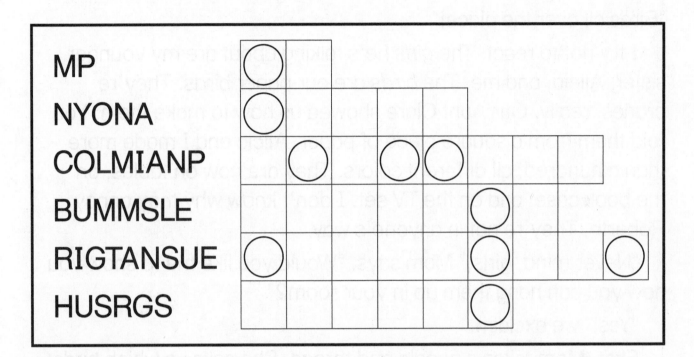

MP

NYONA

COLMIANP

BUMMSLE

RIGTANSUE

HUSRGS

The circled letters can be used to spell two words.
Write the circled letters in the boxes below to spell the answer.

HINT: Someone is shouting and annoying you.
What can you say to complain?

Home Activity Your child reviewed vocabulary words learned earlier in this unit. Talk with your child about the kinds of things that might annoy someone in various situations, such as in a store, a park, a movie theater, or on a bus. For example, people talking loudly in a movie theater. Discuss appropriate ways to deal with these situations, using vocabulary words from this page.

© Pearson Education, Inc., 2

Name _____

Read the story. **Write** the answer to each question.

Our Crane Mobile

My older brother Roberto does complain a lot. "What's the matter with girls?" he mumbles, marching through the TV room. "Birds all over the place!"

I try not to react. The *girls* he's talking about are my younger sister, Alicia, and me. The *birds* are our paper birds. They're cranes, really. Our Aunt Clare showed us how to make them. You fold them from a square piece of paper. Alicia and I made more than a hundred, all different colors. They are now on tables, on the book case, and on the TV set. I don't know why they annoy Roberto. They're not in anyone's way.

"Never mind, girls," Mom says. "Would you like me to show you how you can hang them up in your room?"

"Yes!" we exclaim.

First, Mom takes a needle and thread. She asks us which birds we like best. Then she runs a thread through their backs.

Second, Mom takes some thin sticks. She cuts them with her kitchen scissors. Next, she has us hold the sticks while she ties the prestrung birds on so they hang freely. The birds hang at different heights because the threads are unequal lengths. Sometimes she unties one bird and reties it higher or lower. Then she uses more thread to hang one stick from another.

"I know what this is," I tell Mom. "It's a mobile."

"Isn't it nice, Roberto?" she asks my brother, who is peeking in on us. He just shrugs and disappears.

© Pearson Education, Inc., 2

School + Home

Home Activity Your child recognized causes and effects in a story. Help your child make a list of different types of weather he or she has experienced. Ask your child to tell you the effect each type of weather can have on people.

Name _____

Finally we are done. It is after 8:00 P.M., but we *must* put the mobile in our room. "Before we do, girls, each of you write your signature on a bird. It's a work of art, after all."

The hanging mobile looks beautiful. Every breath of air in the room causes the cranes to swim about slowly.

"Did you know," asks Mom, "that paper cranes mean long life and happiness?"

"They work," I answer. "I'm very happy!"

---

1. What effect do the paper birds have on Roberto at the beginning of the story?

_____

- -

_____

2. What is happening in the middle of the story?

_____

- -

_____

3. Why do the birds hang at different heights?

_____

- -

_____

4. What causes the cranes on the mobile to swim about slowly?

_____

- -

_____

5. What effect do the cranes have on the narrator?

_____

- -

_____

© Pearson Education, Inc., 2

Singular and Plural Pronouns

Circle the pronoun in ( ) that can take the place of the underlined words.

1. Carl thought the <u>water</u> was not cold enough. (he, it)

2. <u>Tony and I</u> made lemonade. (We, They)

3. <u>Mr. Henry and his group</u> signed the petition. (We, They)

Circle the pronouns that name only one. **Underline** the pronouns that name more than one. **Write** the pronouns in the chart.

Dale and I took the petition to the mall. We did not get many people to sign it. A girl walked away when she did not get anything free from us. We also went to the train station. It was not very busy. Then I had a better idea.

Pronouns That Name Only One	Pronouns That Name More Than One

© Pearson Education, Inc., 2

Name _____

Pick a word from the box to finish each phrase.
Write the word on the line.

> climb   knit   wrap   gnash

1. _____ with yarn   2. _____ a gift

3. _____ a ladder   4. _____ your teeth

Write the letters **mb, kn, wr,** or **gn** to complete each word.

5. _____ at   6. _____ ee

7. li _____   8. _____ ist

9. _____ ong   10. thu _____ tack

Read the story.

Matt was going shopping. He needed a new comb. Then there was a knock on the door. Matt turned the knob and opened the door. It was the plumber. He came to fix the pipe that Matt's dog had gnawed on. Matt knew it was the wrong time. The plumber looked at his wristwatch. It was the wrong time. The plumber wrote down the right time. Then he climbed back in his truck. He will come back later.

Home Activity Your child reviewed words that have two letters that stand for one sound such as *gn, wr, mb,* and *kn.* Write the following words and have your child write them on cards and practice spelling them: *gnat, write, lamb, knife.*

© Pearson Education, Inc., 2

Name _____

Consonant Patterns *kn, wr, gn, mb*

Spelling Words					
knock	sign	knee	wrong	write	climb
wrap	wren	gnat	lamb	comb	knob

Read the clues. **Write** the list words in the puzzle.

Across

2. not right

3. _____ at the door

5. written words or marks that
   tell you what to do

6. to go up using your hands
   and feet

Down

1. small songbird

3. a handle

4. part of your leg that bends

Unscramble the list words so the sentence makes sense.
Write the list words.

7. I will **r t w i e** a letter to my grandmother.

8. We saw a young **m l b a** on the farm.

9. What is the difference between a fly and a **t n a g**?

10. Don't forget to **b o c m** your hair.

11. I need to **w p r a** the birthday gift.

7. _____

8. _____

9. _____

10. _____

11. _____

© Pearson Education, Inc., 2

School + Home **Home Activity** Your child has been learning to spell words with *kn, wr, gn,* and *mb*. Scramble spelling list words like the words in items 7–11. Have your child unscramble the words and use them in sentences.

Name _____

Pick a word from the box to finish each sentence.
Write the word on the line.

> chased   chewing   dripping   grabbed
> practice   treat   wagged

1. Max took his dog, Sweetie, to the park. He wanted to

_____

_____

_____ throwing a ball.

_____

_____

2. Sweetie _____ the ball after Max threw it.

3. Sweetie brought the ball back to Max. Max

_____

_____

_____ the ball from Sweetie.

_____

4. Then Max gave Sweetie a bone as a _____.

_____

_____

5. Sweetie was happy _____ on her bone.

6. Then Sweetie jumped into the pond. She was

_____

_____

_____ wet when she got out.

7. Sweetie was so happy. She

_____

_____

_____

her tail all the way home.

© Pearson Education, Inc., 2

School + Home   **Home Activity** Your child reviewed vocabulary words learned in this unit. Ask your child to write sentences about a real or imaginary pet, telling what the pet does. Encourage your child to use as many of the vocabulary words as he or she can.

Name _____

Read the story. **Answer** the questions.

The Space Tent

"Please, Jem," said Mother. "I need you to look after Julie for a few minutes."

"Aw, Mom," answered Jem. "I told Corey I'd come over. We're going to swim in his pool."

"It's early yet," Mother said. "You'll have all the rest of the afternoon."

Jem didn't mind looking after Julie, but he never knew what to do with her. No matter what he tried to do, she wanted to do something different.

He looked at her. She was tearing a newspaper to pieces. Then he had an idea. "Hey, Julie," he said. "Do you want to build a tent? It will be good practice for when we go camping." She looked at him and laughed. He took the newspaper away and gave her a stuffed lamb. She started chewing on it.

"Now you wait here just one minute. Okay?" He dashed to his room. He grabbed a sheet from his closet and came right back. Julie had taken the flowers out of a vase and was giving the lamb a bath. He took the dripping lamb away.

"No, Julie, that's wrong!" he said and wagged his finger at her. He spread the sheet over a table, so that it hung down on all sides. "See? It's a tent. No, wait!" He chased Julie into the kitchen and led her back by the hand. "Now climb under the tent," Jem said, "and I'll give you a treat." He handed her a cracker.

Home Activity Your child analyzed the plot of a story and identified the theme. Have your child tell you what happens at the beginning, middle, and end of the story.

© Pearson Education, Inc., 2

Name _____

Too late he noticed the sheet was his favorite one, with planets and moons and space ships. Well, it wouldn't hurt to use it for a few minutes. It was shady in the tent and quiet. Julie seemed to quiet down. She started to break the cracker into as many crumbs as she could.

"Jem?" called Mother a few minutes later. "Where are you and Julie?" Then she saw Julie. She was happily banging two blocks together. Then she saw the tent. "Well, this was a good idea," she said. "Thank you for keeping Julie out of trouble." Mother lifted the sheet and looked under the tent. There was Jem, curled up on the floor. He was fast asleep.

1. What does Mother ask Jem to do at the beginning of the story?

_____

_____

2. What does Jem do to keep Julie out trouble?

_____

_____

3. What does Mother find when she comes back upstairs?

_____

_____

_____

4. What do you think the author is saying about watching a young child?

_____

_____

_____

_____

© Pearson Education, Inc., 2

Name _____

Using *I* and *Me*

Write *I* or *me* to complete each sentence.

1. Spot pushed _____ with muddy paws.

2. Now Spot and _____ are both muddy.

3. Dad saw Spot and _____.

Circle the word in ( ) that completes each sentence.
Write the sentence.

4. Spot and (I, me) got wet.

_____
_____

5. Spot splashed (I, me) with water.

_____
_____

6. (I, Me) say Spot is a good dog.

_____
_____

© Pearson Education, Inc., 2

Name _____

Write the consonant pattern from the box to correctly complete each word.

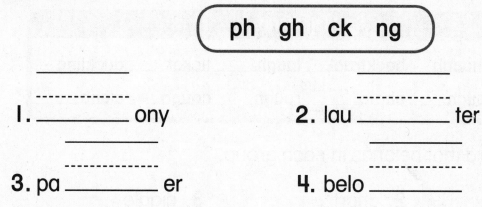

ph   gh   ck   ng

1. _____ ony   2. lau _____ ter

3. pa _____ er   4. belo _____

Pick the word from the box that rhymes with each word.
Write the word on the line.

picket   graphing   enough   ringing

5. rough _____   6. laughing _____

7. ticket _____   8. singing _____

Read the story.

Little Gopher could not stop coughing. He would hack and hack and hack. When he coughed, he sounded like an elephant. So Gopher tried to be tougher. He tried not coughing at all. Gopher's mom told him to take his pills. They would help him stop coughing. Gopher did. They worked. Now Gopher is no longer sick. He said, "Those pills were just the ticket!"

Home Activity Your child reviewed multisyllable words with consonant patterns *ph* as in *photo, gh* as in *laughter, ng* as in *belong,* and *ck* as in *pocket.* Ask your children to use one word with each of these consonant patterns in his or her own sentence.

© Pearson Education, Inc., 2

Name _____

Consonant Patterns *ph, gh, ck, ng*

Spelling Words

phone	enough	backtrack	laugh	ticket	duckling
graph	tough	photo	rough	cough	clang

Write the list word that belongs in each group.

1. cold
   sneeze
   _____
   _____

2. chart
   table
   _____
   _____

3. giggle
   joke
   _____
   _____

4. camera
   picture
   _____
   _____

5. kitten
   puppy
   _____
   _____

6. bang
   crash
   _____
   _____

Circle the hidden list words. **Write** the words.

7. g h p h o n e p l w t

8. r o u g h f f g h i w

9. l f b a c k t r a c k g h

10. y u g e n o u g h r g

11. j o h g t i c k e t l p

12. t g h f t o u g h e p

_____
_____
_____
_____
_____
_____
_____

School + Home **Home Activity** Your child is learning words with the consonant patterns *ph*, *gh*, *ck*, and *ng*. Read a list word to your child. Have your child tell you what letter combination makes the sound without looking at the word.

© Pearson Education, Inc., 2

Name _____

Pick a word from the box to finish each sentence.
Write the word on the line.

> adventure climbed clubhouse exploring
> greatest truest wondered

1. Linda, Joe, and Mira were the _____ of friends.

2. Every week they met at their _____.

3. "Let's go on an _____," said Linda.

4. They went _____ in the woods.

5. They _____ up a hill.

6. "We always have the _____ time," said Joe.

7. They _____ what they would do next week.

 Home Activity Your child reviewed lesson vocabulary words learned earlier in this unit. Ask your child to write a paragraph about what kinds of things he or she would like to do with friends using all or some of the vocabulary words from the box on this page.

Vocabulary 467

© Pearson Education, Inc., 2

Name _____

Read the story. Then follow the directions and answer the questions.

Around the Bend in the River

"Let's go have an adventure," said Rory one day.

"I'm game," I replied. "Shall we go exploring?"

"That sounds like fun," he answered. "Could we go by boat? We've never gone anywhere by boat before."

I'll say this for Rory. Although he's my dog, he does come up with some clever ideas. We didn't have a boat, so we built one. I tied together some old wooden shelves. Then we fastened those to two big old inner tubes. We put up Dad's fishing pole as a mast, and we used a tablecloth for a sail. We named it the *Triumph*. (That was Rory's idea.)

There is a little river behind our house. We slid the *Triumph* into the water. "I already packed us some food," Rory said. He showed me a full picnic basket. So we set sail.

The river got a little bigger and a little faster. Then it was joined by another river. Now it was very big and very fast. "What's around the next bend?" Rory wondered. "Well, I'm going to find out." So he climbed up the mast to look. "Uh-oh," he called down, "I think we're in for our greatest adventure yet!"

Sure enough, there was a waterfall ahead. We sailed right over it. We landed with a great splash in the roaring river below.

"That must be the truest test of a sailor," I gasped.

© Pearson Education, Inc., 2

Home Activity Your child read a fantasy and identified the characters and setting. Have your child explain to you why this is a fantasy. Discuss with your child why he or she liked the character Rory.

Name _____

"No, I think that's coming up yet," Rory answered. Just then our river poured out into the ocean. There we were, sailing on the high seas. They were very rough.

"Do you know what we forgot?" asked Rory. "We have no way to steer this thing. The *Triumph* is just going to sail where it wants to sail."

"That might take us all the way around the world," I answered. "We won't be home until late afternoon at least."

"Then we might as well have our lunch," said Rory. And he started to unpack the basket.

I. Who is telling the story?

_____

- -

_____

2. What is the setting of the story?

_____

- -

_____

3 How would you describe Rory?

_____

- -

_____

4. Why do you think Rory packed food for the trip?

_____

- -

_____

© Pearson Education, Inc., 2

Name _____

Different Kinds of Pronouns

Write the pronoun from the box that can be used in place of the underlined word or words.

| him   They   them |

1. The <u>mice of Mouse School</u> held a Kindness Week. _____

2. The mice children would not tease <u>cats</u>. _____

3. The mice picked <u>Melvin Mouse</u> as leader. _____

Circle the pronoun that can take the place of the underlined word or words.

4. <u>Melvin</u> spoke kind words to the cats.
   She   He   It

5. "You will not tease <u>cats</u>?" asked Cassie Cat.
   we   they   us

6. "That's nice, but <u>this week</u> is Chase Mice Week!"
   she   it   them

© Pearson Education, Inc., 2

Name _____

Write the word in each row that has the same vowel sound as in *saw*.

1. was   laugh   sauce   _____

2. chalk   make   wait   _____

3. arm   caught   save   _____

4. draw   dark   dew   _____

5. haul   cow   cork   _____

6. tough   taught   tail   _____

Read the story.

In August, Audrey and I like to go for walks. We like to talk on our walks. We talk about what we both like to draw. Our art teacher taught us to draw with chalk. Audrey likes to draw tigers with claws. I like to draw snakes that crawl. We both like to draw hawks and astronauts. We go home to draw. We haul out our chalk and begin to draw. Soon we must stop because we are exhausted from walking, talking, and drawing.

© Pearson Education, Inc., 2

Home Activity Your child reviewed words with the vowel sound in *saw* spelled *aw*, *haul* spelled *au*, *caught*, spelled *augh*, and *talk*, spelled *al*. Ask your child to write a word that rhymes with each lword he or she wrote in exercises 1 through 6.

Name _____

Vowel Patterns *aw, au, augh, al*

Spelling Words

talk	because	August	caught	draw	walk
chalk	auto	taught	thaw	fault	launch

Draw a path through the maze. **Follow** the words that have the vowel sound in *fall*. **Write** each word you pass on the path.

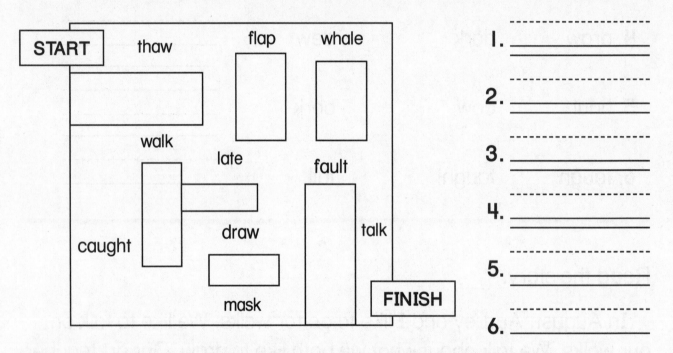

1. _____

2. _____

3. _____

4. _____

5. _____

6. _____

There are stars where the letters that make the vowel sound in *fall* should be. **Write** the list word with the correct letters.

7. b e c ★ ★ s e _____

8. ★ ★ g u s t _____

9. t ★ ★ ★ ★ t _____

10. l ★ ★ n c h _____

11. ★ ★ t o _____

12. c h ★ ★ k _____

Home Activity Your child has been learning to spell words with the vowel patterns *aw, au, augh,* and *al.* Have your child pick a number between 1 and 12. Read the list word that goes with that item number and have your child spell the word without looking at it.

© Pearson Education, Inc., 2

Name _____

Pick a word from the box to finish each sentence.
Write the word on the line.

afternoon   blame   idea
important   signmaker   townspeople

BIG SALE

Kline's Shop

1. One _____, Mr. Kline
decided to have a sale.

2. "It is _____ for everyone to know
about the sale," thought Mr. Kline.

3. Mr. Kline came up with a great _____.

4. Mr. Kline asked the _____
to make big signs.

5. He put them all around town so the
_____
_____ would see them.

6. "If people miss my sale, they cannot _____
me," he said.

Home Activity Your child reviewed vocabulary words learned earlier in this unit. Name each vocabulary word on the page and ask your child to use it in his or her own sentence.

© Pearson Education, Inc., 2

Name _____

Read the story. Then follow the directions and answer the questions.

Mrs. Potts, Signmaker

It all started when Mrs. Potts painted her kitchen. The new color was a nice sky blue. The more she looked at it, though, the unhappier she became. At last she knew what was wrong. Her old orange trash can looked wrong against the blue.

Mrs. Potts went to the store. She bought a new blue trash can and put it in her kitchen. "Yes," she said, "that's much better." Then she wondered, "What shall I do with the old can? I really don't have a place to put it." So she put the old orange can out with the trash. She put it next to her old black outdoor can.

Her town hauled away trash every Friday morning. So Friday afternoon, Mrs. Potts looked out. The old orange can was still there. The workers had taken the trash, but they had left the trash can.

Mrs. Potts didn't blame them. "It's not their fault," she said. "Who throws out a trash can?" She sat down to think. Her old black outdoor can was big and strong. So next Friday, she put the small orange can inside the black outdoor can. Just to be sure, she painted a sign: *Trash. Please take.*

Well, they did. The workers took both cans. Now Mrs. Potts had gotten rid of the old orange indoor can. She still needed an outdoor can though. So she went back to the store and bought another outdoor trash can. This one was brown.

© Pearson Education, Inc., 2

School + Home **Home Activity** Your child identified the main idea in a humorous selection. Read a short story with your child. Have your child tell if the main idea tells a story.

Next Friday, Mrs. Potts put out her new brown outdoor trash can. Into it, she emptied the trash from her new blue can. Then she painted a sign on her new outdoor can: *Property of Mrs. Potts. Do not take!* Can you guess what happened? They left everything!

Next Friday, Mrs. Potts put out her trash. On top of it, she put a sign: *Yes, please, do take the trash, but leave the can. Thank you, Mrs. Potts.*

This time, the workers got it right. They took the trash and left the can. Mrs. Potts saw a note on the can. It was from the workers. It read: *You're welcome, Mrs. Potts. P.S. Nice trash can!*

_____

I. What color did Mrs. Potts paint her kitchen.

_____
- -
_____

2. Look at the second paragraph. Underline the main idea.

3. Look at the fourth paragraph. Write one detail.

_____
- -
_____
- -
_____

4. Look at the fifth paragraph. Underline the main idea.

© Pearson Education, Inc., 2

Name _____

Contractions

Draw a line to match the underlined words with a contraction.

1. "This <u>is not</u> funny," said Lucy.   it's

2. "<u>You have</u> lost my paintbrush," she said.   isn't

3. "Now <u>it is</u> a big problem."   You've

Replace the underlined words with a contraction from the box.

I've   didn't   I'll

_____

- - - - - - - - - - - - - - - - - - - -

4. "I <u>did not</u> lose your paintbrush," said Ken.   _____

_____

- - - - - - - - - - - - - - - - - - - -

5. "I <u>will</u> help you look for it," he said.   _____

_____

- - - - - - - - - - - - - - - - - - - -

6. "I <u>have</u> found it," said Lucy.   _____

© Pearson Education, Inc., 2

Name _____

Persuasion Chart

Fill out this persuasion chart to help you organize your ideas.

Topic

I want to persuade _____

_____
(audience)

to _____
(purpose)

Brainstorm reasons here.

Organize your reasons here.

Least important

_____

_____

_____

Most important

_____

_____

_____

© Pearson Education, Inc., 2

Name _____

Use Persuasive Words

Use the words from the box to complete the letter.

important	best	need	should

July 10, 2011

Dear Dad,

_____

I think our town _____ build a water park.

We could slide down the Zoom Tube and swim in the Swirl

_____

Pool. That would be the _____ thing to

do on hot summer days. People here work hard, and they

_____

really _____ a fun place to go. Also, it is

_____

_____ for families to have a place where

they can spend time together. What do you think?

Your son,

Andrew

© Pearson Education, Inc., 2

Name _____

Adding Words, Phrases, or Sentences

When you revise your letter, add words, phrases, or sentences to make your writing more persuasive. **Follow** the direction to revise the sentences and paragraph.

1. Which word should the writer add to this sentence to make it more persuasive? Write the new sentence.

Our town needs a swimming pool.   home   larger

_____

_____
----

2. Which phrase should the writer add to this sentence to make it more persuasive? Write the new sentence.

The pool is full of leaves.   and dead bugs   from the trees

_____

_____
----

3. Which sentence should the writer add to this paragraph to make it more persuasive? Underline the sentence. Draw an arrow to show where to add the new sentence.

The tennis courts are cracked.   The pool is unsafe too. The old pool is dirty and smelly. It gets too crowded, and it is too small for real swimming. You can cut yourself on the rough concrete. We need a bigger, better pool!

© Pearson Education, Inc., 2

Name _____

Self-Evaluation Guide

Check Yes or **No** about word choice in your letter.

	Yes	No
1. I used one or more words to persuade.		
2. I used one or more good adjectives to describe.		
3. I used exact words instead of vague ones, such as **nice**.		

Answer the questions.

4. What is the best part of your letter?

_____
_____
_____
_____
_____

5. What is one thing you would change about this letter if you could write it again?

_____
_____
_____
_____
_____

© Pearson Education, Inc., 2

Name _____

Read each word.
Find the base word.
Write the base word on the line.

try + -ed = tr**ied**   try + -ing = try**ing**

1. hiked _____   2. skipped _____

3. planning _____   4. shopping _____

5. cried _____   6. liking _____

7. baking _____   8. boxes _____

Find the word that makes sense in the sentences below.
Mark the space to show your answer.

9. Sam is _____ than Luke.
   ○ fast
   ○ faster
   ○ fasting

10. Mia is the _____ person
    I know.
    ○ kinder
    ○ kind
    ○ kindest

Home Activity Your child identified base words with -ed and -ing endings, as in *tried* and *trying*. Read with your child, looking for words with -ed and -ing endings. Have your child pronounce the words and identify the base words.

© Pearson Education, Inc., 2

Name _____

Pick a word from the box to finish each sentence.
Write the word on the line.

| bases   cheers   field   plate   sailed   threw |

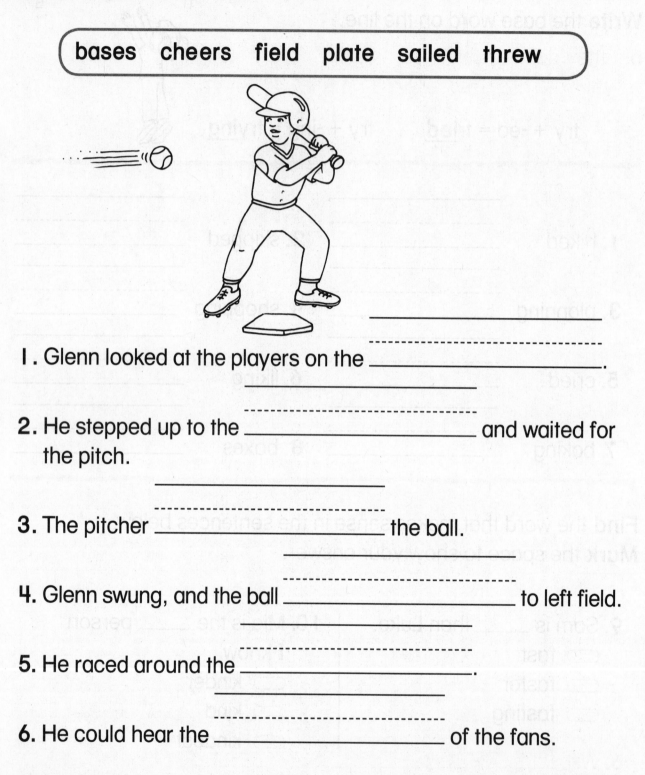

_____

1. Glenn looked at the players on the _____.

_____

2. He stepped up to the _____ and waited for the pitch.

_____

3. The pitcher _____ the ball.

_____

4. Glenn swung, and the ball _____ to left field.

_____

5. He raced around the _____.

_____

6. He could hear the _____ of the fans.

Home Activity Your child used lesson vocabulary words to complete sentences. Ask your child to use the words to write a poem or song about baseball. Help your child write his or her ideas. Encourage your child to perform the piece for other family members.

© Pearson Education, Inc., 2

Name _____

Read the story.
Follow the directions.

Rita and Will both love to play sports, but they do not like the same ones. Rita plays soccer. She enjoys the game because she likes to run. Will likes baseball. Unlike Rita, Will doesn't like to run much. He likes to hit the ball.

1. **Underline** the part of the story that tells how Rita and Will are alike.

2. **Write** the name of the person who likes soccer.

_____

3. **Write** the name of the person who likes baseball.

_____

4. **Write** a sentence to compare and contrast how Rita and Will feel about running.

_____

_____

_____

_____

_____

Use what you know about sports. **Think** about what you read. **List** another sport that Rita and Will might like.

_____

5. Rita _____

_____

6. Will _____

Home Activity Your child read a story and answered questions to compare and contrast two characters and their favorite sports. Ask your child to think about two games or activities he or she enjoys. Discuss what your child likes about them. Ask your child to tell how the activities are alike and different.

© Pearson Education, Inc., 2

Writing • Realistic Story

Read Together **Running Like Jesse Owens**

Rayshaun took his place on the track for the next running event, the 100-meter dash. He thought about his hero, Jesse Owens, who also ran track in high school. Over 80 years ago, Owens tied the world record for the 100-meter dash several times with a time of 9.4 seconds. Rayshaun's best time was 9.8. Could he tie Owen's record today?

The starting gun went off! The runners raced down the track. Rayshaun tried to do his best.

When Rayshaun crossed the finish line, the clock showed 9.7 seconds. Rayshaun had taken a tenth of a second off of his time. He was even closer to Owen's record!

Key Features of a Realistic Story

• Characters and setting seem real.

• Characters do things that could really happen.

• The story has a beginning, middle, and end.

© Pearson Education, Inc., 2

Name _____

Inflected Endings

Spelling Words					
tried	trying	planned	planning	liked	liking
skipped	skipping	heavier	heaviest	lighter	lightest

Write the missing list word. It rhymes with the underlined word.

1. I kept <u>tripping</u> as I was _____ rope.

2. I would have _____ to have <u>biked</u> this afternoon.

3. Have you _____ this <u>fried</u> chicken?

4. The new car belt is <u>tighter</u> and _____.

5. Mom is _____ on <u>canning</u> some tomatoes.

6. <u>Flying</u> is something that is worth _____.

Write the missing list word that combines the words shown.

7. more + heavy _____   8. more + light _____

9. most + heavy _____   10. most + light _____

 Home Activity Your child is learning to spell words with inflected endings. Point to a spelling word. Have your child pronounce and spell the base word and tell whether the base word changed when the ending was added.

© Pearson Education, Inc., 2

Name _____

Find a word that is a homophone in each sentence.
Write the word and its homophone on the line below.

1. Did you know that today is my birthday?

   _____

   -

   _____

2. We have eight members in the band.

   _____

   -

   _____

3. Look who just walked through that door!

   _____

   -

   _____

4. For the costume party, Mark dressed up as a knight.

   _____

   -

   _____

Read the pair of sentences.
Write the correct word from the box on the line.

5. a. I need a new _____ of shoes.

   b. My favorite fruit to eat is a _____ .

pair/pear

© Pearson Education, Inc., 2

School + Home

Home Activity Your child learned about words that sound the same but are spelled differently. Have your child look for homophones in some of his or her favorite storybooks.

Name _____

Using Capital Letters

Days of the week, months of the year, and **holidays** begin with capital letters.

> This year the **Fourth of July** is on **Wednesday.**

Titles for people begin with capital letters.

> **Mrs.** D. J. Davis invited us to a picnic.

Find the words that need capital letters. **Write** the words correctly on the line.

1. On monday, we went to mr. Jung's grocery store.

    _____
    - - - - - - - - - - - - - - - - -
    _____

2. Mom and ms. Jones made potato salad on tuesday.

    _____
    - - - - - - - - - - - - - - - - -
    _____

3. dr. Webb marched in the parade on independence day.

    _____
    - - - - - - - - - - - - - - - - -
    _____

4. The fourth of july is another name for independence day.

    _____
    - - - - - - - - - - - - - - - - -
    _____

5. I wish there were parades in june and august too.

    _____
    - - - - - - - - - - - - - - - - -
    _____

Home Activity Your child learned about using capital letters. Find a calendar. Ask your child to write the names of the days of the week. Remind him or her to use capital letters.

© Pearson Education, Inc., 2

Name _____

Story Chart

Title _____

Characters

Setting

Beginning

↓

Middle

↓

End of Story

© Pearson Education, Inc., 2

Home Activity Your child is learning to write stories, poems, brief reports, nonfiction paragraphs, letters, and other products this year. Ask what your child is writing this week

Name _____

You will be presenting a visual display to help answer the Question of the Week, *Why are sports traditions important in our country?* Use the following steps to help you plan your visual display.

Step 1- Choose which information is interesting to you that you would like to share.

_____

_____

_____

Step 2- Organize the information from Step 1 into groups. Create headings to tell about each group.

_____

My poster headings are _____ .

Step 3- List what type of art you would like to include on your poster.

_____

_____

Step 4- Present the visual display to the class.

© Pearson Education, Inc., 2

Home Activity Your child learned to make a visual display. Ask your child to share what he or she learned about visual displays. Have your child share his or her display with you.

Name _____

Inflected Endings

Read the word puzzle. **Circle** the three words that are spelled wrong. **Write** the words correctly.

Everyone tryed to be first in line.

A girl who skiped rope was first. She is smiling.

A girl who likked wearing bows in her hair is behind a girl who is crying.

Who is last in line?

(Answer: the girl wearing bows in her hair)

Spelling Words	
tried	skipped
trying	skipping
planned	heavier
planning	heaviest
liked	lighter
liking	lightest

1. _____ 2. _____ 3. _____

Circle the word that is spelled correctly.

4.	planing	planning	plainning
5.	heavier	heavyer	hevier
6.	litest	lighttest	lightest
7.	tryying	trying	tring
8.	liking	likeing	likking
9.	skiped	skkipped	skipped
10.	lighter	lightter	ligter

Frequently Misspelled Words

don't

they're

there's

Home Activity Your child is learning to spell words with inflected endings. Pronounce a base word. Ask your child to spell the corresponding -ed and -ing words.

© Pearson Education, Inc., 2

Name _____

field hockey

ice hockey

Look for ways in which ice hockey is like field hockey.
List one way they are **alike.**

1. _____
_____
_____

_____

Look for ways in which ice hockey is **not** like field hockey.
List two ways they are **different.**

2. _____
_____
_____
_____

3. _____
_____
_____

School +Home **Home Activity** Your child described ways in which two sports are alike and different. Use magazines, the newspaper, or the Internet to locate pictures of two other sports, such as soccer and football. Ask your child to name similarities and differences between the two sports.

Comprehension Compare and Contrast **491**

© Pearson Education, Inc., 2

Using Capital Letters

Mark the letter of the word or words that complete each sentence and show the correct use of capital letters.

1. On _____, our teacher had a surprise for us.
   ○ **A** monday
   ○ **B** Monday
   ○ **C** january

2. _____ brought in many small trees.
   ○ **A** mr. fisk
   ○ **B** mr. Fisk
   ○ **C** Mr. Fisk

3. People plant trees on the last Friday in _____ .
   ○ **A** April
   ○ **B** april
   ○ **C** Wednesday

4. He told us it was _____ .
   ○ **A** arbor Day
   ○ **B** Arbor Day
   ○ **C** Arbor day

5. _____ and other parents helped us plant the trees.
   ○ **A** Mrs. Sloan
   ○ **B** mrs. sloan
   ○ **C** mrs. Sloan

6. On _____ , I showed Grandma the trees.
   ○ **A** september
   ○ **B** saturday
   ○ **C** Saturday

© Pearson Education, Inc., 2

Home Activity Your child prepared for taking tests on using capital letters. Look through a newspaper article together. Ask your child to circle days of the week, months, holidays, or titles of people.

Name _____

Read the abbreviation.
Draw a line to the word it stands for.

1. Ave.   Doctor

2. Dr.   November

3. Mr.   Mister

4. Mon.   Avenue

5. Nov.   Street

6. St.   Monday

Write each abbreviation correctly.

7. apr _____   8. mrs _____

9. Mar _____   10. fri _____

Home Activity Your child learned the common abbreviations Ave., Mr., Mrs., Dr., St., and abbreviations for days and months. On some envelopes and business letters addressed to you, point out and read with your child abbreviations such as Mr., Ave., or St. Point out and read abbreviated days and months on letters or e-mailed messages.

© Pearson Education, Inc., 2

Name _____

Pick a word from the box to finish each sentence.
Write the word on the line.

America	birthday	flag	freedom
nicknames	stars	stripes	

1. July 4, 1776, is the _____ of this country.

2. Many people fly the _____ on July 4.

3. Our flag has 13 _____.

4. It has 50 _____.

5. People have many _____ for the flag.

6. No matter what we call it, the flag reminds us of our _____.

7. It stands for our country, the United States of _____.

Home Activity Your child used lesson vocabulary words to complete sentences. Work with your child to write a paragraph describing what he or she most appreciates about this country. Try to include as many vocabulary words as possible.

494 Vocabulary

© Pearson Education, Inc., 2

Read the story.
Write the answer to each question.

A Day to Celebrate

September 15 is a holiday in Japan. It is called Keiro no Hi. This is a day when one shows respect for older people. Keiro no Hi became a national holiday in 1966. Today people in Japan give gifts to people who are 70 years old or older. It is a way to let the older people know they are special and important. Older people may celebrate their long life with their families on this day. In some schools, children make gifts to give to their grandparents. Communities have celebrations, such as sports events, on Keiro no Hi. Tokyo, the largest city in Japan, has a special ceremony for the country's older citizens.

1. What is the topic of this story?

_____

- -

2. What is the purpose of Keiro no Hi?

_____

- -

3. Why do you think the author wrote this story?

_____

- -

_____

- -

School + Home

Home Activity Your child identified the author's purpose for writing informational text. Have your child write about a favorite holiday. Ask your child to choose a reason for writing about the holiday, for example, to give information, to explain something, to entertain.

Comprehension Author's Purpose **495**

© Pearson Education, Inc., 2

Name _____

Writing • Poem or Song

 The American Flag

The American flag is red, white, and blue.
There are fifty stars that cover it, too.
We hang it on houses. We hang it on poles.
It's a symbol of many American goals.
But mostly we know that it means we are free.
"Long may it wave!" we shout loudly with glee.

Key Features of a Descriptive Poem or Song

• It has carefully chosen words arranged in lines.

• It describes something and may have rhymes.

• A song is like a poem that people sing.

© Pearson Education, Inc., 2

Name _____

Abbreviations

Spelling Words					
Mr.	Mrs.	St.	Jan.	Feb.	Aug.
Dr.	Ms.	Rd.	Oct.	Nov.	Dec.

Write the abbreviation for the underlined word in the sentence.

1. I live on Peachtree <u>Street</u>.

2. <u>January</u> is the coldest month.

3. My birthday is in <u>October</u>.

4. <u>Mister</u> Wilson is my teacher.

5. Thanksgiving is in <u>November</u>.

6. I am going to see <u>Doctor</u> Hatcher.

Circle the correct abbreviation in each sentence.

7. Our school is on Countryside   Rd.   Ms.

8. Mrs.   Feb.   Stowe lives across the street from us.

9. Dr.   Dec.   20 is the beginning of our Winter Break.

10. The school year starts on   Aug.   Rd.   20.

11. I get tutored by   Nov.   Ms.   Wilkes.

12. Valentine's Day is on   Feb.   Dr.   14.

© Pearson Education, Inc., 2

Home Activity Your child is learning to spell abbreviations. Show your child a newspaper article. Have him or her point to all the abbreviations in the article.

Name _____

Circle the correct meaning of the underlined word in each sentence. **Use** the other words in the sentence to help. Then **write** a sentence for the multiple-meaning word using a **different** meaning of the word.

1. The <u>band</u> played "America the Beautiful."

    a. strip of material   b. group of musicians

_____

- -

_____

2. We <u>cut</u> through the field instead of walking around it.

    a. to divide with something sharp   b. to cross or pass

_____

- -

_____

3. At that <u>point</u>, everyone left the room.

    a. a particular time   b. sharp end

_____

- -

_____

4. If you throw a rock in the lake, it will <u>sink</u>.

    a. something that is used to hold water used for washing   b. go below

_____

- -

_____

© Pearson Education, Inc., 2

Home Activity Your child used context clues to figure out the correct meaning of words that have more than one meaning. Ask your child to use the multiple-meaning word *fly* in his or her own sentences.

Quotation Marks

Quotation marks (" ") show the beginning and ending of the words someone says. The speaker's name and words such as **said** or **asked** are not inside the quotation marks.

"You're a grand old flag," said George M. Cohan.

"Let's have a parade," said Betsy.

Ross asked, "What kind of parade should we have?"

Add quotation marks to each sentence.

1. I don't know what kind of parade to have, said Betsy.

2. Abe said, We could have a flag parade.

3. What is a flag parade? asked Francis Scott.

4. We could all wear red, white, and blue, George said.

5. Lincoln asked, Could we all carry flags?

6. Betsy said, That's a great idea!

Home Activity Your child learned about quotation marks. Look through a newspaper article with your child. Have him or her circle places where quotation marks are used. Ask your child why quotation marks were needed.

© Pearson Education, Inc., 2

Name _____

Idea Web

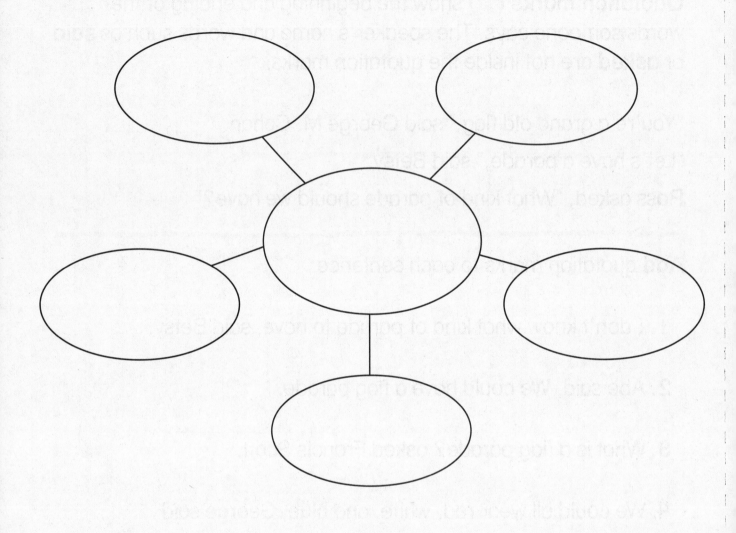

© Pearson Education, Inc., 2

Home Activity Your child is learning to write stories, poems, brief reports, nonfiction paragraphs, letters, and other products this year. Ask what your child is writing this week

Name _____

Look at the tally chart. **Write** the answer to each question.

People Who Saw the Flag Show

Monday	卌
Tuesday	卌 IIII
Thursday	卌 III

1. What information is given on this chart?

_____

- -

_____
                                            - - - - - - - - - - -

2. How many people saw the show on Thursday? _____

3. On Wednesday, 8 people saw the show. Add that information to the chart.

4. On Friday, 7 people saw the show. Add that information to the chart.

5. On what two days did the same number of people see the show?

_____

- -

_____
                                            - - - - - - - - - - -

6. How many more people saw the show
on Tuesday than on Monday?   - - - - - - - - - - -

Home Activity Your child learned how to read a tally chart. Together with your child look at flags of different countries. Make a tally chart about the flags for the following categories: red, white, and blue; stripes; stars; circles; other shapes. Compare the results.

© Pearson Education, Inc., 2

Name _____

Abbreviations

Read the journal entry. **Circle** the three abbreviations that are misspelled.
Write the words correctly.

Dece. 11, 2008
This weekend was a lot of fun. First, I went to
Danny's house. He lives on Lincoln Str. His dad,
Mr. French, drove us to the museum. We both
thought it was really neat. Later, his mom,
Msr. French, picked us up.

Spelling Words	
Mr.	Dr.
Mrs.	Ms.
St.	Rd.
Jan.	Oct.
Feb.	Nov.
Aug.	Dec.

Frequently Misspelled Words

thought

caught

1. _____ 2. _____

3. _____

Circle the abbreviation that is spelled correctly.

4.	Dctr.	Dr.	Dtr.
5.	Janu.	Ja.	Jan.
6.	Rod.	Ro.	Rd.
7.	Aug.	Ag.	Agst.
8.	Mr.	Mstr.	Mtr.
9.	Nmbr.	Nov.	Novr.
10.	Mis.	Mss.	Ms.

Home Activity Your child learned to spell abbreviations. Look through the mail with your child. Have him or her identify abbreviations used for names, streets, and dates.

© Pearson Education, Inc., 2

Name _____

Read the story. **Write** the answer to each question.

Many foods popular in the world today first came from North and South America. Europeans didn't have potatoes or tomatoes or corn before they sailed to the Americas in 1492. That meant there was no tomato sauce in Italy. There were no French fries in France.

Europeans didn't have peanuts, pecans, chocolate, or vanilla either. So there was no peanut butter. Nor was there any pecan pie. How good could dessert have been without chocolate and vanilla?

Other foods that came from the Americas include corn, chili peppers, and avocados. So before 1492 there were no chips and salsa—and certainly no guacamole!

1. What is the topic of this story?

_____

- -

_____

2. What would be a good title for this story?

    Peanuts and Pecans   Food From the Americas

_____

- -

_____

3. Why do you think the author wrote this story?

_____

- -

_____

© Pearson Education, Inc., 2

Home Activity Your child identified the author's purpose for writing informational text. Have your child write about a favorite food. Ask your child to choose a reason for writing about the food, for example, to give information, to explain something, or to entertain.

Quotation Marks

Mark the letter of the correct sentence.

1. ○ **A** "Our flag has many nicknames, said Martha.
   ○ **B** "Our flag has many nicknames," said Martha.
   ○ **C** "Our flag has many nicknames, said Martha."

2. ○ **A** Is the Stars and Stripes one of the names?" asked John.
   ○ **B** "Is the Stars and Stripes one of the names? asked John."
   ○ **C** "Is the Stars and Stripes one of the names?" asked John.

3. ○ **A** "George said, Old Glory is another name for the flag."
   ○ **B** George said, "Old Glory is another name for the flag.
   ○ **C** George said, "Old Glory is another name for the flag."

4. ○ **A** I like the Red, White, and Blue best," Sally said."
   ○ **B** "I like the Red, White, and Blue best," Sally said.
   ○ **C** "I like the Red, White, and Blue best, Sally said."

5. ○ **A** Thomas asked, "Why are there 50 stars?"
   ○ **B** "Thomas asked, Why are there 50 stars?"
   ○ **C** Thomas asked, "Why are there 50 stars?

6. ○ **A** "There is one star for each state in the United States, Sally said."
   ○ **B** "There is one star for each state in the United States," Sally said.
   ○ **C** "There is one star for each state in the United States, Sally said.

© Pearson Education, Inc., 2

Home Activity Your child prepared for taking tests on quotation marks. Ask your child to write a sentence about the flag. Tell him or her to use quotation marks and the name of a person mentioned on this page in the sentence.

Name _____

Circle a word with **-tion, -ture,** or **-ion** to finish each sentence.

na**tion**   mix**ture**

1,000,000
mill**ion**

1. I saw a horse in the _____ .

portion
pasture

2. I watched from one _____ of the yard.

section
suction

3. I moved with _____ .

culture
caution

4. I walked in slow _____ .

motion
station

5. I'd like to see a _____ horses.

million
cushion

Home Activity Your child wrote words that include the syllables *-tion* as in *nation, -ture* as in *mixture,* and *-ion* as in *onion*. Write some other words with *-tion, -ion,* or *-ture,* such as *future, nature, texture, action, station,* and *opinion*. Have your child read each word and identify the final syllable pattern.

© Pearson Education, Inc., 2

Name _____

Pick a word from the box to finish each sentence.
Write the word on the line.

aunt	bank	basket
collects	favorite	present

_____

1. Matt's _____ came to visit on his birthday.

2. Matt's aunt _____ coins.

3. This year she got 50 state quarters from

   the _____.

4. She filled a _____ with the money.

5. Then she gave it to her nephew as a

   birthday _____.

6. It was Matt's _____.

School + Home

Home Activity Your child used lesson vocabulary words to complete sentences. Ask your child to use each word in another sentence. Help your child write the sentences. Have your child draw a picture to illustrate each sentence.

© Pearson Education, Inc., 2

Name _____

Read the story. **Look** at the picture. **Follow** the directions.

    The children were laughing and having fun. A paper piñata hung above them. One at a time, each child took a turn to swing. Finally, the piñata broke open. Candy and small toys fell to the ground. Everyone ran to grab a handful.

Circle the word that best finishes each sentence.

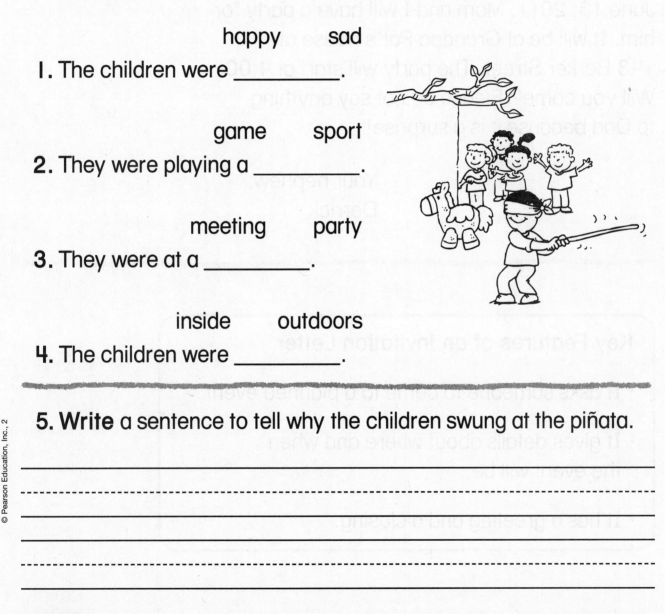

                      happy   sad

1. The children were _____.

                    game   sport

2. They were playing a _____.

                meeting   party

3. They were at a _____.

               inside   outdoors

4. The children were _____.

---

5. **Write** a sentence to tell why the children swung at the piñata.

_____

- -

_____

- -

_____

© Pearson Education, Inc., 2

Home Activity Your child drew conclusions after reading a passage and looking at its illustration. Read your child a favorite book. As you read, pause to discuss what is happening. Ask your child open-ended questions, such as "What's going on now?" and "What's this all about?"

Name _____

Writing · Invitation Letter

An Invitation

Dear Aunt Susan,

   Dad's birthday is next week. On Saturday, June 13, 2011, Mom and I will have a party for him. It will be at Grandpa Pat's house at 143 Barker Street. The party will start at 4:00. Will you come? Please do not say anything to Dad because it is a surprise!

                   Your nephew,
                   Derrick

Key Features of an Invitation Letter

· It asks someone to come to a planned event.

· It gives details about where and when the event will be.

· It has a greeting and a closing.

© Pearson Education, Inc., 2

Name _____

Final Syllables *-tion, -ture*

Spelling Words					
mixture	nation	section	future	picture	action
caution	station	fixture	motion	nature	feature

Write a list word.

It rhymes with **fraction**, but it starts like **apple**.

----

1. _____

It rhymes with **notion**, but it starts like **mop**.

----

2. _____

It rhymes with **mixture**, but it starts like **fan**.

----

3. _____

It rhymes with **station**, but it starts like **nap**.

----

4. _____

It rhymes with **creature**, but it starts like **fix**.

----

5. _____

It rhymes with **fixture**, but it starts like **mat**.

----

6. _____

Write the missing list word.

----

7. Proceed with _____ .

----

8. It's time for a _____ break.

----

9. We went on a _____ walk.

----

10. I get the _____ .

----

11. Where's the sports _____ of the paper?

----

12. It's a job with a _____ .

School + Home **Home Activity** Your child spelled words with *-tion* and *-ture*. Have your child circle *-tion* or *-ture* in each word on this page.

© Pearson Education, Inc., 2

Name _____

Read the sentence. **Write** the meaning of the word in *slanted type*. **Circle** the other words in the sentence that helped you figure out the meaning.

1. We call my Aunt Maria "*Tía* Maria."

_____
----

2. I will invite all of my classmates to my birthday party. We will have fun at the *fiesta*.

_____
----

3. At the end of our visit I said goodbye to my friend. My friend said "*Au revoir*" and then left.

_____
----

4. I do not know his *nombre*. Do you know his name?

_____
----

5. Every morning I say "*Bonjour!*" to my grandmother, and she says good morning.

_____

School + Home

Home Activity Your child learned some words in two other languages. Ask your child to make up his or her own sentences using some of the italicized words on this page.

© Pearson Education, Inc., 2

Prepositions and Prepositional Phrases

A **preposition** is the first word in a group of words called
a **prepositional phrase.**

Preposition	Mamá is cooking <u>for</u> the surprise party.
Prepositional Phrase	Mamá is cooking <u>for the surprise party</u>.

Circle the preposition in each sentence.
Say a new sentence using each preposition.

1. Cecilia smells beans bubbling on the stove.

2. She drew a picture in the sand.

3. Chica and I walk around the front yard.

4. Cecilia fills the living room with balloons.

Write the prepositional phrase in the sentence.
Say other prepositional phrases that could replace it.

5. I like talking with my friends.

_____

_____

© Pearson Education, Inc., 2

Home Activity Your child learned about prepositions. Read a story with your child. Have your child identify prepositional phrases from the story. Tell him or her to point to the preposition.

Name _____

T-Chart

Details	Sentences and Phrases
Who:	
What:	
Where:	
When:	
Why:	

Home Activity Your child is learning to write stories, poems, brief reports, nonfiction paragraphs, letters, and other products this year. Ask what your child is writing this week.

© Pearson Education, Inc., 2

Name _____

Often times, information is gained inside the classroom. Sources of information that you may find inside the classroom are known as **natural sources**. When you use people as a natural source, you must conduct an **interview**.

What are topics you could interview classmates about?

_____

_____

If you conduct an interview with a classmate, should you give the questions or the answers?

_____

_____

If you conduct an interview with a classmate to find information about how he or she gathers information, which natural sources could be included in the response?

_____

_____

_____

© Pearson Education, Inc., 2

Home Activity Your child learned about gathering evidence from natural sources as well as using people as sources of information. Talk with your child about some of the traditions your family celebrates and shares with others. Give your child a topic of a tradition to research. Together with your child make a list of sources you could use to find the answers to your questions.

Name _____

Final Syllables *-tion, -ture*

Spelling Words					
mixture	nation	section	future	picture	action
caution	station	fixture	motion	nature	feature

Read the poster. **Circle** three misspelled words and one word with a capitalization error. **Write** the words correctly.

1. _____

2. _____

3. _____

4. _____

Special double featur!

Packed with ACTION

A superhero of the future saves the naton.

Bring the family saturday at 1:00 P.M.

Circle the word that is spelled correctly. **Write** it.

Frequently Misspelled Words

special

family

really

5. caution   causion   _____

6. nater   nature   _____

7. picture   pichure   _____

8. section   sectshion   _____

© Pearson Education, Inc., 2

School + Home

Home Activity Your child identified misspelled words with *-tion* and *-ture*. Have your child underline these letter combinations in the list words on this page.

Name _____

Read the story. **Ask** yourself what is happening.
Answer each question.

Miss Booker stood by her door.
She heard whispers inside. As she
entered, the children yelled. For
a minute Miss Booker didn't know
what was going on. Then she looked
around. The children were smiling
and had on silly hats. They had
even made a sign for this happy day.

1. Who is Miss Booker? _____

2. Where is she? _____

3. Why didn't she know what was going on?

_____

_____

4. What do you think was on the sign the children made? Why?

_____

_____

_____

_____

Home Activity Your child drew conclusions after reading a story and looking at the illustration. Take turns reading another story with your child. Work together to figure out more about the characters and what happens in the story as you read.

Comprehension Draw Conclusions **515**

© Pearson Education, Inc., 2

Prepositions and Prepositional Phrases

Mark the letter of the preposition in each sentence.

1. We bought wrapping paper from the store.
   - ○ **A** We
   - ○ **B** from
   - ○ **C** store

2. My uncle threw the party at his house.
   - ○ **A** threw
   - ○ **B** party
   - ○ **C** at

3. Tía was the guest of honor.
   - ○ **A** Tía
   - ○ **B** guest
   - ○ **C** of

4. My friends and I danced to the music.
   - ○ **A** to
   - ○ **B** I
   - ○ **C** danced

5. Cecilia hid the basket under the table.
   - ○ **A** hid
   - ○ **B** under
   - ○ **C** basket

6. We ate our food on the patio.
   - ○ **A** on
   - ○ **B** patio
   - ○ **C** our

Home Activity Your child prepared for taking tests on prepositions. Read aloud a newspaper article. Have your child say "Stop" each time he or she hears a prepositional phrase.

© Pearson Education, Inc., 2

Name _____

Add -ness, -less, -ible, or **-able** to each word to make a word from the box. **Write** the new word on the line.

affordable	fearless	fitness	goodness
reversible	terrible	thankless	useless

1. afford

_____

- -

_____

2. fit

_____

- -

_____

3. thank

_____

- -

_____

4. fear

_____

- -

_____

5. good

_____

- -

_____

6. use

_____

- -

_____

Pick a word from the box to match the clue.
Write the word on the line.

7. has two sides you can use

_____

- -

_____

8. very bad, something feared _____

- -

_____

© Pearson Education, Inc., 2

Home Activity Your child wrote words with the suffixes *-ness* as in *sadness*, *-less* as in *careless*, *-ible* as in *reversible*, and *-able* as in *affordable*. Help your child write other words with these suffixes, such as *helpless*, *painless*, *sickness*, *weakness*, *teachable*, and *washable*. Ask your child to read each word and identify the base word (such as *wash* in *washable*).

Name _____

Pick a word from the box to finish each sentence.
Write the word on the line.

campfire	cattle
cowboy	galloped
herd	railroad	trails

1. Tanya read a book about a _____ who lived long ago.

2. He moved the _____ of cattle to market.

3. Sometimes storms scared the _____ .

4. The cowboy and his horse _____ after them.

5. Then the cowboy built a _____ and went to sleep.

6. He led the cattle down dusty _____ .

7. Then the _____ took the cattle to the East.

© Pearson Education, Inc., 2

School + Home

Home Activity Your child used lesson vocabulary words to complete sentences. Have your child use the vocabulary words to tell another story. Help your child write the story. Ask your child to read the story and underline each vocabulary word.

Name _____

Read the story. **Circle** time-order words in the story.
Write 1, 2, 3, 4, 5 to show the correct order of events.

The Pony Express

By 1860, many people had moved to California. The people were eager to get mail from back home, but the mail was slow to come. Mail was carried by stagecoach, and it took about 24 days for it to reach California. But in January 1860, the Pony Express was formed as a faster way to deliver mail. First the Pony Express hired riders to carry the mail on horses. Then the company built stations between St. Joseph, Missouri, and Sacramento, California. The stations were places where new riders and fresh horses took over. Next, on March 31, 1860, a train brought mail from Washington, D.C., and New York to St. Joseph. After that, the first Pony Express rider left St. Joseph on April 3, 1860. Finally, the mail arrived in Sacramento, California, only 10 days later.

_____ The first Pony Express rider left St. Joseph.

_____ A train brought mail to St. Joseph.

_____ The Pony Express hired riders.

_____ The company built Pony Express stations.

_____ The mail arrived in Sacramento, California.

© Pearson Education, Inc., 2

Home Activity Your child identified words in a story that show sequence and placed events in the correct order. Ask your child to tell events that take place on a holiday such as the Fourth of July. Make sure your child tells the events in the correct order. Encourage your child to use order words.

Name _____

Writing • Compare-and-Contrast Text

Line Leader

One job at school is line leader. This job is much like the job of the cowboy. The jobs are the same because both the line leader and the cowboy are in front of a group. They both show the group which way to go. The jobs are different, though. A line leader leads children, but a cowboy leads a group of cattle. A line leader walks along hallways in a school, but a cowboy walks along a dusty trail.

Key Features of a Compare-and-Contrast Text

- It tells how two things are alike and how they are different.

- It uses clue words to show likenesses and differences.

© Pearson Education, Inc., 2

Name _____

Suffixes *-ness, -less*

Spelling Words					
kindness	careless	goodness	useless	fearless	darkness
sadness	sickness	helpless	thankless	fitness	weakness

Write a list word that means the same as each word or phrase.

sorrow   being fit   being good

1. _____   2. _____   3. _____

without help   being kind   not rewarded

4. _____   5. _____   6. _____

Write a list word to finish each sentence.

7. Grandma has a _____ for sweets.

8. His _____ caused a high fever.

9. I stumbled in the _____ .

10. It's _____ to look for his ring in the lake.

11. The _____ firefighters rescued the little boy.

12. I was _____ and dropped my model airplane.

School + Home **Home Activity** Your child used spelling words in sentences. Have your child make up new sentences using the list words.

© Pearson Education, Inc., 2

Name _____

Read each sentence. **Choose** the meaning of the underlined word from the box and write it on the line. **Use** the other words in the sentence to help.

in the sky	given payment
good manners	told	safe to eat

1. The teacher <u>related</u> the story to the class.

_____

- -

_____

2. Sandy showed such <u>decorum</u> by acting in a polite and kind way.

_____

- -

_____

3. In most jobs you are <u>compensated</u> for your work.

_____

- -

_____

4. The sun, moon, and stars are all <u>celestial</u> bodies.

_____

- -

_____

5. The inside of a banana is <u>edible</u>, but the skin is not.

_____

- -

_____

Home Activity Your child used context clues to figure out the meanings of unfamiliar words. Have your child tell you how he or she figured out the meanings of the words in the sentences.

© Pearson Education, Inc., 2

Using Commas

- **Commas** are used in addresses:

    St. Louis, MO 63119

- **Commas** are used in dates:

    May 10, 1946   Thursday, December 16

- **Commas** are used to begin and end a letter:

    Dear Grandpa,
    Love,
    Tony

- **Commas** are used to separate three or more things in a sentence.

    Tony bought stamps, paper, and a pen.

Add commas to the letter where they are needed.

> 307 Hillside Drive
> Dallas TX 75220
>
> June 28 2011
>
> Dear Marie
>   I will come to Texas for a visit in July. I hope we can go to a ranch again. I love riding. Could we go on a short trail ride? See you soon.
>
>   Your cousin
>   Anna

Home Activity Your child learned about using commas. Collect pieces of mail. Look at the ads and the addresses on the envelopes. Have your child point out places where commas are used.

© Pearson Education, Inc., 2

Name _____

Venn Diagram

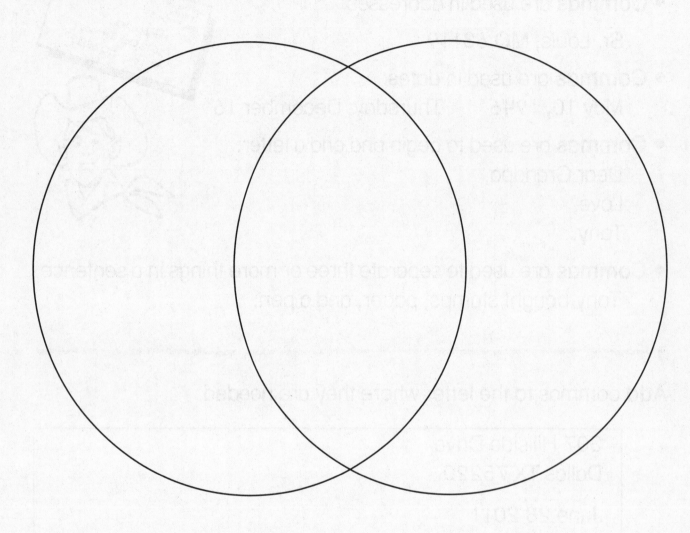

© Pearson Education, Inc., 2

Home Activity Your child is learning to write stories, poems, brief reports, nonfiction paragraphs, letters, and other products this year. Ask what your child is writing this week.

Name _____

Today, you will decide which sources of information might be relevant to answer your questions about the Question of the Week, *What can we learn about cowboy traditions?* Use the following steps to help you choose a relevant source to answer your questions.

Step 1- Make sure it is clear what you want to learn about your topic. Write some of your inquiry questions below.

_____   _____

_____   _____

_____   _____

Step 2- Review the many sources of information that you have learned about this year. Write down four sources.

_____   _____

_____   _____

_____   _____

Step 3- Circle the sources that you think will help you answer your inquiry questions. Find these sources and use them to answer your inquiry questions.

Step 4- Are you able to find answers to all of your inquiry questions? If not, work with a partner to think about other sources you might use. Or, think about how a source might be more focused to answer your questions. For example, if you chose to search the Internet, do you need to enter a new search topic?

© Pearson Education 2

 School + Home **Home Activity** Your child learned how to decide what sources of information might be relevant to answer his or her inquiry questions. Visit a Media Center or Library and discuss the various information sources that are available. Discuss with your child why some sources might be better than others.

Name _____

Suffixes *-ness*, *-less*

Spelling Words					
kindness	careless	goodness	useless	fearless	darkness
sadness	sickness	helpless	thankless	fitness	weakness

Read the story. **Circle** three spelling mistakes. **Write** the words correctly. **Write** the run-on sentence as two separate sentences.

Frequently Misspelled Words
again
very
then

Last night I heard a scratchy noise in the darknes. My fearless sister got up she turned on the light. My hamster was scratching under my bed. I hadn't put him back in his cage. I won't be so carless agin!

1. _____ 2. _____ 3. _____

4. _____

_____

Circle the word that is spelled correctly. **Write** it.

5. sickness _____   6. usless _____
   sicknes   useless

7. weakness _____   8. sadness _____
   weekness   sadnes

Home Activity Your child identified misspelled words with *-ness* and *-less*. Have your child say a list word and then spell the base word and the suffix separately.

© Pearson Education, Inc., 2

Name _____

Read the story. **Underline** time-order words and phrases. **Circle** the dates. **Write 1, 2, 3, 4, 5** to show the correct order of events.

Arctic Explorer

Have you heard of Matthew Henson? He was a famous explorer. Henson helped discover the North Pole together with Robert Peary. Peary and Henson worked together for many years. They made several tries at reaching the North Pole. Each time, they would take a ship to Greenland. Then they would set out across the Arctic on foot. They used dogsleds to carry their gear.

Their first trip was in 1890. They didn't get very far. Next, in 1900, they made it farther north than anyone had before. Then, in 1906, they went even farther north, beating their own record. Finally, in 1909, Henson and Peary made it to the North Pole. Many years later, in 2000, the National Geographic Society gave Henson its highest honor—the Hubbard Medal.

_____ Henson and Peary make it to the North Pole.

_____ Henson and Peary make it farther north than anyone else.

_____ Henson and Peary make their first trip.

_____ The National Geographic Society give Henson a medal.

_____ Henson and Peary beat their own record.

© Pearson Education, Inc., 2

School + Home **Home Activity** Your child identified words in a story that show sequence and placed events in the correct order. Ask your child to tell events that take place on a typical school day. Make sure your child tells the events in the correct order. Encourage your child to use order words.

Name _____

Using Commas

Mark the letter of the group of words, the address, or the date that uses commas correctly.

1. ○ A Littleton, CO 80120
   ○ B Littleton CO, 80120
   ○ C Littleton C,O 80120

2. ○ A November, 12 2007
   ○ B November 12 2007,
   ○ C November 12, 2007

3. ○ A Dear Aunt, Betty
   ○ B Dear, Aunt Betty
   ○ C Dear Aunt Betty,

4. ○ A ski sled, and skate
   ○ B ski, sled, and skate
   ○ C ski, sled and skate,

5. ○ A boots, hat, and mittens
   ○ B boots, hat and mittens,
   ○ C boots hat, and mittens

6. ○ A Your niece Monica,
   ○ B Your niece, Monica
   ○ C Your, niece Monica

© Pearson Education, Inc., 2

Home Activity Your child prepared for taking tests on using commas. Ask your child to name three objects in the room. Have your child write a sentence using the objects. For example, *I see a chair, a picture, and a rug.*

Name _____

Read the clues.
Write **mis-, mid-, micro-,**
or **non-** to finish the words.

<u>mid</u>air   <u>mis</u>place
<u>non</u>fat   <u>micro</u>scope

1. middle of the week

_____

- - - - - - - - - - - - - - -
_____week

2. an error

_____

- - - - - - - - - - - - - - -
_____take

3. true story

_____

- - - - - - - - - - - - - - -
_____fiction

4. act badly

_____

- - - - - - - - - - - - - - -
_____behave

5. peaceful

_____

- - - - - - - - - - - - - - -
_____violent

6. about July 1

_____

- - - - - - - - - - - - - - -
_____year

7. an error in printing

_____

- - - - - - - - - - - - - - -
_____print

8. something that makes
sound louder

_____

- - - - - - - - - - - - - - -
_____phone

9. makes no sense

_____

- - - - - - - - - - - - - - -
_____sense

10. a wrong act

_____

- - - - - - - - - - - - - - -
_____deed

© Pearson Education, Inc., 2

Home Activity Your child wrote words with the prefixes *mid-* (as in *midair*), *mis-* (as in *misplace*), *micro-* (as in *microscope*), and *non-* (as in *nonfat*). Together name other words with these prefixes, such as *midsize*, *midweek, mislead, misfile, nonstop,* and *nontoxic.* Write the words. Ask your child to say them and identify the prefixes.

Name _____

Read the story. **Pick** a word from the box to complete each sentence. **Write** the word on the line.

> microphone   slogan   rallies
> speeches   election   assembly

Carlos spoke at the school _____ on Thursday morning. He spoke right into the

_____

_____, as his teacher had taught him. Carlos

was running for president in the school _____.
All the students running for president made

_____

_____ that day. Carlos had already spent hours

speaking at _____. He and his neighbor had

_____

written his _____ on posters and clothing. They spent very little money. Now his only question was "Who will win?"

Home Activity Your child used lesson vocabulary words to complete a story. Ask your child to use the vocabulary words to make up his or her own sentences.

© Pearson Education, Inc., 2

Name _____

Read the story. **Follow** the directions.

Emma Loves to Swim

Emma is a great swimmer. When she was a baby, she learned to do the dog paddle. This way of swimming is called the dog paddle because it's how a dog swims. When Emma was older, she learned to do the backstroke. During a backstroke, a swimmer lies on his or her back. Then the swimmer moves one arm at a time back and over his or her head. In school, Emma joined a swim team and won a medal for swimming the fastest backstroke. Later, Emma learned to swim a stroke called the butterfly. To do the butterfly, a swimmer lies face down in the water. Then the swimmer moves his or her arms like a windmill. The butterfly is a hard stroke to do, but Emma won several butterfly races. Emma feels like she has butterfly wings when she swims this way.

I. What is a fact about the dog paddle?

_____

- -

2. Underline details in the story that tell about the backstroke.

3. What is a fact about how a swimmer begins the butterfly stroke?

_____

- -

_____

- -

_____

© Pearson Education, Inc., 2

Home Activity Your child read a story that is realistic fiction and identified facts and details in it. Ask your child to tell a few facts and details about another sport.

Comprehension Facts and Details **531**

Name _____

Writing • Persuasive Statement

 A School Flag

Writing Prompt: Write a persuasive statement about a change in a tradition that would make your school better.

We are proud of our country and state. So we always fly the American and Texas flags in front of the school. We are proud of our school too. Yet we do not have a flag to show it. I think we should make a school flag now. In the future, we can fly it so that everyone will know how we feel.

It would be easy to make a flag. The eagle is our school symbol. We could put it on the flag. Some parents can sew it, and other parents can set the pole. We can have bake sales after school to raise the money to pay for the fabric and the pole. Once the school flag is flying, the community will see that we love our country, state, and school!

© Pearson Education, Inc., 2

School + Home **Home Activity** Your child is learning to write in response to a test prompt. Ask your child to tell you why this is a good example of a persuasive statement.

Name _____

Prefixes *mis-*, *mid-*

© Pearson Education, Inc., 2

Spelling Words					
midair	misplace	mislead	midway	misprint	midday
midweek	misbehave	midyear	mismatch	misdeed	mistake

Write a list word by adding **mis-** or **mid-** to each base word.

match

1. _____

print

2. _____

week

3. _____

air

4. _____

behave

5. _____

deed

6. _____

year

7. _____

way

8. _____

Write the list word to complete each phrase.

9. _____ your keys

10. make a _____

11. _____ people

12. _____ nap

Home Activity Your child spelled words with the prefixes *mis-* and *mid-*. Take turns with your child using the words in sentences.

Name _____

Write the meaning of each underlined word.
Use the dictionary page to help.

cover [ku ver] *v.* put
something over, *n.* a lid or
a cloth
patch [pach] *v.* to fix or
repair, *n.* a small square of
material

post [pōst] *v.* to display
or to place, *n.* a pole
raise [rāz] *v.* to lift,
n. an increase in pay
share [shar] *v.* to let use,
n. a part of something

1. Please <u>cover</u> your mouth when you cough.

_____
- -
_____

2. They will <u>post</u> the sign on the tree at the end of the block.

_____
- -
_____

3. Hal just got a <u>raise</u> at his job.

_____
- -
_____

4. She put a <u>patch</u> over the hole in her sweater.

_____
- -
_____

5. Ellen likes to <u>share</u> her toys with her friends.

_____
- -
_____

Home Activity Your child used a dictionary to figure out the correct meanings of words that have more than one meaning. Ask your child to tell you the clues in each sentence that helped him or her choose the correct meaning from the dictionary page.

© Pearson Education, Inc., 2

Commas in Compound Sentences

Sometimes sentences have ideas that go together. These sentences can be combined using a comma and a connecting word, such as **and** or **but**. The combined sentence is called a **compound sentence.**

I want to be the mayor. I want to help people.
I want to be the mayor, and I want to help people.

I wanted to vote for president. I was too young.
I wanted to vote for president, but I was too young.

Use the word in ( ) and a comma to combine each pair of sentences. **Write** the new sentence on the lines.

1. Our flag has stars. It has stripes. (and)

   _____

   -

   _____

2. States have flags. Each is different. (but)

   _____

   -

   _____

3. The flag goes up the pole in the morning. It comes down after school. (and)

   _____

   -

   _____

   -

   _____

© Pearson Education, Inc., 2

School + Home
Home Activity Your child learned about commas in compound sentences. Ask your child to combine these sentences, using a comma and the word *and: Our flag has red stripes. It has white stars.*

Name _____

Scoring Rubric: Persuasive Statement

	4	3	2	1
Focus/Ideas	The statement is well-focused on an idea with three supporting facts, reasons, or examples.	The statement is focused on an idea with two supporting facts, reasons, or examples.	The statement is loosely focused on an idea with one supporting fact, reason, or example.	The statement is unfocused and lacks supporting facts, reasons, or examples.
Organization	Details are presented in a clearly organized way.	Details are presented in an organized way.	Some of the details are organized.	The details are not organized.
Voice	The writing uses a strong, persuasive tone and knowledge.	The writing uses a persuasive tone.	The writing sometimes uses a persuasive tone.	The writing does not use a persuasive tone.
Word Choice	The writer uses vivid and persuasive words.	The writer uses some persuasive words.	The writer uses few persuasive words.	The writer uses dull words.
Sentences	The sentences are complete and varied in length.	Most sentences are complete and varied in length.	Some sentences are complete and varied in length.	Few sentences are complete or varied in length.
Conventions	There are no spelling, capitalization, or punctuation errors.	There are few spelling, capitalization, or punctuation errors.	There are some spelling, capitalization, or punctuation errors.	There are many spelling, capitalization, or punctuation errors.

© Pearson Education, Inc., 2

Home Activity Your child is learning to write a persuasive statement. Ask your child to explain the topic. Then have your child tell his or her main idea statement and supporting details. Your child's writing will be evaluated based on this four-point scoring rubric.

Name _____

Often times, information is gained inside the classroom. Sources of information that you may find inside the classroom are known as **natural sources.** When you use people as a natural source, you must conduct an **interview.**

Who are natural sources that you could interview?

_____

- -

_____

What is a question you would ask a classmate if you wanted to learn about his or her favorite game?

_____

- -

_____

What is a question you would ask your teacher if you wanted help on understanding an assignment?

_____

- -

_____

What is a question you would ask your principal if you wanted to learn about school rules?

_____

- -

_____

© Pearson Education 2

Home Activity Your child learned about gathering evidence from natural sources as well as using people as sources of information. Talk with your child about some of the traditions your family celebrates and shares with others. Give your child a topic of a tradition to research. Together with your child make a list of sources you could use to find the answers to your questions.

Name _____

Prefixes *mis-*, *mid-*

Read the notice. **Circle** three spelling mistakes and a word with a capitalization error. **Write** the words correctly.

> **Notice:** There was a missprint in last week's newsletter. The class book fair will **not** be misweek. It will be after school on friday. We are sorry about the mistake. We didn't mean to mislead you. We hope evry student can come!

Spelling Words	
midair	misplace
mislead	midway
misprint	midday
midweek	misbehave
midyear	mismatch
misdeed	mistake

1. _____

2. _____

3. _____

4. _____

Frequently Misspelled Words

every

whole

could

Circle the word that is spelled correctly. **Write** the word.

5. midway   middway

6. misbehav   misbehave

7. mislead   misleed

8. misplace   misplase

5. _____

6. _____

7. _____

8. _____

© Pearson Education, Inc., 2

Home Activity Your child identified misspelled words with *mis-* and *mid-*. Pronounce a list word. Have your child spell the base word and the prefix separately.

Name _____

Read the story. **Follow** the directions.

Baking Muffins

Lin loved to bake with her mother. Every Saturday morning, they baked together. This Saturday they were making blueberry muffins. Lin laid all the ingredients out on the counter.

"Do we have everything?" her mother asked. "Flour, baking powder, salt, eggs, oil, yogurt, and blueberries?"

Lin nodded. Together they mixed the flour with baking powder, salt, and blueberries. Next, they mixed the eggs, oil, and yogurt together. Then, they combined the two. "Mix lightly!" Lin's mother warned. "Too much mixing will make the muffins tough."

"Okay," said Lin. She glanced at the recipe. "Now they have to bake for 25 minutes."

Soon the kitchen smelled wonderful. Later, Lin bit into a still-warm muffin. She thought she had never tasted anything so good!

I. What happens in this story?

_____

- -

2. **Underline** the details in the story that tell how to bake muffins.

3. What fact does the recipe state about baking the muffins?

_____

- -

© Pearson Education, Inc., 2

Home Activity Your child read a realistic fiction story and identified facts and details in it. Ask your child to list a few facts and details about something he or she loves to do.

Comprehension Facts and Details **539**

Commas in Compound Sentences

Mark the letter of the compound sentence that shows how to correctly combine the two sentences.

1. Everyone can vote for president. You must be 18 years old.
   - ○ **A** Everyone can vote for president, you must be 18 years old.
   - ○ **B** Everyone can vote for president, but you must be 18 years old.
   - ○ **C** Everyone can vote for president but, you must be 18 years old.

2. There have been many presidents. None of them were girls.
   - ○ **A** There have been many presidents, none of them were girls.
   - ○ **B** There have been many presidents and, none of them were girls.
   - ○ **C** There have been many presidents, but none of them were girls.

3. There are popular votes. There are electoral votes.
   - ○ **A** There are popular votes, and there are electoral votes.
   - ○ **B** There are popular votes and, there are electoral votes.
   - ○ **C** There are popular votes, there are electoral votes.

4. Many students voted for Thomas. Grace won the election.
   - ○ **A** Many students voted for Thomas and Grace won the election.
   - ○ **B** Many students voted for Thomas, but Grace won the election.
   - ○ **C** Many students voted for Thomas but, Grace won the election.

© Pearson Education, Inc., 2

Home Activity Your child prepared for taking tests on commas in compound sentences. Ask your child to choose one of the numbered pairs of sentences on this page and to combine the two sentences to make a compound sentence.

Name _____

Cross off any word in each box that is NOT a base word with the added ending shown at the top of the box.

-s	-es	-ed
his	reaches	red
hers	cheese	sailed
mess	presses	pointed
birds	punches	rested
walks	dresses	bed
does	lessons	cricket

-ing	-er	-est
talking	teacher	tallest
ring	another	west
string	shorter	fastest
ringing	banner	best
playing	lower	smartest
drinking	lighter	longest

Read the story.

The tallest boy in our class is David. He is also the smartest. One day David was playing in the schoolyard. He did not want to share the basketball. He just wanted to shoot baskets by himself. Then David tripped. He fell and scraped his knee. His pants were ripped. David didn't feel smarter than the rest of us then. We helped him up. We all played basketball. Sometimes it's better to have friends than to be the smartest one in school. Now David knows this too.

Home Activity Your child identified base words and endings *-s*, *-es*, *-ing*, *-er*, and *-est*. Have your child make up four sentences using the words *talk, talks, talked,* and *talking*. Check your child's work to make sure each word is used correctly in each sentence.

© Pearson Education, Inc., 2

Name _____

Inflected Endings

Spelling Words					
tried	trying	planned	planning	liked	liking
skipped	skipping	heavier	heaviest	lighter	lightest

Circle the word that best completes the sentence.

1. Morgan   liked   liking   his mother's chicken noodle soup.

2. I am   tried   trying   to beat the high score.

3. My teacher   planned   planning   a class picnic for the last day of school.

4. The flute is the   lighter   lightest   instrument in our band.

5. Arnold is   skipped   skipping   rocks down at the lake.

6. My backpack is much   heavier   heaviest   than Ryan's backpack.

Write the words in the box in ABC order.

7. _____

8. _____

9. _____

10. _____

11. _____

12. _____

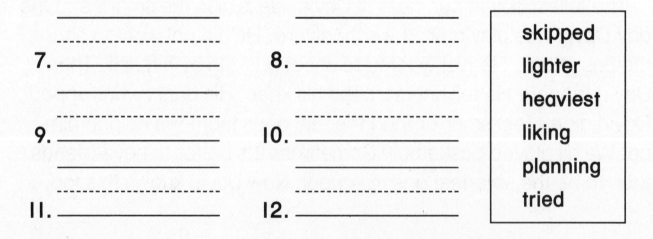

skipped

lighter

heaviest

liking

planning

tried

© Pearson Education, Inc., 2

Home Activity Your child spelled words with inflected endings. Write words with these endings on a sheet of paper. Have your child read each word and explain the rule for adding the ending. For example, for the word *stopped*, double the final consonant before adding *-ed* to the base word. If your child needs help, suggest to use a resource to find the correct spelling.

Pick a word from the box to finish each sentence.
Write the word on the line.

> bases   cheers   field
> plate   sailed   threw

1. All the _____ were loaded.

2. The batter stood at the _____.

3. Jay _____ the ball to the batter.

4. The batter hit a home run out of the _____.

5. The ball _____ over my head, and the batter ran safely to home plate.

6. There were _____ from the crowd.

Home Activity Your child reviewed lesson vocabulary learned in this unit. Have your child pretend to be a sports newscaster as he or she reads the sentences.

© Pearson Education, Inc., 2

Name _____

Read the story.
Answer the questions.

Help the Flood Victims

The Gift of Giving

Juan and his family had just moved to a new town. Juan was beginning to make some friends in his new neighborhood, but he missed his old friends. Last week there was a flood in his old town. Many people lost their homes and were living in tents in open fields.

Juan wanted to raise money to help the people in his old town. But since he was new in this town, he felt strange asking people he did not know for help.

"How can I ask them for money?" he asked his mother.

"It is not easy, but you will find that most people will want to help," she said. "First, you must make a plan. I will help you find a place where the money will do the most good."

Juan still felt strange, but he wanted to try to do something to help the flood victims. He and his sister Maria decided to go to stores in the neighborhood. The first stop was Flynn's Food Store.

"What can I do for you?" asked Mr. Flynn.

"Well, we're not here to buy anything, but we'd like to ask you something. Would you like to help the people that were hurt by the flood?" Juan asked. Then he explained to Mr. Flynn what his plan was.

"If a young man like yourself can do something like this, I want to do the same," Mr. Flynn exclaimed. "How about we work together?"

"Sure!" cheered Juan.

© Pearson Education, Inc., 2

School + Home **Home Activity** Your child compared and contrasted characters in the story. Make a list with your child of ways people can help others in need. Compare and contrast the different ways.

Name _____

Mr. Flynn and Juan threw a party to raise money for the people in the flood area. Many of Mr. Flynn's customers offered money. Others offered clothing and canned food.

"I am so proud of you," Juan's mother cried. "I never told you, but when I was a little girl, a hurricane destroyed our home. We had nothing but the clothes we were wearing. We had nowhere to go, and little food and water. People around the world heard about the hurricane and sent food and medicine. So you see, many people help others without thinking about themselves. You have done just that!"

1. How are Juan and Mr. Flynn alike?

_____

- -

_____

- -

_____

2. How is what Juan is doing different than something his mother did when she was a child?

_____

- -

_____

- -

_____

3. What is a way Juan's mother says people are alike?

_____

- -

_____

- -

_____

© Pearson Education, Inc., 2

Using Capital Letters

Find the words that need capital letters. **Write** the words correctly on the line.

1. july and august are two summer months when baseball is played.

   _____

   -

2. Many games are played on saturday and sunday.

   _____

   -

3. dr. Shea and ms. Wallace took me to a Chicago Cubs game.

   _____

   -

Underline the words that need capital letters. **Write** the words you underlined.

   _____

   -

4. We went to the game on labor day. _____

   _____

   -

5. The game was on a monday. _____

   _____

   -

6. We saw mr. Ernie Banks there. _____

© Pearson Education, Inc., 2

Name _____

Day I Unit 6 Week I   Just Like Josh Gibson

Copy the sentences. Make sure your letters and words are spaced correctly.

We won't go to Vienna.

_____
- -
_____

You don't know Uncle Will.

_____
- -
_____

Day 2 Unit 6 Week 2   Red, White, and Blue

Copy the sentences. Make sure your letters are written smoothly.

Beth and Pam like shopping.

_____
- -
_____

Rob hiked the Forest Trail.

_____
- -
_____

© Pearson Education, Inc., 2

Home Activity Your child practiced writing all cursive letters. Each day have your child copy a sentence from a favorite storybook using his or her best cursive handwriting.

Handwriting   547

Name _____

Day 3 Unit 6 Week 3   A Birthday Basket for Tía

Copy the sentence. Make sure your lowercase and uppercase letters are the correct size.

Gail has a terrible cold.

Day 4 Unit 6 Week 4   Cowboys

Copy the sentence. Make sure your letters are slanting the same way.

Xavier Zorbo has a question.

Day 5 Unit 6 Week 5   Grace for President

Copy the sentence. Make sure your letters and words are spaced correctly.

Look at Dan's microscope.

© Pearson Education, Inc., 2

Name _____

Draw a line to match the word with its abbreviation.

1. Mister   Ave.

2. Avenue   Mr.

3. Street   Dr.

4. Doctor   St.

Write the abbreviation for the underlined word.

_____

5. <u>January</u> 12   _____

_____

6. <u>Monday</u> morning   _____

_____

7. last <u>December</u>   _____

_____

8. next <u>Wednesday</u>   _____

Read the story.

On Dec. 12, Mr. and Mrs. Walters had to go to the doctor. They both needed to get flu shots. So on Mon. they both went to see Dr. Lin on Allen St. When they got there, the door was locked. Mr. Walters pushed the door, but it would not open. Mrs. Walters looked in the window. No one was inside. Then Mrs. Smith walked by. She told Mr. and Mrs. Walters that Dr. Lin did not come in on Mondays. Mr. Walters looked at his notebook. It said he had to go to the doctor on Tues., Dec. 12!

© Pearson Education, Inc., 2

Home Activity Your child practiced using and reading common abbreviations such as *Ave., St., Mr., Mrs.,* and *Dr.* Have your child write his or her birthday, address, and today's date, using as many abbreviations as possible for the month, day, and address.

Name _____

Abbreviations

Spelling Words					
Mr.	Mrs.	St.	Jan.	Feb.	Aug.
Dr.	Ms.	Rd.	Oct.	Nov.	Dec.

Read the clues. **Write** the list word.

1. title for a man _____

2. month after July _____

3. the first month _____

4. something you drive on _____

5. title for a woman _____

6. month before March _____

Write the abbreviation for the underlined word in each sentence.

7. <u>December</u> is my favorite month. _____

8. Justin lives on Rosebud <u>Road</u>. _____

9. We are going to a baseball game in <u>October</u>. _____

10. <u>Mister</u> White walks his dog every day. _____

11. Thanksgiving is in <u>November</u>. _____

12. <u>Doctor</u> Lopez works in a hospital. _____

© Pearson Education, Inc., 2

School + Home

Home Activity Your child learned to spell abbreviations. Have your child point to each abbreviation, say the word it represents, and then write it.

Name _____

Pick a word to match each clue. **Write** the word on the line.

> birthday   flag   freedom
> nicknames   stars   stripes   America

_____

1. The _____ flies high on a pole.

2. I like to watch the _____ sparkle and shine in the night sky.

3. Happy _____ to you!

4. Many people fought for the country's _____.

5. A zebra has many _____.

6. Fran has red hair. Fran's friends call her "Red." Leo loves to eat peanuts. Leo's dad calls him "Peanut." "Red" and "Peanut" are _____

_____

7. Another name for our country is _____.

Write a nickname you might give a friendly white dog with black spots. _____

© Pearson Education, Inc., 2

School + Home **Home Activity** Your child reviewed lesson vocabulary learned in this unit. Ask your child to make up a poem about the U.S. flag using as many words in the box as possible. Your child can illustrate the poem with a picture.

Vocabulary   551

Name _____

Read the story. **Write** the answer to each question.

Celebrating Hawaii

The people of Hawaii have many ancient customs. Two of these customs are dancing the hula and giving leis.

Hawaiians have been dancing the hula for thousands of years. In the early days, both men and women danced the hula. The dancers did not wear grass skirts then. They did wear skirts, but the skirts were made from bark.

The ancient hula was often performed to chanting, called *mele*, in which sounds were repeated over and over. Sometimes the dancers danced to music played on ancient instruments. Hawaiians used coconuts, gourds, and small logs to make instruments that they would beat or shake.

A hula dancer's movements told a story. The dances would express the history, customs, and ceremonies of Hawaii. Sometimes the dancing gave thanks for the people's blessings. The ancient hula was a serious kind of dancing. Dance teachers taught young dancers the correct way to dance this hula.

Another important custom of the Hawaiian people is to make, wear, and give away leis. A lei is a necklace of flowers—real flowers. Beautiful flowers of bright colors grow all over Hawaii.

The people who make leis usually string flowers, but sometimes they string shiny green leaves. They may also make leis with shells, nuts, or feathers.

When visitors came to Hawaii in the 1900s, the Hawaiians gave them leis as a way to welcome them to the islands. They would

© Pearson Education, Inc., 2

Home Activity Your child read a nonfiction story and identified the author's purpose in writing it. Reread the story with your child. Ask your child why he or she thinks the author told readers about the ancient hula.

Name _____

place the lei around the visitor's neck. Today visitors to Hawaii are still welcomed with leis.

No one should refuse to accept and wear a lei. To do so would hurt the feelings of the person who gives it. Leis are so important to Hawaiians that May 1 is called Lei Day. It's a holiday.

1. What is the topic of this story?

_____

_____

2. What do you think was the author's purpose in writing this story? Underline the answer below.

to tell a funny story

to explain how to make something

to give information

3. Why do you think the author told the reader about chanting?

_____

_____

_____

4. What facts about Hawaii did you learn as you read the story? Tell two things that you learned.

_____

_____

_____

_____

© Pearson Education, Inc., 2

Name _____

Quotation Marks

Write each sentence. **Add** quotation marks.

1. Where do we see flags? asked Lewis.

   _____

   -

2. Clark said, There is one on our porch.

   _____

   -

3. I see one in the classroom, Molly said.

   _____

   -

Add quotation marks to each sentence.

4. Flags are on the streetlights in town, said Paul.

5. Jackie asked, Is there a flag on the flagpole at school?

6. I saw a flag on a car, Eleanor said.

7. Paul said, I did not see the flag.

8. Are you sure there was a flag? asked Jackie.

© Pearson Education, Inc., 2

Name _____

Pick a final syllable from the box to correctly complete each word. **Write** the syllable on the line.

> -tion   -ture   -ion

1. contrac_____

2. sta_____

3. men_____

4. mill_____

5. cush_____

6. bill_____

7. mix_____

8. cul_____

9. ac_____

10. pic_____

Read the story.

Sam stood inside the train station. He looked at all the pictures of trains on the wall. Sam was waiting for his friend. It seemed like a million years since he had last seen Ted. Meanwhile, Ted was on the train. He was looking out at the scenery. Ted was in the section of the train that had big windows. The seats had soft cushions. Ted's train had crossed the whole nation. When his train pulled in, Ted could see Sam waiting with a big smile. He knew his future, living in the same town as Sam, was going to be great.

© Pearson Education, Inc., 2

Home Activity Your child reviewed words ending with the syllables *ion, tion,* and *ture.* Have your child read each word he or she completed in 1 through 10 above, and then use the word in a sentence.

Phonics 555

Name _____

Final Syllables *-tion*, *-ture*

Spelling Words					
mixture	nation	section	future	picture	action
caution	station	fixture	motion	nature	feature

Find two rhyming words in each box. **Circle** the words.
Write the words.

mixture	future	action
feature	section	caution
nature	fixture	motion

future	section	nature
caution	picture	nation
station	motion	feature

1. _____   2. _____   3. _____   4. _____

Write the missing letters to make a list word.

5. a division or slice ___ ___ ___ t i o n

6. a painting or photograph ___ ___ ___ t u r e

7. the process of doing something ___ ___ ___ t i o n

8. what will be ___ ___ ___ t u r e

9. movement ___ ___ t i o n

10. care to avoid danger ___ ___ ___ t i o n

11. everything on Earth not made
    by people ___ ___ t u r e

12. something that stands out ___ ___ ___ t u r e

© Pearson Education, Inc., 2

Home Activity Your child learned to spell words that end with *-tion* and *-ture*. Take turns thinking of other words with these letter combinations. Use a magazine or book if necessary.

Name _____

Pick a word from the box to finish each sentence.
Write the word on the line.

> aunt basket collects
> favorite present

1. Tim _____ stamps.

2. It is his _____ thing to do.

3. He saves all his stamps in a _____.

4. Tim's _____ gave him a book
   about stamps.

5. Tim was very happy with his _____.

Write a sentence using the word *bank*.

6. _____

_____

_____

Home Activity Your child reviewed lesson vocabulary learned earlier in this unit. Ask your child what kinds of things he or she collects or would like to collect. Then have your child write a paragraph about collecting things, using some of the vocabulary words.

© Pearson Education, Inc., 2

Read the story. **Answer** the questions.

The Family Tree

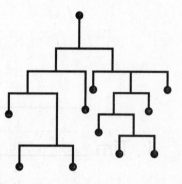

Every year the West family has a large family picnic. There are always baskets full of different foods. It is Mary West's favorite summer picnic. She gets to see her aunts and uncles and play with her cousins.

"This would be a good time to learn about our family tree," Mrs. West said.

"Where is the tree planted?" Mary asked.

"It's not the kind of tree that grows in the earth," Aunt Jill laughed. "It's a chart that shows a family's history."

"Like a real tree, it has branches. The branches show all the people in the family," explained Mr. West.

"I like to climb trees. Can I be on the top?" Mary asked.

"Sorry, the youngest family members are at the bottom of the tree," answered Mrs. West.

The West family began working on their family tree. Mary learned a lot about her family. The birthday present her grandmother always sent was handmade clothes. Mary learned that at one time, her grandmother owned a clothing store.

"Remember how Grandma always talked about her mother?" Mr. West asked. "She was a teacher in a one-room schoolhouse."

"The first West to go to college," Aunt Jill said proudly.

© Pearson Education, Inc., 2

Home Activity Your child drew conclusions about characters in a story. Have your child tell if Mary has a big or small family and why he or she thinks so.

Name _____

The tree showed the people on both sides of Mary's family. The West family is her father's side. The Jacobs family is her mother's side. Mary discovered that the Jacobs family came to the United States from Russia.

"Do we have family in Russia?" asked Mary.

"My cousin Rachel is still in Russia," answered Mrs. West.

"Can we invite her to the picnic next year?" asked Mary excitedly.

"What a great idea!" said Mrs. West.

Mr. and Mrs. West collected all the information for the family tree.

"Can I keep adding branches to the tree?" asked Mary.

"Sure, and as time goes on, you won't be on the bottom anymore!" Mrs. West added.

---

1. How do you know Mary is interested in her family tree?

_____
_____
_____

2. Why do you think the family is proud of their grandmother's mother?

_____
_____
_____
_____

3. How might Cousin Rachel get to the picnic next year?

_____
_____
_____

© Pearson Education, Inc., 2

Name _____

Prepositions and Prepositional Phrases

Underline the preposition in each sentence.

1. I went to the store.

2. I bought streamers for the party.

3. We will decorate in the morning.

4. I am getting help from my mom.

Write the prepositional phrase in each sentence. **Say** each sentence with a different prepositional phrase.

5. Tía is my aunt from Mexico.

_____

- -

_____

6. I visit her after school.

_____

- -

_____

7. I like dancing with my family.

_____

- -

_____

8. I helped my mom in the kitchen.

_____

- -

_____

© Pearson Education, Inc., 2

Name _____

Write *less* or *ness* on the line to finish each word correctly.

1. help_____   2. dark _____

3. fear _____   4. use _____

5. sad_____   6. care _____

Circle the word that has the correct suffix.

7. affordless   affordible   affordable

8. terribleness   terrible   terrable

9. enjoyable   enjoyible   enjoyness

10. horrable   horrible   horribless

Read the story.

Dr. Ruth was very likeable. A visit to her office was never terrible. As Adam sat in the exam room, he felt comfortable and was fearless. When Dr. Ruth came in, she told Adam laughable stories. The whole exam was short and painless. Then Adam told Dr. Ruth a laughable story. He said that he had a remarkable fitness plan. His fitness plan was to use heavy forks whenever he ate. Dr. Ruth laughed, but she said it was a very sensible plan.

© Pearson Education, Inc., 2

Home Activity Your child wrote words that end with the suffixes *-less, -ness, -able,* and *-ible* and read a story. Have your child write a sentence or short story using these words: *useless, happiness, likeable, terrible.*

Name _____

Suffixes -ness, -less

Spelling Words					
kindness	careless	goodness	useless	fearless	darkness
sadness	sickness	helpless	thankless	fitness	weakness

Write the list word that means the **opposite**.

1. cruelty _____

2. strength _____

3. light _____

4. afraid _____

5. happiness _____

6. health _____

Unscramble the list words.

7. g d n e o s o s _____

8. s e u s s l e _____

9. h e p l e s l s _____

10. k n a h l e t s s _____

11. t i n s f e s _____

12. r e l e c s a s _____

© Pearson Education, Inc. 2

Home Activity Your child learned to spell words with *-ness* and *-less*. Have your child write a short story using five of the list words.

Name _____

Pick a word from the box to finish each sentence.
Write the word on the line.

> campfire   cattle   cowboy
> galloped   herd   railroad   trails

1. The _____ rides a horse.

2. He cooks food over a _____.

3. He takes the _____ across the plains.

4. There were no roads, only dusty _____.

5. Sometimes a _____ of cattle would run off.

6. The cowboy _____ on his horse to get them back.

7. The cattle went in pens near the _____ tracks.

© Pearson Education, Inc., 2

Home Activity Your child reviewed lesson vocabulary words learned earlier in this unit. Ask your child to write about a day in a cowboy's life using these vocabulary words.

Vocabulary   563

Read the story. **Follow** the directions.

The Great Wheel

Have you ever ridden on a Ferris wheel? The first Ferris wheel was built more than 100 years ago for a World's Fair in Chicago.

The people in charge of creating the fair wanted to show off something grand at the fair. A group of men met to discuss their ideas. In the audience at this meeting was a young engineer with the long name of George Washington Gale Ferris.

Ferris had the idea of building a Great Wheel. You might think the Ferris wheels you've seen are big, but the wheel Ferris wanted to build was much bigger. It would be a GIANT wheel!

But first Ferris had to have his design approved. So in 1892, he took his plans to another meeting. Those at the meeting said Ferris was a fool. They told him his wheel would be impossible to build. But Ferris did not give up, and in the end, his idea was approved.

Then Ferris went to work immediately to build his wheel. Next, in June of 1893, Ferris arranged to test his finished wheel. He wanted to see if the enormous wheel would run before he hung cars on it. The wheel already weighed more than 2 million pounds! Would a wheel that heavy actually turn? Yes! The wheel passed the test easily.

So Ferris ordered 36 cars for his Great Wheel. The cars were huge. Each car weighed 26,000 pounds and was big enough to hold 60 passengers. Finally, Ferris hung the cars, and the wheel was ready.

© Pearson Education, Inc., 2

Home Activity Your child identified the order of events in a story. Have your child tell you what happened in a movie he or she has seen recently. Ask your child to tell the events in the order in which they happened. Encourage your child to use time-order words.

Name _____

At last, in the fall of 1893, the World's Fair opened to the public. There was a grand ceremony on opening day with speakers, music, and crowds of visitors. The last speaker was George Washington Gale Ferris. After his speech, he blew a golden whistle to signal the start-up of the wheel. Everyone watched in awe and cheered excitedly as the magnificent wheel turned. The Great Wheel was a great success.

1. **Circle** the words in the story that give clues to the order in which the events happened.

2. **Write** the numbers **1, 2, 3, 4, 5, 6** to show the correct order of events.

_____ Ferris goes to work to build his Great Wheel.

_____ Ferris's idea is approved.

_____ The World's Fair opens in 1893.

_____ Ferris orders cars for his wheel.

_____ Ferris tests his wheel to see if it will turn.

_____ Ferris hangs cars on his wheel.

© Pearson Education, Inc., 2

Name _____

Using Commas

Write parts of a letter. **Use** commas where they are needed.

1. Chicago IL 60616

2. March 18 2012

3. Dear Pedro

Write each sentence. **Use** commas where they are needed.

4. I visited the ranch on May 12 2012.

5. We rode ate and played.

6. I got back to the ranch on Monday July 2.

© Pearson Education, Inc., 2

Name _____

Write a prefix from the box to finish each word. You will need to use each prefix more than one time.

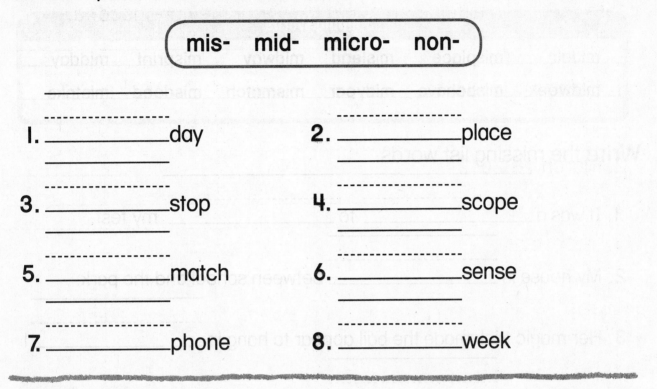

mis- mid- micro- non-

1. _____day

2. _____place

3. _____stop

4. _____scope

5. _____match

6. _____sense

7. _____phone

8. _____week

Read the story.

Here it was midweek. It was a sunny midday on Wednesday, and Keisha still couldn't go out. She really didn't mean to misbehave. She just couldn't put up with her little brother's nonsense anymore. He kept asking for juice over and over. They had no juice. He was yelling nonstop. What she did was more of a microscopic mistake than a misdeed. That's what Keisha thought. All she did was open a quart of nonfat milk and put it on the tray of her little brother's high chair.

© Pearson Education, Inc., 2

Home Activity Your child wrote words with the prefixes *mis-, mid-, micro-,* and *non-* and read a story. Write the following words and have your child read the word, tell you the prefix, and what the word means: *mismatch, midnight, microchip, nonviolent.*

Name _____

Prefixes *mis-, mid-*

Spelling Words					
midair	misplace	mislead	midway	misprint	midday
midweek	misbehave	midyear	mismatch	misdeed	mistake

Write the missing list words.

_____   _____

1. It was a _____ to _____ my test.

2. My house is _____ between school and the park.

3. Her magic trick made the ball appear to hang in _____!

4. Lunch is the _____ meal.

5. The puppy is learning not to _____ and chew Dad's shoes.

Circle the hidden list words.

```
a  m  m  i  s  m  a  t  c  h  x  m
r  i  m  i  s  p  r  i  n  t  u  i
y  s  a  z  s  z  w  g  u  i  j  d
s  l  q  m  i  d  y  e  a  r  z  w
h  e  w  d  t  i  e  o  u  j  m  e
k  a  r  x  r  f  b  e  p  a  q  e
h  d  e  g  h  c  x  y  d  q  b  k
```

mislead

midyear

misdeed

misprint

midweek

mismatch

© Pearson Education, Inc., 2

Home Activity Your child learned to spell words with the prefixes *mis-* and *mid-*. Have your child make up new sentences using the list words.

Name _____

Write a word from the box to complete each sentence.

> microphone   slogan   rallies
> speeches   election   assembly

1. When students run for school president, students vote in the
   _____
   school _____.

2. The students running for president may speak at a school
   _____
   _____.

3. Usually, speakers will speak into a _____.

4. Sometimes _____ are held before
   an election.

5. Students give _____, telling why they
   should be president.

6. They make up _____ such as
   "Bob can do the job."

Home Activity Your child reviewed vocabulary learned earlier in this unit. Tell your child to pretend that he or she is running for class president. Have your child write a short description of what happens using as many of the vocabulary words as possible.

© Pearson Education, Inc., 2

Name _____

Read the story. **Follow** the directions.

The Butterfly Place

Rich and Flo had an exciting visit to The Butterfly Place. They saw hundreds of butterflies there. The guide told them that there are about 28,000 kinds of butterflies.

The butterflies were flying around in a big building with a glass ceiling. Sometimes the butterflies floated very close to Rich and Flo. One butterfly even landed on Flo's head!

The ceiling was glass so the warm sun could shine in. The heat in the building was kept at the correct temperature for butterflies. Butterflies need warmth. If the temperature is lower than 86°F, butterflies cannot fly. That's why they're active in the day and sleep at night.

Rich and Flo learned that some butterflies are very small with a wingspan of only 1/8 inch. Others are large with a wingspan of almost 12 inches. Butterfly wings are covered with scales. These scales are beautiful colors and form interesting patterns. But the scales can be rubbed off the wings.

The guide explained that a butterfly does not grow once it comes out of its chrysalis. Rich and Flo were surprised to learn that most butterflies only live from two to four weeks.

As they were walking around, Rich wondered, "Can butterflies see?"

"They see three colors," the guide said, "red, yellow, and green."

Then Flo asked, "Do they make sounds?"

© Pearson Education, Inc., 2

School + Home

Home Activity Your child learned to identify facts and details from a story. Read part of a short biography written at your child's level. Work together to make a list of facts about the person.

Name _____

"Most butterflies make no sounds," the guide answered. "But a few will make loud clicks with their wings."

When it was time to leave, the visitors to The Butterfly Place thanked the guide for telling them about butterflies. As Rich and Flo walked out, they checked to make sure no butterflies were going along with them!

I. About how many kinds of butterflies are there?

_____

- -

_____

2. What is the correct temperature for butterflies?

_____

- -

_____

3. What is the wingspan of the smallest butterflies?

_____

- -

_____

4. How long do most butterflies live?

_____

- -

_____

5. Underline a fact about what butterflies see.

© Pearson Education, Inc., 2

Commas in Compound Sentences

Use the word in ( ) and a comma to combine each pair of sentences. **Write** the new sentence on the lines.

1. The election is today. We will vote. (and)

    _____

    -

    _____

    -

    _____

2. Sam wanted to vote. She has the flu. (but)

    _____

    -

    _____

    -

    _____

Add a comma where it is needed. **Circle** the word that joins the two sentences.

3. Our teacher made a box and we put our votes in.

4. Each vote was secret but some tried to peek.

5. Mrs. Lee counted the votes and she made a tally chart.

6. We will find out who won but we must wait.

Home Activity Your child prepared for taking tests on compound sentences. Have your child tell you three compound sentences about his or her day.

© Pearson Education, Inc., 2

Name _____

KWL Chart

Fill out this KWL chart to help you organize your ideas.
Write your ideas in sentences.

What I <u>K</u>now	What I <u>W</u>ant to Know	What I <u>L</u>earned

© Pearson Education, Inc., 2

Name _____

Writing Trait: Organization

Paragraph

- All the sentences in a paragraph must tell about the same idea.
- The sentences in a paragraph must be in an order that makes sense.
- One sentence in a paragraph gives the main idea, and the other sentences give details about the main idea.
- The first sentence of a paragraph is indented.

Read the sentences below. **Cross out** the sentence that does not tell about the same idea. **Write** the other sentences in the correct order to make a paragraph. **Indent** the first sentence.

Chris swung her bat at the ball.
She waited for the first pitch.
Chris raced to first base.
Her team won five games.
Whack! The bat hit the ball.
It was Chris's turn to bat.

_____

_____

_____

_____

_____

_____

© Pearson Education, Inc., 2

Name _____

Deleting Words, Phrases, or Sentences

When you revise, you might delete words, phrases, or sentences to make your writing clearer and less wordy. Here are some rules to help you.

• Delete a word that means the same as another word: ~~great~~ big, tiny ~~little.~~
• Delete a phrase that isn't needed: ~~sort of~~ warm.
• Delete any sentence that isn't about the topic.

Follow the directions.

I. Draw a line through the word that is not needed in this sentence.

We play basketball inside when it's freezing cold outside.

2. Draw a line through the phrase that is not needed in this sentence.

The rules of basketball have kind of changed.

3. Delete the sentence that does not belong in this paragraph. Draw a line through the sentence. Tell why you deleted it.

   The game of basketball has had many changes over the years. The old wooden hoops are made of metal now. The ball is bigger than it used to be. The rules of the game have also changed. The Chicago Bulls are my favorite team. Basketball has changed, but it is still exciting.

_____

_____

_____

© Pearson Education, Inc., 2

Name _____

Self-Evaluation Guide

Check Yes or **No** about paragraphs in your research report.

	Yes	No
I. I organized my facts in paragraphs.		
2. The sentences in my paragraphs are in an order that makes sense.		
3. The sentences in each paragraph tell about the same idea.		

Answer the questions.

4. What is the best part of your research report?

_____

- -

_____

- -

_____

- -

_____

5. What is one thing you would change about this research report if you could write it again?

_____

- -

_____

- -

_____

- -

_____

© Pearson Education, Inc., 2